THE ESSENTIALS OF THE
ISLAMIC FAITH

The Essentials of the

ISLAMIC FAITH

M. Fethullah Gülen

Translated by Ali Ünal

TUGHRA
BOOKS

New Jersey

Published by Tughra Books
335 Clifton Ave
Clifton, NJ, 07011

www.tughrabooks.com

For other titles by Gülen http://fgulen.org

Library of Congress Cataloging-in-Publication Data for the previous edition

Gülen, M. Fethullah,
        [İnancın Gölgesinde. English.]
        Essentials of the Islamic Faith / M. Fethullah Gülen.
        p. cm.
        Includes index.
        ISBN 9757388327
        1. Islam--Doctrines. 2. Islam--Essence, genius, nature
        3. Islam--Appreciation   I. Title.
BP165.5 G8513 2000
297.2--dc21
00-010841

ISBN: 978-1-932099-85-0 (Paperback)
ISBN: 978-1-59784-063-7 (Hardcover)

TABLE OF CONTENTS

ABOUT THE AUTHOR

Born in Erzurum, in eastern Turkey, in 1938, M. Fethullah Gülen is an Islamic scholar and thinker, and a prolific writer and poet. He was trained in the religious sciences by several celebrated Muslim scholars and spiritual masters. Gülen also studied the principles and theories of modern social and physical sciences. Based on his exceptional skills in learning and focused self-study, he soon surpassed his peers. In 1958, after attaining excellent examination results, he was awarded a state preacher's license, and was quickly promoted to a post in Izmir, Turkey's third largest province. It was here that Gülen started to crystallize his theme and expand his audience base. In his sermons and speeches he emphasized the pressing social issues of the times: his particular aim was to urge the younger generation to harmonize intellectual enlightenment with wise spirituality and a caring, humane activism.

Gülen did not restrict himself to teaching in the inner cities. He traveled around the provinces in Anatolia and lectured not only in mosques, but also at town meetings and corner coffee houses. This enabled him to reach a more representative cross-section of the population and to attract the attention of the academic community, especially the student body. The subject matter of his speeches, whether formal or informal, was not restricted explicitly to religious questions; he also talked about education, science, Darwinism, about the economy and social justice. It was the depth and quality of his speeches on such a wide range of topics that most impressed the academic community, and won their attention and respect.

Gülen retired from formal teaching duties in 1981, having inspired a whole generation of young students. His efforts, dating from the 1960s, especially in educational reform, have made him one of the best-known and respected figures in Turkey. From 1988 to 1991 he gave a series of sermons as preacher emeritus in some of the most famous mosques in major population centers, while continuing to deliver his message in the form of popular conferences, not only in Turkey, but also in the West.

MAIN IDEAS

In his speeches and writings Gülen envisions a twenty-first century in which we shall witness the birth of a spiritual dynamic that will revitalize long-dormant moral values; an age of tolerance, understanding, and international cooperation that will ultimately lead, through inter-cultural dialogue and a sharing of values, to a single, inclusive civilization. In the field of education, he has spearheaded the establishment of many charitable organizations to work for the welfare of the community, both within and without Turkey. He has inspired the use of mass media, notably television, to inform the public, of matters of pressing concern to them, individually and collectively.

Gülen believes the road to justice for all is dependent on the provision of an adequate and appropriate universal education. Only then will there be sufficient understanding and tolerance to secure respect for the rights of others. To this end, he has, over the years, encouraged the social elite and community leaders, powerful industrialists as well as small businessmen, to support quality education. With donations from these sources, educational trusts have been able to establish many schools in Turkey and other countries.

Gülen has stated that in the modern world the only way to get others to accept your ideas is by persuasion. He describes those who resort to force as being intellectually bankrupt; people will always demand freedom of choice in the way they run their affairs and in their expression of their spiritual and religious values. Democracy, Gülen argues, in spite of its many short-comings, is now the only viable political system, and people should strive to modernize and consolidate democratic institutions in order to build a society where individual rights and freedoms are respected and protected, where equal opportunity for all is more than a dream.

INTERFAITH AND INTERCULTURAL ACTIVITIES

Since his retirement, Gülen has concentrated his efforts on establishing a dialogue among the factions representing different ideologies, cultures, religions, and nations. In 1999, his paper "The Necessity of Interfaith Dialogue" was presented to the Parliament of World's Religions in Cape Town, December 1-8. He maintains that "dialogue is a must" and that people, regardless of nation or political borders, have far more in common than they realize.

Given all of this, Gülen considers it both worthwhile and necessary for a sincere dialogue to be established in order to increase mutual understanding. To this end, he has helped to establish the Journalists and Writers Foundation (1994), whose activities to promote dialogue and tolerance among all strata of the society have been warmly welcomed by people from almost all walks of life. Again to this end, Gülen visits and receives leading figures, not only from among the Turkish population, but from all over the world. Pope John Paul II at the Vatican, the late John O'Connor, Archbishop of New York, Leon Levy, former president of The Anti-Defamation League are among many leading representatives of world religions with whom Gülen has met to discuss dialogue and take initiatives in this respect. In Turkey, the Vatican's Ambassador to Turkey, the Patriarch of the Turkish Orthodox Church, the Patriarch of the Turkish Armenian community, the Chief Rabbi of the Turkish Jewish community and many other leading figures in Turkey have frequently met with him, portraying an example of how sincere dialogue can be established between people of faith.

In his meeting with Pope John Paul II at the Vatican (1998), Gülen presented a proposal to take firm steps to stop the conflict in the Middle East via collaborative work on this soil, a place where all three religions originated. In his proposal, he also underlined the fact that science and religion are in fact two different aspects that emanate from the same truth: "Humankind from time to time has denied religion in the name of science and denied science in the name of religion, arguing that the two present conflicting views. All knowledge belongs to God and religion is from God. How then can the two be in conflict? To this end, our joint efforts directed at inter-religious dialogue can do much to improve understanding and tolerance among people."

Gülen released a press declaration renouncing the September 11th terrorist attacks on the USA, which he regarded as a great blow to world peace that unfairly tarnished the credit of believers: ". . . terror can never be used in the name of Islam or for the sake of any Islamic ends. A terrorist cannot be a Muslim and a Muslim cannot be a terrorist. A Muslim can only be the representative and symbol of peace, welfare, and prosperity."

Gülen's efforts for worldwide peace have been echoed at conferences and symposiums. "The Peaceful Heroes Symposium" (April 11-13, 2003) at the University of Texas, Austin, produced a list of peacemakers over 5,000 years of human history. Gülen was mentioned among contemporary heroes of peace, in a list which includes names such as Jesus, Buddha, Mohandas Gandhi, Martin Luther King, Jr., and Mother Teresa.

The Muslim World, a journal devoted to the study of Islam and Christian-Muslim relations, published a special issue (Volume 95, Number 3, July 2005) entitled "Islam in Contemporary Turkey: the Contributions of Fethullah Gülen" with papers by scholars in the field.

Rice University, Houston, TX, hosted a first-time conference "Islam in the Contemporary World: The Fethullah Gülen Movement in Thought and Practice," November 12-13, 2005. Participants from different countries discussed the personage of

Gülen and his activities in addition to the dynamics of the movement, all from a variety of angles.

Gülen contributes to a number of journals and magazines. He writes the lead article for several magazines. A number of his publications have been translated into world languages.

The educational trusts inspired by Gülen have established countless non-profit voluntary organizations—foundations and associations—within and without Turkey supporting many scholarships.

Though a well-known public figure, Gülen has always shied away from involvement in formal politics. Gülen's admirers include leading journalists, academics, TV personalities, politicians, and Turkish and foreign state authorities. They see in him a true innovator and unique social reformer who practices what he preaches. They see him as a peace activist, an intellectual, a religious scholar, a mentor, author and poet, a great thinker and spiritual guide who has devoted his life to seeking the solutions for society's ills and spiritual needs. They see the movement he helped to nurture as a movement dedicated to education, but an education of the heart and soul as well as of the mind, aimed at reviving and invigorating the whole being to achieve competence and providing goods and services useful to others.

CHAPTER 1

The Existence and Unity of God

THE EXISTENCE AND UNITY OF GOD

The existence of God is too evident to need any arguments. Some saintly scholars have even stated that God is the most manifest being, but that those lacking insight cannot see Him. Others have said that His Self-manifestation's intensity conceals Him from direct perception.

However, the massive influence of positivism and materialism on science and on all people of recent centuries makes it necessary to discuss such arguments. As this now-prevalent "scientific" worldview reduces existence to what can be perceived directly, it blinds itself to the far vaster invisible dimensions of existence. To remove the resulting veil, we will review briefly several traditional demonstrations of God's necessary existence.

Before doing so, let us reflect on one simple historical fact: Since the beginning of human life, the overwhelming majority of humanity has believed that God exists. This belief alone is enough to establish God's existence. Unbelievers cannot claim to be smarter than believers. Some of the most innovative scientists, scholars, researchers have been—and are—believers, as are the field's experts: all Prophets and saints.

In addition, people usually confuse the non-acceptance of something's existence with the acceptance of its non-existence. While the former is only a negation or a rejection, the latter is a judgment that requires proof. No one has ever proven God's non-existence, for to do so is impossible, whereas countless arguments prove His existence. This point may be clarified through the following comparison.

Imagine a palace with 1,000 entrances, 999 of which are open and one of which appears to be closed. Given this, it would be unreasonable to claim that the palace is inaccessible. Unbelievers confine their (and others') attention only to the door that is seemingly closed.

The doors to God's existence are open to everybody, provided they sincerely intend to enter through them. Some of those doors—demonstrations for God's existence—are as follows:

TRADITIONAL ARGUMENTS FOR GOD'S EXISTENCE

- *Everything is contingent, for it is equally possible that they will exist or not exist.* Anything can exist any time and anywhere, in any form, and with any character. Nothing or no one has a role in determining the way, time, and place of its coming into existence, or its character and features. So, there must be a power that chooses between a thing's existence and non-existence, giving it unique characteristics. This power must be infinite, have absolute will and all-comprehensive knowledge. Necessarily, it is God.

- *Everything changes.* Therefore it is contained in time and space, meaning that it begins and ends. That which has a beginning needs one with no beginning to bring it into existence, for it cannot originate itself, as this would require an infinite regression of originators. As reason cannot accept such a situation, an originator who is infinitely self-existent, self-subsistent, and unchanging is needed. This original originator is God.

- *Life is a riddle* (scientists cannot explain it with material causes or discover its origin) *and transparent* (it displays a creative power). Given this, life declares: "God created me." (See Chapter I Endnote)

- *Everything that exists, and the universe as a whole, display a magnificent harmony and order in themselves and in their interrelationships.* The existence of one part necessitates the existence of the whole, and the whole requires the existence of all parts for its own existence. For example, a deformed cell may destroy an entire body. Similarly, a pomegranate requires the collaborative and cooperative existence of air, water, soil, and the sun, as well as their mutual and well-balanced cooperation for its existence. This harmony and cooperation point to a creator of order, who knows the relationships and characteristics of everything, and who can order everything. The creator of order is God.

- *All of creation exhibits an overwhelming artistry of dazzling worth.* Yet it is brought into being, as we see it, with great ease and speed. Furthermore, creation is divided into countless families, genera, species, and even smaller groups, each of which exists in great abundance. Despite this, we see nothing but order, art, and ease in creation. This shows the existence of one with an absolute power and knowledge, who is God.

- *Whatever has been created has a purpose.* Take the example of ecology. Everything, no matter how apparently insignificant, has a significant role and purpose. The chain of creation up to humanity, its last link, is clearly directed to a final purpose. A fruit-bearing tree's purpose is to yield fruit, and its whole life is directed toward that goal. Similarly, the "tree of creation" yields humanity as its final and most comprehensive fruit. Nothing is in vain; rather, every item, activity, and event has many purposes. This requires a wise one who pursues certain purposes in creation. Since only humanity can understand those purposes, the wisdom and purposiveness in creation necessarily point to God.

- *All living and non-living beings cannot meet almost any of their own needs on their own.* For example, the universe can operate and maintain itself only by such universal laws as growth and reproduction, gravitation and repulsion. But these so-called "natural laws" have no actual external, visible, or material existence; they are nominal. How can something nominal, completely devoid of knowledge and consciousness, be responsible for such a miraculous creation that requires absolute power and absolute knowledge, wisdom, choice, and preference? So, one who has all of these attributes has established these "natural laws" and uses them as veils to cover His operations for a certain purpose.

- Plants need air and water, as well as heat and light, to survive. Can they fulfill their own needs? Humanity's needs are infinite. Fortunately, all of our essential needs, from our beginning in the womb to death, are met by someone who is able to meet them and chooses to do so. When we enter this world, we find everything prepared to meet all the needs of our senses and intellectual and spiritual faculties. This clearly shows that one who is infinitely merciful and knowledgeable provides for all created beings in the most extraordinary way, and causes all things to collaborate to that end.

- *All things in the universe, regardless of distance, help each other.* This mutual helping is so comprehensive that, for example, almost all things, among them air and water, fire and soil, the sun and the sky, help us in an extraordinarily prearranged manner. Our bodily cells, members, and systems work together to keep us alive. Soil and air, water and heat, and bacteria cooperate with each other to benefit plants. Such activities, which display knowledge and conscious purpose, by unconscious beings show the existence of a miraculous arranger. That one is God.

- *Before humanity began to overpollute the air, water and soil, the natural world was cleansed and purified continually.* Even now, it still preserves its original purity in many regions, mostly where modern life has not yet taken hold. Have you ever wondered why nature is so clean? Why are forests so clean, even though many animals die in them every day? If all flies born during the summer survived, the Earth would be covered completely with layers of dead flies. Nothing is wasted in nature, for each death is the beginning of a new birth. For example, a dead body decomposes and is integrated into the soil. Elements die and are revived in plants; plants die in the stomachs of animals and people and are promoted to a higher rank of life. This cycle of death and revival is one factor that keeps the universe clean and pure. Bacteria and insects, wind and rain, black holes and oxygen in organic bodies all sustain the universe's purity. This purity points to the All-Holy One, Whose attributes include cleanliness and purity.

- *Innumerable human beings have lived since Adam and Eve were created.* Despite their common origin—a sperm and ovum, formed from the same foods consumed by parents—and their being composed of the same structures or elements or organisms, every person has a unique countenance. Science cannot explain this. It cannot be explained by DNA or chromosomes since this difference dates back to the first differentiation of individuals in the world. Moreover, this difference is not only in countenances; all human beings are unique in character, desire, ambition, and ability, and so on. While members of animal species are almost the same and display no difference in behavior, each human individual is like a different species that has his or her own world within the larger world of humanity. This obviously shows one with an absolutely free choice and all-encompassing knowledge: God.

- *We need about 15 years to direct our lives and to understand what is good and bad.* But many animals have such knowledge very soon after they are born. For example, ducklings can swim as soon as they hatch, and ants start digging nests in the ground when they leave their cocoons. Bees and spiders quickly learn how to make their honeycombs and webs, respectively, which are marvels of handiwork that we cannot reproduce. Who teaches young eels born in the waters of Europe to find their way to their ancestral home in the Pacific? The migration of birds remains a mystery? (See Chapter I Endnote) How can you explain such astounding facts other than by attributing them to the teaching or directing of one who knows everything, and has arranged the universe and its inhabitants in a way that every creature can direct its life?

- *Despite enormous scientific advances, we still cannot explain life.* Life is the gift of the Ever-Living One, Who "breathes" a spirit into each embryo. We know little about the spirit's nature and relation with the body, but our ignorance does not mean that the spirit does not exist. The spirit is sent to this world to be perfected and to acquire a state appropriate for the other life.

- *Our conscience is the center of our inclinations toward right and wrong.* Everybody feels this conscience occasionally, and most people are inclined to turn to God on certain occasions. For us, this inclination and belief in Him are intrinsic. Even if we consciously deny God, our unconscious belief in Him occasionally shows itself. The Qur'an mentions this in several verses:

> It is He Who enables you to travel on the land and the sea; and when you are in the ship, and the ships run with a favorable wind and they rejoice in it, there comes upon them a strong wind, and waves come on them from every side and they think that they are encompassed. Then they cry unto God, making their faith pure for Him only, (saying): "If you deliver us from this, we truly will be thankful." (10:22)

> Then [Abraham] broke them [the idols] into pieces, all except the large one, so that they might turn to Him. [When they returned and saw this] they said: "Who has done this to our gods? Surely it must be some evildoer." They said: "We have heard a youth talk of them; he is called Abraham." They said: "Then [at once] bring him before the eyes of the people, so that they may testify." [When Abraham was there] they said: "Is it you who has done this to our gods, O Abraham?" He said: "Nay, their chief has done it, so ask them, if they can speak." At once they turned to themselves and said: "You, you are the wrongdoers." Then they were utterly confounded, and said: "O Abraham! You know that these do not speak." Abraham said: "Do you then worship, besides God, those things that cannot profit in anything at all, nor harm you? Woe unto you, and all that you worship instead of God! Do you not use your intelligence?" They said: "Burn him (immediately) and protect your gods, if you are doing anything." (21:58-68)

So, the human spirit and conscience are a strong argument for the existence of One God.

- *Human beings are innately disposed to good and beauty, virtue and moral values, and are adverse to evil and ugliness.* Therefore, unless corrupted by external factors and conditions, we naturally seek universal good and moral values. These turn out to be the same virtues and morality promulgated by all Divine revealed religions. As history witnesses, humanity has always had some kind of religion. Just as no other system has superseded religion in human life, the Prophets and religious people always influenced us the most and have left indelible marks on us. This is another irrefutable proof for the existence of One God.

• *We feel many intuitions and emotions that are messages from immaterial realms.* Among them, the intuition of eternity arouses in us a desire for eternity, which we strive to realize in various ways. However, this desire can be realized only through belief in and worship of the Eternal One Who inspired it. True human happiness lies in satisfying this desire for eternity.

• *If a few liars come to us several times and tell us the same things, we may, in the absence of reliable information, believe them.* But when tens of thousands of Prophets who never lied, hundreds of thousands of saints, and millions of believers, all of whom have adopted truthfulness as a most essential pillar of belief, and then agree on God's existence, is it reasonable to reject their testimony and accept the individual reports of a few liars?

• *The proofs for the Qur'an's Divine origin are also proofs for God's existence.*[1] The Qur'an teaches with great emphasis and focus, as indeed do the Bible's Old and New Testaments, the existence of One God. In addition, tens of thousands of Prophets have been sent to guide humanity to truth. All were justly renowned for their truthfulness and other praiseworthy virtues, and all gave priority to preaching the existence and Oneness of God.

ARGUMENTS FOR DIVINE UNITY [2]

• *Everything that exists displays God's Unity.* For example, of the innumerable arguments for His existence and Unity, consider life: He makes everything out of one thing and makes one thing out of many things. He makes an animal's countless bodily members and systems out of a fertilizing sperm-bearing fluid and water. One who can do this must be an Absolutely All-Powerful One. One Who transforms with perfect orderliness all substances contained in innumerable types of vegetable or animal foods into particular bodies and bodily parts, weaving from them a unique skin for each, is surely an All-Powerful and Absolutely All-Knowing One.

- *Air displays His Unity.* As a marvelous conductor, air conducts innumerable sounds, voices, images, and many other things simultaneously, without confusion, and without one hindering the other. This shows that there is One, without partner, Who created, controls, and administers all things according to His Wisdom.

- *The universe resembles a tree that has grown from a seed containing a comprehensive program for its life cycle.* Everything is closely interrelated. For example, a particle in the eye's pupil has relationships with and duties toward the eye, as well as with the head; the powers of reproduction, attraction, and repulsion; veins and arteries; motor and sensory nerves that circulate the blood and operate the body; and with the rest of the body. This clearly shows that the whole body, including every particle, is the work of an Eternal, All-Powerful One, and operates under His command.

An air molecule may visit any flower or fruit and work within it. If this wandering molecule were not subjugated and obedient to the Absolutely All-Powerful One's command, it would have to know all the systems and structures of all flowers and fruits, and how they are formed, right down to their peripheral lines. Thus, this air molecule displays Divine Unity like a sun, as do its counterparts in light, soil, and water. And, as we know, science says that the building blocks of everything are hydrogen, oxygen, carbon, and nitrogen.

The seeds of all flowering and fruit-bearing plants are composed of hydrogen, oxygen, carbon, and nitrogen. They only differ due to the program deposited in them by Divine Destiny. If we put several kinds of seeds in a flowerpot filled with soil, which has its own particular elements, each plant will assume its unique wonderful form and shape. If their particles were not subjugated to and directed by One Who knows each thing's features, structures, life cycles, and conditions of its life, One Who endows everything with what is suitable and necessary for it; and to Whose Power everything is subjected without resistance, there would be quite a problem.

Put simply, without God's activity, each soil particle would have to contain "immaterial factories" determining all plants' future lives. It also would need to have as many workshops as there are flowering and fruit-bearing plants, so that each could bring each unique item into being. Or, each plant would have an all-encompassing knowledge and power so that it could create itself. Thus, in the absence of One God, there would have to be as many deities as there are soil particles. Such a belief is untenable.

Each particle contains two further true witnesses to the Maker's necessary existence and Unity. First, a particle can perform many significant activities although it is absolutely powerless. Second, by acting in conformity with the universal order, each particle displays a universal consciousness although it has no life. Each particle testifies through its own impotence to the necessary existence of the Absolutely All-Powerful One, and by acting in conformity with the universal order to His Unity.

• *Each person is a miniature universe, a fruit of the tree of creation or the universe, and a seed of this world, for each of us contains samples of most living species.* It is as if each person were a drop distilled from the universe, having the most subtle and sensitive balance. To create such a living being and to be its Lord requires having total control of the universe.

Given this, we understand that the following things represent stamps unique to the Creator of all things, the All-Majestic Lord of the universe: making a honeybee a small index of most things; inscribing most of the universe's features in humans; including the program for a fig tree's life cycle in a tiny fig seed; exhibiting the works of all Divine Names manifested throughout the universe in the human heart; and recording in our memory, located in a lentil-sized place, enough information to fill a library, as well as a detailed index of all events in the universe.

- *All life is a symphony of mutual helping.* Just like a living body's members and organs, systems and cells, all parts of the universe support and help each other. For example, air and water, soil and the sun, work together so that a single apple can come into existence. Like a factory's components or a palace's building blocks, creatures support and aid each other, and cooperate to meet each other's needs in perfect orderliness. Joining efforts, they serve living beings. Elements in the soil aid plants by helping them come into existence and survive. Most animals live on plants, and people live on plants and animals. Thus, elements form the basic foundation of a living being's physical constitution.

  By obeying this rule of mutual assistance, which is in force throughout the universe—from the sun and moon, night and day, winter and summer to plants helping needy and hungry animals, animals helping humanity, nutritious substances helping infants, and fruits and food particles helping the body's cells—they demonstrate that they are acting through the power of a single, Most Munificent Upbringer, and at the command of a single, Most Wise Administrator.

- *The universal providence and favor of this universal wisdom are clearly apparent in everything's purposeful creation.* This, along with providence's comprehensive mercy and the universal sustenance required by that mercy to provide all living beings with food, form a seal of Divine Unity so brilliant that anyone can see and understand it.

  All beings, especially those that are alive, must satisfy their demands and needs to remain alive. This is true whether the being in question is universal or particular, an individual or a species. But they cannot fulfill even their smallest need. Rather, all their requirements are met in an unexpected way and from an unexpected place, with perfect order and timing, in a suitable fashion, and with perfect wisdom. All of this shows the existence of an All-Wise Nurturer of Majesty, an All-Compassionate Provider of Grace.

- *Consider the sun.* From planets to drops of water, glass fragments, and sparkling snowflakes, a radiant effect particular to the sun is apparent. If you do not agree that the tiny suns seen in these innumerable things are only reflections, you must accept the existence of a sun in each drop of water, glass fragment, and transparent object facing the sunlight. Is this not absurd?

If such images or reflections are not attributed to the sun, you must accept the existence of innumerable suns in place of the one sun. Is this logical? Similarly, if everything is not attributed to One God, the Absolutely All-Powerful One, you must accept that there are as many deities as there are particles in the universe. How can you believe such a thing?

- *During spring and summer, God raises to life countless plant and animal species, each member of which is unique.* The process is so ordered that there is no confusion despite infinite intermingling. He "inscribes" on the Earth's face individual members of countless species without fault or forgetfulness, mistake or deficiency. Everything is done in a most well-balanced well-proportioned, well-ordered, and perfect fashion. This points to One of Majesty, an All-Powerful One of Perfection, an All-Wise One of Grace and Beauty, One Who has infinite Power, all-encompassing Knowledge, and Will to govern the universe.

Consider what happens during spring and summer. The amount of Divine activity during those seasons is absolutely miraculous in terms of extent, speed, and liberality, as well as in terms of generosity and order, beauty and creation. Only One with an infinite knowledge and boundless power could own such a "seal." That seal certainly belongs to One Who is everywhere although He is nowhere since He is not bound with time and space, all-present and all-seeing. Nothing is hidden or difficult for Him, and particles and stars are the same to His Power.

- *Seeds sown in a field show that both the field and the seeds belong to their owner.* Likewise, the fundamental elements of life (e.g., air, water, and soil) are universal and present everywhere despite their simplicity and same nature. Plants and animals are found everywhere, despite their essentially similar nature vis-à-vis the diverse conditions of life.

All of these are controlled by a single miracle-displaying Maker. Every flower, fruit, and animal is a stamp, a seal, or a signature of that Maker. Wherever they are found, each proclaims in the tongue of its being: "The One Whose stamp I bear made this location. The One Whose seal I carry owns this place. The One Whose signature I indicate wove this land." In other words, only the one who holds all elements in His Power can own and sustain the least of creatures. Anyone can see that only One Who exercises Lordship over all plants and animals can own, sustain, and govern the simplest of them.

Truly, in the tongue of similarity to other individuals, each individual being says: "Only one who owns my species can own me." In the tongue of spreading over the planet with other species, each species says: "Only one who owns the planet can own us." In the tongue of being bound to the sun and of its mutual relationships with the heavens, the Earth and the other planets say: "Only one who owns all these can own me." If apples were conscious and someone said to one of them: "You are my work of art," that apple would retort: "Be quiet! If you can form all apples, rather if you can dispose freely of all fruit-bearing trees on this planet and all gifts of the All-Merciful One coming from the treasury of Mercy in shiploads, only then can you claim to own me."

Since each fruit depends on one law of growth from one center, it is equally easy and cheap to produce one or many fruits. In other words, for multiple centers to produce one fruit would be as hard and expensive as equipping the tree, and to produce the equipment necessary for one soldier would require all the factories needed to supply an army. The point is clear: When a single result related to numerous individuals depends on multiple centers, there are as many difficulties as there are individuals involved. Thus, the extraordinary ease seen in all species arises from unity.

The correspondence and similarity in basic features and forms seen in all members of a species, and within all divisions of a genus proves that they are the work of a single Maker, for they are "inscribed" with the same Pen and bear the same seal. The absolute ease observed in their coming into existence necessarily and inevitably requires that they be the work of One Maker. Otherwise, it would be so hard to bring them into existence that genus and species in question would not exist.

To conclude: When attributed to Almighty God, all things become as easy as one thing; when attributed to causes, one thing becomes as difficult as all things. As a result, the extraordinary cheapness and ease observed in the universe, as well as the endless abundance, display the stamp of Unity. If these abundant and cheap fruits were not owned by the One of Unity, we could not purchase them even if we gave the whole world. How could we pay for the purposeful and conscious cooperation of soil and air, water and sunlight, the sun's heat and the seed, and many other things that make a pomegranate's existence possible? All of these factors are unconscious and controlled by a Single Maker, Who is Almighty God. The cost of a single pomegranate or any other fruit is the whole universe.

• *Life, which manifests Divine Grace, is an argument and proof for Divine Unity, as well as a sort of manifestation of It.* Death, which manifests Divine Majesty, is an argument and proof for Divine Oneness.

For example, bubbles on a river's surface show the sun's image, light, and reflection, as do all transparent objects. These facts testify to the sun's existence. Despite the bubbles' occasional disappearance (e.g., when they pass under a bridge), the splendid continuation of the sun's manifestations and its light's uninterrupted display on successive bubbles proves that the sun's images (which appear, disappear, and are then renewed) come from one enduring, perpetual sun manifesting itself from on high. Therefore, the appearance of these sparkling bubbles demonstrate the sun's existence, and their disappearance displays its continuation and unity.

In the same way, beings in continuous flux testify through their existence and life to the necessary existence and Oneness of the Necessarily Existent Being. They testify to His Unity, eternity, and permanence through their decay and death. Beautiful, delicate creatures that are renewed and recruited, along with the alternation of day and night, as well as seasons, and the passage of time show the existence, Unity, and permanence of an elevated, everlasting One with a continuous display of beauty. Their decay and death, together with the apparent causes for their lives, demonstrate that the (material or natural) causes are only veils. This decisively proves that these arts, inscriptions, and manifestations are the constantly renewed arts, changing inscriptions, and moving mirrors of an All-Beautiful One of Majesty.

- *Obviously, the perfect design and adornment of a perfect palace indicate a master builder's perfect acts.* This starts the following series of relationships: Perfect acts show the builder's perfect titles (which specify his or her rank), which shows the builder's perfect attributes (the origin of his or her art), which show master's perfect abilities and essential capacity, which show the perfection of the master's essential nature.

In the same way, the faultless works and art in all well-ordered beings point to the perfect acts of an Effective, Powerful Agent. This fact starts another chain: Such perfect acts point to that Majestic Agent's perfect Names, which point and testify to the perfect Attributes of the Majestic One known with the Names, which points and testifies to the perfection of the essential capacity and qualities of the Perfect One qualified by those attributes, which points to the perfection of the One having such capacity and qualities that all the types of perfection in the universe are signs of His Perfection, hints of His Majesty, and allusions to His Beauty. They are pale, weak shadows in comparison with His Perfect Reality.

FALSE ARGUMENTS ABOUT THE ORIGIN OF EXISTENCE

Mediaeval European conceptions about the universe's nature and existence were underpinned by the Catholic Church's authority. The Church, relying upon a Divine Revelation (the Bible) that had been altered over time, considered modern science a threat to its authority and so viewed it with great hostility. The resulting science–religion rift deepened steadily until the two became irreconcilable. Eventually, religion was relegated to a domain of blind belief and consolatory rituals considered alien to science. Thus, science no longer had to defer to the Divine Revelation's authority. The Darwinian account of evolution sealed and popularized the idea that existence was self-originated and self-sustained, a process that had unfolded by itself according to laws that would one day be understood fully (and therefore to some degree could be manipulated) by humanity.

Not all scientists maintain that natural causes or so-called laws of nature can explain all phenomena. Before discussing this issue, we should point out that all the Prophets, regardless of place or time, agree on how existence originated and is sustained and all other essential issues pertaining to life and existence. While a considerable number of scientists agree with the Prophets, scientists and philosophers who favor naturalism and materialism differ greatly in their explanations. Some attribute creativity and eternity, as well as life and consciousness, to matter. Others argue that nature is eternally self-existent and that everything can be explained by natural causes and laws. Still others, unable to explain the origin of life, fall back on such notions as chance and necessity.

The next section discusses the impossibility of explaining existence without affirming God's Existence and Unity.

Nature, Natural Laws, and Causes

- *Natural laws have nominal, not real, existence.* They are propositions tendered as explanations of particular events or phenomenon, and allude to imaginary forces inferred from the motions or relationships of events or phenomena. The laws of gravity, reproduction and growth in living organisms, magnetic attraction and repulsion, and others are not entities whose existence can be verified by our external senses or scientific instruments. For example, whatever truth the law of gravity may have, can we claim that the real universe (the one in which this law operates) has (or must) come about because of it? Is it reasonable to ascribe anything's existence, let alone intelligent and conscious living beings, to propositions?

- *Natural laws and causes are inferred from the motions or relationships of events or phenomena observed in the universe.* Therefore, as they depend upon external factors, they are neither self-dependent nor self-existent.

- *The existence of the universe, as well as all its events or phenomena, is contingent.* So nothing in it must exist, for it is equally possible for each thing to exist or not to exist. There is an almost limitless number of cells in an embryo that a food particle can visit. Anything whose existence is contingent cannot be eternal, for someone has to prefer its existence over its non-existence or merely potential existence.

- *As all contingent entities are contained in time and space, they have a beginning.* Anything that begins must certainly end, and so cannot be eternal.

- *Natural causes need each other to bring about an effect.* For example, an apple needs an apple blossom to exist, a blossom needs a branch, a branch needs a tree, and so on, just as a seed needs soil, air, and moisture to germinate and grow. Each cause is also an effect and, unless we accept as many deities as the number of causes, we must look to a single cause outside the chain of cause and effect.

- *For a single effect to come into existence, an infinite number of causes must collaborate in such a coordinated and reliable way that they become "natural laws."* Consider this: In order to exist, an apple requires the cooperation of air and soil, sunlight and water, the 23° inclination of the Earth's axis, and the complex rules of germination and growth for seeds and plants. Could so many deaf and blind, ignorant and unconscious causes and laws come together by themselves to form a living organism? Do you really think that they could form human beings, all of whom are alive and conscious, intelligent and responsible, and able to answer questions about their intentions and actions?

- *A tiny seed contains a huge tree.* A human being, the most complex creature, grows from an ovum fertilized by a microscopic sperm. Is there an appropriate relation or acceptable proportionality between cause and effect here? Can extremely weak and simple, ignorant and lifeless causes result in very powerful and complex, intelligent and vigorously living effects?

- *All natural phenomena and processes have opposites:* north and south, positive and negative, hot and cold, beautiful and ugly, day and night, attraction and repulsion, freezing and melting, vaporization and condensation, and so on. Something that has an opposite, that needs its opposite to exist and to be known, cannot be a creator or originator.

- *Although all causes necessary for an effect are present, that effect does not always come into existence.* Conversely, something happens or comes into existence without any causes that we can recognize or understand as such. Also, the same causes do not always engender the same effects. This is why some scientists reject causality as a way of explaining things and events.

- *Among causes, humanity is the most capable and eminent,* for we are distinguished with intellect, consciousness, willpower, and many other faculties and inner and outer senses and feelings. Yet we are so weak and helpless that even a microbe can cause us great pain. If even we have no part in our own coming into existence, and no control over our body's working, how can other causes have creativity?

- *Materialists take the conjunction of events for causality.* If two events coexist, they imagine that one causes the other. Seeking to deny the Creator they make claims like: "Water causes plants to grow." They never ask how water knows what to do, how it does it, and what qualities it has that enable plants to grow?

Does water possess the knowledge and power to grow plants? Does it know the laws or properties of plant formation? If we attribute a plant's growth to the laws of nature, do they know how to form plants? Some sort or amount of knowledge, will, and power are absolutely necessary to make the least thing. Therefore, should not an all-encompassing knowledge, and an absolute will and power be necessary to make this complex, amazing, and miraculous universe about which we still know so little?

Consider a flower. Where does its beauty come from, and who designed the relationship between it and our senses of smell and seeing and faculty of appreciation? Can a seed, soil or sunlight, all of which are unconscious, ignorant, and deaf, do such things? Do they have the knowledge, power, or will to make even a flower, let alone to make it beautiful? Can we, this planet's only conscious and knowledgeable beings, make a single flower? A flower can exist only if the whole universe exists first. To produce a flower, therefore, one must be able to produce the universe. In other words, its creator must have absolute power, knowledge, and will. All of these are attributes of God alone.

Matter and Chance

Our argument against natural laws and causes being somehow self-existent, self-sustaining, and even in some sense eternal, holds true for those views attributing creativity to chance and matter.

Whether defined according to the principles of classical physics or new physics, matter is obviously changeable and susceptible to external interventions. Thus it cannot be eternal or capable of origination. Also, as matter is deaf and blind, lifeless and ignorant, powerless and unconscious, how can it be the origin of life and knowledge, power and consciousness? Something cannot impart to others what it does not possess itself.

There is such abundant evidence of purposive arrangement, organization, and harmony in the universe that it is irrational to speak of chance or coincidence as its cause. For example, a human body contains trillions of cells, and a single cell contains about 1 million proteins. The possibility of a protein occurring by chance is infinitesimally small. Without One to prefer its existence and to create it; Who has an absolute and all-comprehensive knowledge to prearrange its relations with other proteins, the cell, and all bodily parts; and then to place it just where it must be, a single protein could not exist. Science will find its true path only when its practitioners admit that this One—God—is the Creator of all things.

The following simple scientific experiment helps us understand this significant argument:

> Overbeck and his co-workers at the Baylor College of Medicine in Houston were trying to practice some gene therapy techniques by seeing if they could convert albino mice into colored ones. The researcher injected a gene essential to the production of the pigment melanin into the single-cell embryo of an albino mouse. Later they bread that mouse's offspring, half of which carried the gene on one chromosome of a chromosome pair. Classic Mendelian genetics told them that roughly a quarter of the grandchildren should carry the gene on both chromosomes—should be "homozygous," in the language of genetics—and should therefore be colored.
>
> But the mice never got a chance to acquire color. "The first thing we noticed," says Overbeck, "was that we were losing about 25% of the grandchildren within a week after they were born." The explanation:
>
> The melanin-related gene that his group injected into the albino mouse embryo had inserted itself into a completely unrelated gene. An unfamiliar stretch of DNA in the middle of a gene wrecks that gene's ability to get its message read. So in the mice, it seems whatever protein the gene coded for went unproduced, whatever function the protein had went undone, and the stomach, heart, liver, and spleen all wound up in the wrong place. Somehow, too, the kidneys and pancreas were damaged, and that damage is apparently what killed the mice.
>
> Overbeck and his colleagues have already located the gene on a particular mouse chromosome and are now trying to pin down its structure. That will tell them something about the structure of the protein the gene encodes, how the protein works, and when and where it is produced as the gene gets "expressed," or turned on, "Is the gene expressed everywhere, or just on the left side of the embryo or just on the right side?" Overbeck wonders, "And when does it get expressed?"

These questions will take Overbeck far from the gene-trans-
fer experiment. "We think there are at least 100,000 genes," he
points out, "so the chances of this happening were literally one
in 100,000." [3]

It will take thousands of tests, and therefore thousands of
mice, for such an experiment to succeed. However, there is no trial and error in nature. Any tree seed placed in the soil germinates
and becomes a tree, unless something prevents it from doing so.
Likewise, an embryo in the womb grows into a living, conscious
being equipped with intellectual and spiritual faculties.

The human body is a miracle of symmetry and asymmetry.
Scientists know how it develops in the womb. What they cannot figure out is how the building-block particles reaching the
embryo distinguish between right and left, determine the specific organ's location, insert themselves in their proper places, and
understand the extremely complicated relations and requirements
among cells and organs. This process is so complicated that if a
single particle required by the right eye's pupil ended up in the
ear instead, the embryo could be damaged or even die.

In addition, all animate beings are made from the same elements coming from soil, air, and water. They also are similar to each
other with respect to their bodily members and organs. And yet they
are almost completely unique with respect to bodily features and vis-
age, character, desire, and ambition. This uniqueness is so reliable
that you can be identified positively just by your fingerprints.

How can we explain this? There are the two alternatives:
Either each particle possesses almost infinite knowledge, will, and
power; or One Who has such knowledge, will, and power creates
and administers each particle. However far back we go in an
attempt to ascribe this to cause and effect and heredity, these two
alternatives remain valid.

Even if the universe's existence is attributed to that which is
not God (e.g., evolution, causality, nature, matter, or coincidences
and necessity), we cannot deny one fact: Everything displays,
through its coming into existence and subsistence and death, both
an all-comprehensive knowledge as well as an absolute power and

determination. As we saw in Overbeck's experiment, one misplaced or misdirected gene may ruin or terminate life. The interconnectedness of everything, from galaxies to atoms, is a reality into which every new entity enters and wherein it must know its unique place and function.

Is there a better demonstration of the existence and free operation of an all-comprehensive knowledge, an absolute power and will, that particles of the same biochemical constituents should produce, through the subtlest adjustments in their mutual relationships, unique entities and organisms? Is it satisfactory to explain this as heredity or coincidence, seeing that all such explanations rest on the same all-encompassing knowledge, absolute power, and will?

We must not be misled by the apparent fact that everything happens according to a certain program, plan, or process of causes. Such things are veils spread over the flux of the universe, the ever-moving stream of events. Laws of nature may be inferred from this process of causes, but they have no real existence. Unless we attribute to nature (or to matter or coincidence and necessity) what we normally would attribute to its Creator, we must accept that it is, in essence and reality, a printing mechanism and not a printer, a design and not a designer, a passive recipient and not an agent, an order and not an orderer, a collection of nominal laws and not a power.[4]

To understand better why these cannot have any part in existence, let's analyze the purpose, harmony, and interrelatedness in creation by observing some plain facts. Morrison draws our attentions to some of these:

The bulk of the Earth is now reduced to very permanent dimensions and its mass has been determined. Its speed in its orbit around the sun is extremely constant. Its rotation on its axis is determined so accurately that a variation of a second in a century would upset astronomical calculations. Had the bulk of the Earth been greater or less, or had its speed been different, it would have been farther from or nearer to the sun, and this different condition would have profoundly affected life of all kinds, including man.

The earth rotates on its axis in twenty-four hours or at the rate of about one thousand miles an hour. Suppose it turned at the rate of a hundred miles an hour. Why not? Our days and nights would then be ten times as long as now. The hot sun of summer would then burn up our vegetation each long day and every sprout would freeze in such a night. The sun, the source of all life, has a surface temperature of 12,000 degrees Fahrenheit, and our Earth is just far enough away so that this "eternal fire" warms us just enough and not too much. If the temperature on Earth had changed so much as fifty degrees on the average for a single year, all vegetation would be dead and man with it, roasted or frozen. The Earth travels around the sun at the rate of eighteen miles each second. If the rate of revolution had been, say, six miles or forty miles each second, we would be too far from or too close to the sun for our form of life to exist.

The Earth is tilted at an angle of 23°. This gives us our seasons. If it had not been tilted, the poles would be in eternal twilight. The water vapor from the ocean would move north and south, piling up continents of ice and leaving possibly a desert between the equator and the ice.

The moon is 240,000 miles away, and the tides twice a day are usually a gentle reminder of its presence. Tides of the ocean run as high as fifty feet in some places, and even the crust of the Earth is twice a day bent outward several inches by the moon's attraction. If our moon was, say, fifty thousand miles away instead of its present respectable distance, our tides would be so enormous that twice a day all the lowland of all the continents would be submerged by a rush of water so enormous that even the mountains would soon be eroded away, and probably no continent could have risen from the depths fast enough to exist today. The Earth would crack with the turmoil and the tides in the air would create daily hurricanes.

Had the crust of the Earth been ten feet thicker, there would be no oxygen, without which animal life is impossible; and had the ocean been a few feet deeper, carbon dioxide and oxygen would have been absorbed and vegetable life on the surface of the land could not exist. If the atmosphere had been much thinner, some of the meteors which are now burned in the outer atmosphere by the millions every day would strike all parts of the Earth.

Oxygen is commonly placed at 21 per cent [in the atmosphere]. The atmosphere as a whole presses upon the Earth at approximately fifteen pounds on each square inch of surface at sea level. The oxygen which exists in the atmosphere is a part of this pressure, being about three pounds per square inch. All the rest of the oxygen is locked up in the form of compounds in the crust of the Earth and makes up 8/10 of all the waters in the world. Oxygen is the breath of life for all land animals and is for this purpose utterly unobtainable except from the atmosphere.

The question arises how this extremely active chemical element escaped combination and was left in the atmosphere in the almost exact proportion necessary for practically all living things. If, for instance, instead of 21 per cent oxygen were 50 per cent or more of the atmosphere, all combustible substances in the world would become inflammable to such an extent that the first stroke of lightning to hit a tree would ignite the forest, which would almost explode... If free oxygen, this one part in many millions of the Earth's substance, should be absorbed, all animal life would cease.

When a man breathes, he draws in oxygen, which is taken up by the blood and distributed through his body. This oxygen burns the food in every cell very slowly at a comparatively low temperature, but the result is carbon dioxide and water vapor, so when a man is said to sigh like a furnace, there is a touch of reality about it. The carbon dioxide escapes into his lungs and is not breathable except in small quantities. It sets his lungs in action and he takes his next breath throwing into the atmosphere carbon dioxide. All animal life is thus absorbing oxygen and throwing off carbon dioxide. Oxygen is further essential to life because of its action upon other elements in the blood as well as elsewhere in the body, without which life processes would cease.

On the other hand, as is well known, all plant life is dependent upon the almost infinitesimal quantity of carbon dioxide in the atmosphere which, so to speak, it breathes. To express this complicated photosynthetic chemical reaction in the simplest possible way, the leaves of the trees are lungs and they have the power when in the sunlight to separate this obstinate carbon dioxide into carbon and oxygen. In other words, the oxygen is given off and the carbon retained and combined with the hydrogen of the water brought up by the plant from its roots. By magical chemistry, out of these elements "nature" makes sugar, cellulose and numerous other chemicals, fruits and flowers [all in different smell, taste, color and shape according to the kind of plant or tree. Can this infinite difference or variation be attributed to tiny seeds that are blind, ignorant and unconscious?] The plant feeds itself and produces enough more to feed every animal on Earth. At the same time, the plant releases the oxygen we breathe without which life would end in five minutes. So all the plants, the forests, the grasses, every bit of moss, and all else of vegetable life, build their structure principally out of carbon and water. Animals give off carbon dioxide and plants give off oxygen. If this interchange did not take place, either the animal or vegetable life would ultimately use up practically all of the oxygen or all of the carbon dioxide, and the balance being completely upset, one would wilt or die and the other would quickly follow.

Hydrogen must be included although we do not breathe it. Without hydrogen water would not exist, and the water content of animal and vegetable matter is surprisingly great and absolutely essential. Oxygen, hydrogen, carbon dioxide, and carbon, singly and in their various relations to each other are the principal biological elements. They are the very basis on which life rests.

We pour an infinite variety of substances into this chemical laboratory—the digestive system, which is the greatest laboratory of the world—with almost total disregard of what we take in, depending on what we consider the automatic process to keep us alive. When these foods have been broken down and are again prepared, they are delivered constantly to each of our billions of cells, a greater number than all the human beings on Earth. The delivery to each individual cell must be constant, and only those substances which the particular cell needs to transform them into bones, nails, flesh, hair, eyes, and teeth are taken up by the proper cell. Here is a chemical laboratory producing more substances than any laboratory which human ingenuity has devised. Here is a delivery system greater than any method of transportation or distribution the world has ever known, all being conducted in perfect order. From childhood until, say, a man is fifty years of age, this laboratory makes no serious mistakes, though the very substances with which it deals could literally form over a million different kinds of molecules—many of them deadly. When the channels of distribution become somewhat sluggish from long use we find weakened ability and ultimate old age.

When the proper food is absorbed by each cell, it is still only the proper food. The process in each cell now becomes a form of combustion, which accounts for the heat of the whole body. You cannot have combustion without ignition. Fire must be lighted, and so [you are provided with] a little chemical combination which ignites a controlled fire for the oxygen, hydrogen, and the carbon in the food in each cell, thus producing the necessary warmth and, as from any fire, the result is water vapor and carbon dioxide. The carbon dioxide is carried away by the blood to the lungs, and there it is the one thing that makes you draw in your breath of life. A person produces about two pounds of carbon dioxide in a day, but by wonderful processes gets rid of it. Every animal digests food, and each must have the special chemicals it individually needs. Even in minute detail, the chemical constituents of the blood, for instance, differ in each species. There is, therefore, a special formative process for each.

In case of infection by hostile germs, the system also continuously maintains a standing army to meet, and usually overcome invaders and save the entire structure of the man from premature death. No such combination of marvels does or can take place under any circumstances in the absence of life. And all this is done in perfect order, and order is absolutely contrary to chance.[5]

Does all this require and point to One Who knows us thoroughly—all our needs, environment, and bodily mechanisms—One Who is All-Knowing and does as He wishes? In Morrison's words: "Purpose seems fundamental in all things, from the laws that govern the universe to the combinations of atoms which sustain our lives. Atoms and molecules in living creatures do marvelous things and build wonderful mechanisms, but such machines are useless unless intelligence sets them in objective motion. There is the directive Intelligence which science does not explain, nor does science dare say it is material."[6]

Why God Created Natural Laws and Causes

In the next world, the realm of Power, God will execute His Will directly. As there will be no "causes," everything will happen instantaneously. But here, in the realm of Wisdom, the Divine Name the All-Wise requires the Divine Power to operate behind the veil of causes and laws for several reasons, among them the following.

- Opposites are mingled in this world: truth with falsehood, light with darkness, good with evil, and so on. Since our human nature inclines toward both good and evil, we are tested to see whether or not we will use our free will and other faculties in the way of truth and good. Divine Wisdom requires that causes and laws should conceal the operations of Divine Power. If God had willed, He could train the planets with His "hands" in a way that we could see, or He could have them administered by visible angels. If this were the case, we would not need to speak of the laws or causes involved. To communicate His Commandments, He could speak to each individual directly, without sending Prophets. To make us believe in His existence and Oneness, He could write His Name with stars in the sky. But then our earthly existence would not be an arena of trial. As a result of this trial, since the time of Adam and Eve good and evil flow through this world into the next to fill its two mighty pools of Paradise and Hell.

- Like a mirror's two sides, existence has two aspects or dimensions: one visible and material, the realm of opposites and (in most cases) imperfections; and a spiritual realm that is transparent, pure, and perfect. There can be—and actually are— events and phenomena in the material dimension that we do not like. Those who cannot perceive the Divine Wisdom behind all things may criticize the Almighty for such events and phenomena. To prevent that, God made natural laws and causes veil His acts. For example, in order that we should not criticize either God or His Angel of Death for our own or others' deaths, God placed disease and natural disasters (among other agents or causes) between Himself and death.

Due to this world's essential imperfection, we experience many deficiencies and shortcomings. In absolute terms, every event and phenomenon is good and beautiful in itself and in its consequences. Whatever God does or decrees is good, beautiful, and just. Injustice, ugliness, and evil are only apparent or superficial, and arise from human error and abuse. For example, a court may rule against us unjustly, but we should know that Destiny permitted it because of a concealed crime belonging to us. Whatever befalls us usually is due to self-wronging or an evil we have done. However, those who cannot understand the Divine Wisdom behind events and phenomena may impute the resulting apparent ugliness or evil, imperfection and shortcoming, directly to God, although He has no defect or imperfection.

To prevent such a mistake, His Glory and Grandeur require that natural causes and laws conceal His acts, while belief in His Unity demands that those causes and laws not be ascribed to any creative power.

- If God Almighty acted here directly, we could not have developed science, known happiness, or be free of fear and anxiety. Thanks to God's acting behind natural causes and laws, we can observe and study patterns in phenomena. Otherwise, each event would be a miracle. The regular flux and mutability of events and phenomena makes them comprehensible to us, and so awakens our desire to wonder and reflect, which is a principal factor in science. For the same reason, to some degree we can plan and arrange our affairs. What would our lives be like if we were not sure that the sun would rise tomorrow?

- Whoever has such attributes as beauty and perfection desires to know them and make them known. God owns absolute beauty and perfection and, being independent of all things, needs nothing. He also owns a holy and transcendent love, and has a sacred desire to manifest His Beauty and Perfection. If He manifested His Names and Attributes directly, we could not endure them. He therefore manifests them behind causes and laws, and by degrees within the confines of time and space, so that we can build a connection with them, and reflect on and perceive them. The gradual manifestation of Divine Names and Attributes is also a reason for our curiosity and wonder about them.

These four points constitute only some of the reasons why God acts through natural laws and causes.

ENDNOTE: God, the All-Knowing, All-Determining, and All-Powerful

In his book *Man Does Not Stand Alone* A.C. Morrison draws our attention to the many beauties and complicated phenomena in the nature:

Life is a sculptor and shapes all living things; an artist that designs every leaf of every tree, that colors the flowers, the apple, the forest, and the plumage of the bird of paradise. Life is a musician and has taught each bird to sing its love songs, the insects to call each other in the music of their multitudinous sounds.

Life has given to man alone mastery over combined sound vibrations and has furnished the material for their production.

Life is an engineer, for it has designed the legs of the grasshopper and the flea, the coordinated muscles, levers and joints, the tireless beating heart, the system of electric nerves of every animal, and the complete system of circulation of every living thing.

Life is a chemist that gives taste to our fruits and spices and perfume to the rose. Life synthesizes new substances which Nature has not yet provided to balance its processes and to destroy invading life... Life's chemistry is sublime, for not only does it set the rays of the sun to work to change water and carbonic acid into wood and sugar, but, in doing so, releases oxygen that animals may have the breath of life.

Life is a historian, for it has written its history page by page, through the ages, leaving its record in the rocks, an autobiography which only awaits correct interpretation.

Life protects its creations by the abundance of food in the egg and prepares many of its infants for active life after birth, or by conscious motherhood stores food in preparation for her young. Life produces life-giving milk to meet immediate needs, foreseeing this necessity and preparing for events to come.

Matter has never done more than its laws decree. The atoms and molecules obey the dictates of chemical affinity, the force of gravity, the influences of temperature and electric impulses. Matter has no initiative, but life brings into being marvelous new designs and structures.

What life is no man has yet fathomed; it has no weight or dimensions... Nature did not create life; fire-blistered rocks and a saltless sea did not meet the necessary requirements. Gravity is a property of matter; electricity we now believe to be matter itself; the rays of the sun and stars can be deflected by gravity and seem to be akin to it. Man is learning the dimensions of the atom and is measuring its locked-up power, but life is illusive, like space. Why?

Life is fundamental and is the only means by which matter can attain understanding. Life is the only source of consciousness and it alone makes possible knowledge of the works of God which we, still half blind, yet know to be good. [A. C. Morrison, *Man Does Not Stand Alone* (New York: 1945), 31-6.]

Morrison writes further:

The robin that nested at your door goes south in the fall, but comes back to his old nest the next spring. In September, flocks of most of our birds fly south, often over a thousand miles of open ocean, but they do not lose their way. The homing pigeon confused by new sounds on a long journey in a closed box, circles for a moment and then heads almost unerringly for home. The bee finds its hive while the wind waving the grasses and trees blot out every visible guide to its whereabouts. This homing sense is slightly developed in man, but he supplements his meager equipment with instruments of navigation. The tiny insects must have microscopic eyes, how perfect we do not know, and the hawks, the eagle and the condor must have telescopic vision. Here again man surpasses them with his mechanical instruments.

If you let old Dobbin alone he will keep to the road in the blackest night. The owl can see the nice warm mouse as he runs in the cooler grass in the blackest night.

The ordinary scallop whose muscle we eat has several dozen beautiful eyes very like ours, which sparkle because each eye has unnumbered little reflectors which are said to enable it to see things right side up. These reflectors are not found in the human eye. Were these reflectors developed because of the absence of superior brain power in the scallop? As the number of eyes in animals ranges from two to thousands, and all are different, Nature would have had a big job in developing the science of optics unless [God, the All-Knowing, All-Determining, and All-Powerful had predestined and predetermined everything].

The honeybee is not attracted by the gaudy flowers as we see them, but sees by the ultra-violet light, which may make them even more beautiful to bees. From the rays of slower vibrations to the photographic plate and beyond are realms of beauty, joy and inspiration. The honeybee workers make chambers of different sizes in the comb used for breeding. Small chambers are constructed for the workers, larger ones for the drones, and special chambers for the prospective queens. The queen bee lays unfertilized eggs in the cells designed for males, but lays fertilized eggs in the proper chambers for the male workers and the possible queens. The workers, who are the modified females, having long since anticipated the coming of the new generation, are also prepared to furnish food for the young bees by chewing and predigesting honey and pollen. They discontinue the process of chewing, including the predigesting, at a certain stage of development of the males and females, and feed only honey and pollen. The females so treated become the workers.

The dog with an inquiring nose can sense the animal that has passed. No instrument of human invention has added to our inferior sense of smell, and we hardly know where to begin to investigate its extension.

All animals hear sounds, many of which are outside our range of vibration, with an acuteness that far surpasses our limited sense of hearing.

The young salmon spends years at sea, then comes back to its own river, and, what is more, it travels up the side of the river into which flows the tributary in which it was born. If a salmon going up a river is transferred to another tributary it will fight its way down to the main stream and then turn up against the current to finish its destiny. There is, however, a much more difficult problem in the exact reverse to solve in the case of the eel. These amazing creatures migrate at maturity from all the ponds and rivers everywhere—those from Europe across thousands of miles of ocean—all go to the abysmal deeps south of Bermuda. There they breed and die. The little ones, with no apparent means of knowing anything except that they are in a wilderness of water, start back and find their way to the shore from which their parents came and thence to every river, lake and little pond, so that each body of water is always populated with eels.

Animals seem to have telepathy. Who has not watched with admiration the sandpiper flying and wheeling till every white breast shows in the sunlight at the same instant? A female moth placed in your attic by the open window will send out some subtle signal. Over an unbelievable area, the male moths of the same species will watch the message and respond in spite of your attempts to produce laboratory odors to disconcert them.

Vegetation makes subtle use of involuntary agents to carry on its existence—insects to carry pollen from flower to flower and the winds and everything that flies or walks to distribute seed. At last, vegetation has trapped masterful man. He has improved nature and she generously rewards him. But he has multiplied so prodigiously that he is now chained to the plow. He must sow, reap, and store; breed and cross-breed; prune and graft. Should he neglect these chores starvation would be his lot, civilization would crumble, and Earth return to her pristine state. [A.C. Morrison, *Man Does Not Stand Alone* (New York: 1945), 49-57]

Are all these habits or distinctive "instinctive" acts, which must have their origin deep at the beginning of life on Earth, the result of chance or of an intelligent provision? Should we reflect on why certain animals are more developed than human beings in having certain faculties? Among all living creatures that have roamed the Earth none has a record of reasoning power which may compare with that of humanity. What we call nature is utterly blind and senseless, unconscious and ignorant. Men and women, who are the only intelligent beings on Earth, can do nothing other than to try to explain all these miraculous phenomena; they cannot even control their own bodies. Does all this not display a supreme determination, all-encompassing knowledge, and an absolute power and thereby One Who has these?

CHAPTER 2

The Invisible Realm of Existence

THE INVISIBLE REALM OF EXISTENCE

S ince our sensory powers are limited, it is not wise to deny the existence of realms beyond our senses. Also, what we know about existence is far less than what we do not know about existence. Our sciences are still in their "childhood," and the future will witness dazzling scientific discoveries and developments.

Sciences are supported by theories and develop through trial-and-error investigation of those theories. Numerous "facts" that were once considered true are now known to be incorrect. We accept unquestionably, and with no scientific basis, the existence of many things. Since the beginning of time, most people have believed in the existence of spirits and angels, jinn and Satan. So, it seems more scientific to allow their existence in theory and then investigate it. Denying their existence is unscientific, insofar as such a judgment or conclusion must be based on concrete proof. But no one can prove and therefore scientifically claim that invisible realms do not exist.

Many physical qualities (e.g., heat and cold) and abstract qualities (e.g., beauty and charm, and feelings of joy, sorrow, and love) can be experienced directly and measured to some degree. Materialists attribute these to biochemical processes in the brain, and some scientists (like psychologists and psychiatrists) still try to explain them by natural or physical laws. However, our non-physical side (namely, each person's feelings, beliefs, potentialities, desires, and so on) is too profound to be explained by physics, chemistry, or biology. Believers can (and do) observe that the stronger their belief, the deeper and more regular their worship; and the higher their morality, the more radiant and lovable their faces appear to be. Can such things be explained in merely physical terms?

ARGUMENTS FOR THE EXISTENCE OF INVISIBLE BEINGS

Let's consider some positive arguments for the existence of spirit beings.

- *Matter serves life, not the other way around.* Science cannot explain life or how organic matter acquires life. Although matter appears to be the basis for or serves as a receiver of life, it is clearly not its originator. So, life is sent from the immaterial dimensions of existence. God infuses it into matter or inorganic substances via something immaterial and invisible. We call this spirit. The particular features of each spirit makes each individual unique although they are formed of the same physical elements.

- *Life does not depend on matter.* On the contrary, life makes a tiny body greater than a huge one. For example, life makes a fly or a bird greater than a mountain. Life enables a honeybee to claim the Earth as its garden, establish relations with all flowers, and enter into transactions with them. Again, the more refined matter is, the more developed and active life becomes. Life's development and activity has nothing to do with physical size. A fly or a flea is more active and has sharper senses than a camel or rhinoceros.

- *This world is the arena in which God manifests His Will through natural causes.* Life is the result of the direct manifestation of His Name the Ever-Living. Thus, as long as science insists on its positivistic, even materialistic, viewpoint, it will never penetrate the mystery of life. (See Chapter II Endnote)

- *Angels are pure spiritual beings that represent the purely good aspect in existence, while Satan and his minions represent the purely evil aspect.* God is One and Infinite, without opposite. All other beings and existents have an opposite. Therefore, angels represent our good aspect while Satan represents our evil aspect. Angels invite us to our purely spiritual or "angelic" aspect, while Satan tempts toward evil. The resulting struggle, both in us and in the universe as a whole, has been ongoing since the beginning of existence. Everyone feels a stimulus toward good and evil at the same time. The former comes from the angels or our unpolluted spirit; the latter comes from Satan collaborating with our carnal self, which represents our animal aspect.

- *This spirit–body relation is similar to the relation between electrical power and a factory run by electricity.* If there is no electricity, the factory is reduced to heap of junk. Likewise, when the spirit leaves the body because of some rupture or disconnection (e.g., illness or death), we become no more than a mass of tissue and bone that decomposes in soil. This shows that our real existence and uniqueness depend on this spirit.

- *We accept the existence of natural laws and forces unquestionably, and even go so far as to attribute all phenomena to them.* We ascribe a tiny seed's growth into a huge, elaborate tree to the law of germination and growth in that seed, and the universe's incredible balance to the laws of gravitation and repulsion. But we ignore the absolute will, knowledge, power, and wisdom necessary for the universe's very existence, operation, and balance. The One Who has absolute Will, Knowledge, Power, and absolute Wisdom uses such powerful invisible beings (angels) as winds or gales, and others much more powerful than natural forces or laws, behind natural forces and laws to make them operative.

- *In addition to religious scholars, almost all Muslim philosophers and even all Oriental philosophers agree that angels and spirit beings exist.* They just have different names for them. The Peripatetic (*Mashshaiyyun*) school of philosophy, although quite inclined toward rationalism and even materialism, admitted the existence of angels on the grounds that each species has a spiritual, incorporeal essence. The Illuminists (*Ishraqiyyun*) also accepted the existence of angels, calling them (wrongly) the "Ten Intellects and Masters of Species." On the other hand, followers of all Divine religions, guided by Divine Revelation, believe that there is an angel in charge of each type of existence, and name them accordingly: the Angel of the mountains, the Angel of the seas, the Angel of rain, and so on. Even naturalists and materialists, who restrict themselves to what they see, admit the existence of angels, which they call pervasive forces.[1]

- *All Prophets, numbering 124,000 in reliable religious sources, report the existence of angels, spirit beings, jinn, and Satan.* All saints and religious scholars agree on this invisible realm's existence. We hardly need to say that two experts of a field are preferable to thousands of non-specialists. In addition, it is an established fact that once a matter is confirmed by two people, its denial by thousands of others has no weight. Furthermore, all people of religion and followers of almost all religions accept the existence of such beings.

  All Divine Scriptures record the existence of spirit beings and the human spirit, as well as the story of Satan and how he tempts us. Above all, can one doubt the report of the Qur'an and the testimony and experiences of Prophet Muhammad?[2] The proofs of the Qur'an's Divine authorship, the mission of Prophethood, and the Prophethood of Muhammad and all other Prophets also prove the invisible realm's existence and thus the existence of spirit, angels, jinn, and Satan.

  The best and most rational way of establishing the existence of such beings is expounded by Islam, described by the Qur'an, and was seen by the Prophet during his Ascension through the heavens. The Qur'an explains the meaning of angelic existence so reasonably that anyone can understand it. In brief, it says that humanity is a community responsible for carrying out the Divine Commandments issuing from the Divine Attribute of Speech, and that angels are a community whose "working class" carry out the Divine Laws of nature issuing from the Attribute of Will. They are God's honored servants who do whatever He commands. The existence of angels and other spirit beings can be established by proving the existence of one angel. As denying one amounts to denying the entire species, accepting one requires accepting the entire species.

- *A consensus has formed, especially among followers of religions, that there have always been people who can see and converse with angels, jinn, Satan, and other spirit beings.* Had angels not existed, had one angel never been seen or their existence established through observation, how could such a widespread belief continue? If this belief were not based on strong evidence, could it have come down to us despite changing ideas and beliefs and the passage of time? Therefore, we can conclude that religious belief in the existence of such beings is based on the experiences of the Prophets and saints. Such accounts have been narrated by reliable sources.

THE SPIRIT AND ITS IDENTITY

The Spirit is from the World of Divine Commands

There are many other worlds than those we commonly think of, such as those of plants, animals, human beings, and of the world of jinn. Our visible, material world addresses itself to our senses. From tiny particles to galaxies, this world is the realm where God Almighty gives life, fashions, renews, changes, and causes things to die. Science concerns itself with these phenomena.

Above this visible, material world is the immaterial world of Divine Laws or Commands. To learn something about this world, consider how a book, a tree, or a human being comes into existence. The main part of a book's existence is its meaning. Regardless of how excellent the printing machine is or how much paper we have, a book cannot exist without meaning. In the case of a tree, the essence of life and the law of germination and growth (with which it is endowed) stimulates its seed to germinate underground and grow into a tree. We can observe the entire growth process with our own eyes. If this invisible essence and these unobservable laws did not exist, there would be no plants.

Similarly, menstruation prepares a womb every month for insemination. This process is dictated by a (biological) law. Out of the millions of sperms heading for the womb, only one reaches and fertilizes the ovum. After this, another (biological) law takes over: menstruation stops until birth. An embryo's multistage development into a new individual is the third process governed by other (biological or embryological) laws. This process is mentioned in the Qur'an quite explicitly:

> We created man from a quintessence of clay. We then placed
> him as a drop in a place of rest firmly fixed. Then We made the
> drop into a leech-like structure suspended on the wall of the
> womb, and then of that leech-like structure We made a chewed-
> like substance. Then We made out of that chewed-like sub-
> stance bones (skeletal system). Then We clothed the bones with
> flesh (muscles). Then We developed out of it another creation.
> So blessed be God the best to create. (23:12-15)

The Qur'an says that this process takes place within three
veils of darkness: *He created you in the wombs of your mothers, in
stages, one after another, in three veils of darkness* (39:6). These three
veils of darkness are the belly, the womb, and the caul or mem-
brane; the constituents of the fetal membranes; or the decidua's
three regions: *decidua basalis, decidua capsularis,* and the *decidua
parietalis.* Or rather, the verse includes all of these meanings.

We derive the existence of such laws from the almost never-
changing repetition of these processes. Likewise, by observing
the (natural) phenomena around us, we derive the existence of
many other laws, such as gravitation and repulsion, and the freezing and vaporization of water.

Like these laws, the spirit is also a law issuing from the world of
Divine Laws or Commands. This is stated in the Qur'an: *Say: "The
spirit is of my Lord's Command"* (17:85). But it is unique in one
way: It is a living, conscious law. If the spirit were stripped of life
and consciousness, it would be "regular" law; if "regular" laws
were given life and consciousness, each one would become a spirit.

Science cannot define or perceive the spirit. While matter or
anything in the material world is composed of atoms, and atoms
are made up of more minute particles, the spirit is a simple, non-
compound entity. We cannot see it, but we can know it through
its manifestations in this world. Although we accept its existence and observe its manifestations, we cannot know its nature.
Such ignorance, however, does not mean that it does not exist.

We see with our eyes, as they are our instruments of sight.
The main center of sight is located in the brain. But the brain
does not see. You do not say: "My brain sees"; rather, you say:
"I see." It is the individual who sees or hears or senses. But what

is this "I"? Is it something composed of a brain, a heart, and other organs and limbs? Why can we not move when we die, although all our organs and limbs are there? Does a factory operate by itself, or does something else (i.e., electrical energy) cause it to work? Any defect or error in a factory that causes a disconnect between it and its electrical energy can reduce a once highly productive and invaluable factory to a heap of junk. Is such a relation at all comparable to that between the spirit and the body?

When the body's connection with the spirit is cut by death, the body is reduced to something that must be disposed of quickly before it begins to rot and decompose.

The spirit is not an electrical power, but rather a conscious, powerful thing that learns, thinks, senses, and reasons. It develops continually, usually in parallel with the body's physical development, as well as mentally and spiritually through learning and reflection, belief, and worship. The spirit determines each individual's character, nature, or identity. As a result, although all human begins are substantially made of the same elements, each individual is unique.

The Spirit Commands Our Inner Faculties

According to the Qur'an, God has given a particular nature to each creature: *All that is in the heavens and Earth submits to Him, willingly or unwillingly, and they will be returned to Him* (3:83); and *Glorify the Name of your Lord, the Most High, Who has created (all things) and well proportioned (them); Who has assigned for each a particular form and a particular way to follow and ordained their destinies, and guided (them)* (87:1-3).

Whatever exists in the universe, including the human body, acts according to the primordial nature God Almighty assigned to it. This is why we observe a strict determinism in how the universe operates. What we call natural laws are no more than names we give to a thing's or a creature's God-given primordial nature.

The primordial nature of things does not deceive. For example, since God orders the Earth to revolve around its own axis as well as the sun, it always does so. A seed says in the tongue of its being or primordial nature: "I will germinate underground in proper conditions and grow into a plant," and it does what it says. Water declares that it freezes at 0°C and vaporizes at 100°C, and does what it declares.

Similarly, the human conscience, as long as it remains sound, does not lie. If it is not deluded by the carnal self or harmful desires, it deeply feels the existence of God and finds peace through believing in and worshipping Him. Thus, the spirit directs or commands our conscience and other faculties. It seeks the world from which it came, and yearns for its Creator. Unless it is stunted and spoiled by sin, it will find the Creator and attain true happiness in Him.

The Spirit Has Deep Relations With the Past and the Future

Animals have no conception of time, for their God-given primordial nature causes them to live only for the present, without feeling any pain for the past or anxiety for the future. On the other hand, we are deeply influenced by such pain and anxiety, for our spirit is a conscious, sentient entity. The spirit is never satisfied with this mortal, fleeting world, and our accomplishments or possessions (e.g., money, status, satisfied desires) cannot make it content. Rather, especially when considered for their own sakes or for that of the carnal self alone, such things only increase its dissatisfaction and unhappiness, for the spirit finds rest only through belief, worship, and remembrance of God.

Every person feels a strong desire for eternity. This desire cannot come from the physical dimension of our existence, for our mortality precludes any feeling of and desire for eternity. This desire of eternity originates in the eternal dimension of our existence, which is inhabited by our spirit. Our spirit causes us to lament: "I am mortal but do not desire what is mortal. I am impotent but do not desire what is impotent. What I desire is an eternal beloved (who will never desert me), and I yearn for an eternal world."

The Spirit Needs Our Body in This World

The spirit, a non-compound entity issuing from the world of Divine Commands, must use material means to be manifested and function in this world. As the body cannot contact the world of symbols or immaterial forms, the spirit cannot contact this world if there is no human heart, brain, or other bodily organs and limbs to mediate. The spirit functions through the body's nerves, cells, and other elements. Therefore, if one or more bodily systems or organs goes awry, the spirit's relation with them is disconnected and can no longer command it. If the failure or "illness" causing this disconnection severs the spirit's relation with the entire body, what we call death occurs.

Although some coarse, meaningless hand, or finger movements can be produced by stimulating certain areas of the brain, these movements are like confused, meaningless sounds produced by pressing piano keys at random. They are automatic bodily responses to stimulation, and are produced by the body's automatic functioning. Therefore, the body needs the spirit, which is conscious and has free will, to produce meaningful movements.

Although such psychoanalysists as Freud offered various explanations for dreams, dreams cannot only be the subconscious mind's jumbled activities. Almost everyone has had dreams that have come true. Many scientific or technological discoveries have been made because of true dreams. So, as we will discuss later, dreams point to the existence of something within us that can see in a different way while we are sleeping. This something is the spirit.

Although the spirit sees with our eyes, smells with our nose, hears with our ears and so on, there are many examples of people who somehow manage to see with their fingers or the tips of their nose, and smell with their heels.

The Spirit Manifests Itself Mostly on a Person's Face

Truly, our face is a window opened on our inner world, for its features disclose our character. Psychologists assert that almost all of our movements, even coughing, reveal our character. The face's ability to reveal one's character, abilities, and personality resulted in physiognomy, the art of judging character from facial features. The spirit determines these features.

Our body's cells are renewed continuously. Every day, millions of cells die and are replaced. Biologists say that all bodily cells are renewed every 6 months. Despite this continuous renewal, the face's main features remain unchanged. We recognize individuals from their unchanging facial features and fingerprints. The cells of a finger change due to such renewal or injury and bruise, but their prints never change. Each individual's unique spirit makes these distinguishing features stable.

Our Spirit Makes us Unique

Our body experiences ceaseless change throughout its existence. This change is directed toward physical growth and development until a certain period, gradually becoming stronger and more perfect. When this growth stops at a certain point, decay begins. Unlike our body, we can grow continuously in learning and development, decay spiritually and intellectually, or stop and change direction while developing or decaying. Our moral, spiritual, and intellectual education does not depend on our bodily changes.

Furthermore, our moral, spiritual, and intellectual differences have nothing to do with our physical structure. Although we are composed of the same substantial, physical or material elements, we are morally and intellectually unique. Which part of us receives this moral and intellectual education, and which part is trained physically? Does physical training have any relation to learning or moral and intellectual education? Are physically well-developed people smarter and more moral than others?

If physical training or development does not affect our scientific, moral, and intellectual level, why should we not accept the spirit's existence? How can we attribute learning and moral and intellectual education to some biochemical processes in the brain? Are those processes quicker in some people? Are some smarter because they have quicker processes, or are the processes quicker because some study and thus become smarter? What relation do these processes have with our spiritual and moral education and development? How can we explain the differences regular worship makes to one's face? Why are believers' faces more radiant than those of unbelievers?

Our physical changes engender no parallel changes in our character, morality, or thinking. How can we explain this, other than by admitting that the spirit exists and is the center of thinking and feeling, choosing and deciding, learning and forming opinions and preferences, and is the cause of unique characters?

Our Spirit Feels and Believes or Denies

All people have innumerable, complex feelings: love and hate, happiness and sadness, hope and despair, ambition and the ability to imagine, relief and boredom, and so on. We like and dislike, appreciate and disregard, experience fear and timidity as well as courage and enthusiasm. We repent, become excited, and long for various things. If we look through a dictionary, we find hundreds of words that express human feelings. Moreover, we do not all "feel" the same way. We may reflect on what is going on around us, the beauty of creation, develop ourselves through learning, compare and reason, and thus believe in the Creator of all things. Worshipping and following His Commandments causes us to develop morally and spiritually until finally we are perfected. How can we explain such phenomena other than by admitting that each human being has a conscious spirit? Can we attribute them to chemical processes in the brain?

Are We Only Physical Bodies?

If we are only a physical entity of blood and bones, flesh and tissues, and attribute all our movements to biochemical processes in the brain, why should we obey any laws? We have established that our physical body is renewed every 6 months. If we were tried for a murder we committed a year ago, would not the following conversation be entirely logical, given the above understanding?

> Judge: When did you commit the crime?
> Defendant: One year ago.
> The judge announces the verdict: Since the murder was committed a year ago and the defendant's cells, including those of his trigger finger, have been completely replaced, and since it is therefore impossible to punish the actual murderer, the jury has voted for acquittal.

How can anyone be merely a physical entity? Can their movements, feelings, thoughts, beliefs, and decisions be the results of the brain's biochemical processes? Such assertions are untenable. The main part of our being is our living and conscious spirit. This part of our body feels, thinks, believes, wills, decides, and uses the body to enact its decisions.

The Spirit is the Basis of Human Life

God acts in this world through causes. However, there are many other worlds or realms: the world of ideas, symbols or immaterial forms, the inner dimensions of things, and spirits, where God acts directly and where matter and causes do not exist. The spirit is breathed into the embryo directly, making it a direct manifestation of the Divine Name the All-Living, and therefore the basis of human life. Like natural laws, which issue from the same realm as the spirit, the spirit is invisible and known through its manifestations.

In this world, matter is refined in favor of life. A lifeless body, regardless of size, such as a mountain, is lonely, passive, and static. But life enables a bee to interact with almost the entire world so that it can say: "This world is my garden, and flowers are my business partners." The smaller a living body is, the more active, astonishing, and powerful life becomes. Compare a bee, a fly, or even a micro-organism with an elephant. The more refined matter is, the more active and powerful the body becomes. For example, wood produces flame and carbon when it burns, and water vaporizes when heated. We come across electrical energy in the atomic and subatomic worlds. We cannot see it, but we are aware of its presence and power through its manifestations.

This means that existence is not limited only to this world; rather, this world is only the apparent, mutable, and unstable dimension of existence. Behind it lies the pure, invisible dimension that uses matter to be seen and known. As the spirit belongs to that dimension, it is therefore pure and invisible.

The arguments for the spirit's existence also affirm the Creator's existence. They are as follows:

- Just as our body, which God creates from elements, needs the spirit to govern it, the universe (and what it contains) needs God to bring it into existence and to command and govern it.

- Each body has one spirit that makes it alive and governs it. So, there must be a single Lord, without partner, to create and govern the universe. Otherwise, disaster and confusion is inevitable.
- The spirit is not located in any specific place or part of the body. It may even leave the body and, as in the case of dreams, continue its relation with the body by means of a specific cord attached to the body. Likewise, God Almighty is not contained by time or space. He is always present everywhere and nowhere, whereas the spirit is in the body and is contained by time and space.
- There is only one sun, and the world is very far from it. However, the sun is present everywhere through its heat and light, and via reflection it can appear in every transparent thing. Therefore, we can say that the sun is nearer to things than things are to themselves. The spirit has the same relation with the body, as well as with all of its separate cells. This analogy may help us to understand God's relation with existence. He controls and directs all things at the same time like a single thing, and although we are infinitely distant from Him, He is nearer to us than we are to ourselves.
- The spirit is invisible, and its nature is unknown. In the same way, we cannot think of or imagine God as He really is, for His Essence cannot be known. Like the spirit, God Almighty is known via the manifestations of His Names, Attributes, and Essence.

Our Spirit Has Its Own Cover

When the spirit leaves the body at death, it retains this cover, which is like a body's "negative." It is called by many names: the envelope of light, the person's ethereal figure, energetic form, second body, astral body, double (of that person), and phantom.

DEATH AND THE SPIRIT AFTER DEATH

All human beings have an intrinsic feeling of eternity, and so feel imprisoned in the narrow confines of the material world and yearn for eternity. Whoever can hear our conscious nature will hear it pronouncing eternity over and over again. If we were given the whole universe, we would still hunger for the eternal life for which we were created. This natural inclination toward eternal happiness comes from an objective reality: the existence of eternal life and our desire for it.

Death and Angels of Death

The spirit uses the body as an instrument, and thus governs and controls it in a comprehensive manner. When the appointed hour of death comes, any illness or failure in the body's functions is an invitation to the Angel of Death (the Archangel Azra'il). In reality, God causes people to die. However, He employs Azra'il to take the souls, so that people should not complain about Him, as death might seem disagreeable to many. He also uses illness or other calamities as another veil between Azra'il and death so that people should not curse the Archangel.

Since all angels are created from light, Azra'il can be present and assume any form in innumerable places at once and do many things simultaneously and perfectly. Like the sun giving heat and light to all things in the world at the same time, and being present through its images in innumerable transparent objects, Azra'il can take millions of souls at the same moment with great ease.

Archangels like Gabriel, Michael, and Azra'il have subordinates that resemble them and are supervised by them. When good, righteous people die, certain angels come to them with smiles and radiant faces. They are followed by Azra'il and his subordinates charged with taking the souls of the good. The Qur'anic verses: *By those who pluck out violently; by those who draw out gently* (79:1-2), indicate that those angels who take the souls of the righteous differ from those who take the souls of the wicked. The latter are plucked out violently, and have sour, frightened faces at death.

Those who believe and live righteous lives are greeted with scenes from the places reserved for them in Paradise. Prophet Muhammad stated that the souls of such people are drawn out as gently as the flowing of water from a pitcher. Better than that, martyrs do not feel death's agony and do not know that they are

dead. Instead, they consider themselves to have been transferred
to a better world and enjoy perfect happiness. Prophet Muhammad
told Jabir ibn 'Abd Allah ibn 'Amr, who was martyred at the
Battle of Uhud:

> Do you know how God welcomed your father? He welcomed
> him in such an indescribable manner that neither eyes have seen
> it nor ears heard it, nor minds conceived of it. Your father said:
> "O God, let me return to the world so that I can explain to those
> left behind how pleasant martyrdom is." God replied: "There is
> no return. Life is lived only once. However, I will inform them
> of your circumstances," and He revealed: *Never think of those
> slain in the way of God to be dead; rather they are alive and are pro-
> vided in the Presence of their Lord.* (3:169)

Prophet Muhammad, the most advanced in worshipping God,
advised prescribed prayers while he was dying. So did 'Umar,
the second Caliph. Khalid ibn Walid was one of the few invin-
cible generals in world history. Just before his death, he asked
those beside him to bring his sword and horse. People like 'Uthman
(the third Caliph), 'Ali (the fourth Caliph), Hamza, and Mus'ab
ibn 'Umayr dedicated themselves to the cause of Islam and died
as martyrs. Those who lead lives of dissipation die while fre-
quenting drinking or gambling tables, brothels, and other unsa-
vory places.

Should We Fear Death?

Believers and those who do righteous deeds do not need to fear
death. Although death seems to bring decomposition, extinguish
life, and destroy pleasure, in fact it represents a Divine discharge
from the heavy duties of worldly life. It is a change of residence,
a transferal of the body, an invitation to and the beginning of
everlasting life.

Just as the world is continually enlivened through acts of
creation and predetermination, so is it continually stripped of life
through other cycles of creation, determination, and wisdom.
The dying of plants, the simplest level of life, is a work of Divine
artistry, just like their living, but one that is more perfect and

better designed.[3] When a fruit's seed dies in the soil, it seems to decompose and rot away. But in reality, it undergoes a perfect chemical process, passes through predetermined states of reformation, and ultimately grows again into an elaborate, new tree. So a seed's death is really the beginning of a new tree, a new, more perfect and elaborate life.

Since the death of fruits, vegetables, and meat in our stomachs causes them to rise to the degree of human life, in this sense their death can be regarded as more noble than their lives. Since the dying of plants is so perfect and serves so great a purpose, our deaths, given that we are the highest form of life, must be much more perfect and serve a still greater purpose. After we have been buried, we certainly will be brought into eternal life.

Death releases us from the hardships of worldly life—a turbulent, suffocating, narrow dungeon of space that gradually becomes more unbearable through old age and affliction—and admits us to the infinitely wide circle of the Eternal, Beloved One's mercy. There, we may enjoy the everlasting company of our beloved ones and the consolation of a happy, eternal life.

THE SPIRIT IN THE INTERMEDIATE WORLD

Following death, the spirit is taken to the Presence of God. If it led a good, virtuous life and refined itself, the angels charged with taking it there wrap it in a piece of satin and bear it, through the heavens and all inner dimensions of existence, to His Presence. During this journey, angels welcome it in every mansion or station it passes and ask: "Whose spirit is this? How beautiful it is!" The angels conveying it introduce it with the most beautiful titles it had while in the world, and answer: "This is the spirit of the one who, for example, prayed, fasted, gave alms, and bore all kinds of hardship for God's sake." Finally, God Almighty welcomes it and tells the angels: "Take it back to the grave where its body is buried, so that it can answer the questions of Munkar and Nakir, the interrogating angels."

Whatever misfortune we experience is usually the result of our own sins. If believers are sincere but cannot always refrain from sin, God, out of His Mercy, allows misfortune to strike so that they may be purified. God may subject them to great agony during death, either to forgive their still unpardoned sins or to promote them to higher (spiritual) ranks, but then take their spirit very gently. If, despite all misfortune and death agonies there are still some unforgiven sins, these people are punished in the grave and so will not be punished in Hell. As the grave is the first station on the journey toward eternal life, it features a preliminary interrogation by two angels about what kind of life the deceased led. Almost everyone, except Prophets, is subjected to some suffering.

It is recorded in reliable books that 'Abbas, the uncle of the Prophet, desired very much to see 'Umar in his dream after the latter had died. When he saw him six months later, he asked him: "Where were you until now?" 'Umar replied: "Don't ask me that! I have just finished accounting (for my life)."

Sa'd ibn Mu'adh was among the greatest Companions. When he died, Archangel Gabriel told God's Messenger: "The Divine Throne trembled when Sa'd died." Innumerable angels took part in his funeral. After Sa'd, may God be pleased with him, was buried, the Messenger said in amazement: "Glory to God! What (will happen to others) if the grave squeezes (even such people like) Sa'd?"

In the grave, everyone is questioned by the angels Munkar and Nakir. They ask: "Who is your Lord? Who is your Prophet? What is your religion?" and many other questions. If the deceased were believers, they can answer these questions. Otherwise, they cannot. The questions continue concerning their deeds in the world.

The spirit's relationship with the body differs according to which world it inhabits. In this world, the spirit is confined within the prison of the body. If the evil-commanding self and bodily desires dominate it, the spirit inevitably deteriorates and spells the person's final doom. Those who use their willpower in the way taught by God, discipline their evil-commanding selves, nourish their spirits (via belief, worship, and good conduct), and are not enslaved by bodily desires will find their spirits refined, purified, and furnished with laudable qualities. Such people will find happiness in both worlds.

After burial, the spirit waits in the intermediate world between this one and the Hereafter. Although the body decomposes, its essential particles (called *ajb al-dhanab, which literally means coccyx, in a hadith*) do not rot. We do not know whether ajb al-dhanab is a person's genes or something else. Regardless of this ambiguity, however, the spirit continues its relations with the body through it. God will make this part, which is formed of the body's essential particles, atoms, or all its other particles already dispersed in the soil, conducive to eternal life during the final destruction and rebuilding of the universe. He also will use it to re-create us on the Day of Judgment.

The intermediate world is the realm where the spirit feels the "breath" of the bliss of Paradise or the punishment of Hell. If we led a virtuous life in the world, our good deeds (e.g., prayers, recitations, acts of charity) will appear as amiable fellows. Also, windows onto heavenly scenes will be opened for us and, as stated in a *hadith*, our grave will become like a garden of Paradise. However, if some of our sins still remain unpardoned, regardless of how virtuous we were, we may suffer some punishment in the intermediate world until we become deserving of Paradise. Unbelievers who indulged in sin will be met by their deeds, which will assume the forms of bad fellows and vermin. They will see scenes of Hell, and their graves will become like a pit of Hell.

When we are alive, our spirit suffers pain and feels joy and happiness. Although it feels pain apparently through the nervous system and uses this extremely complicated system to communicate with all bodily parts, scientists still do not understand how it interacts with the body, especially with the brain. Any bodily failure that causes death can make the nervous system disfunctional. However, it has been established scientifically that certain brain cells survive for a while after death. Scientists try to receive signals from such cells. If they succeed in doing so and can decipher those signals, it will be useful, especially in criminology, in solving unsolved crimes. For example, the Qur'an tell us how, during the time of Prophet Moses, God revived a dead person, who identified his killer:

> When Moses said to his people: "God commands you to sacri-
> fice a cow" ... they sacrificed her, a thing they had scarcely done.
> And when you killed a living soul, and disputed thereon—God
> disclosed what you were hiding—so We said: "Smite him with
> part of it"; even so He brings to life the dead, and He shows you
> His signs, that haply you may have understanding. (2:67, 71-73)

As the spirit suffers pain and feels happy, and as it continues
its relation with the body (via those essential bodily particles
that do not rot) in the intermediate world, it is meaningless to
discuss whether the spirit, the body, or both will enjoy Paradise
or suffer Hell.

Since the spirit lives the worldly life together with the body
and shares all its joys and sorrows, God will resurrect people
both bodily and spiritually. The Ahl al-Sunna wa al-Jama'a[4]
agree that the spirit and the body will go either to Paradise or
Hell together. God will build bodies in forms unique to the
Hereafter, where everything will be alive: *This life of the world is
but a pastime and a game. Lo! the home of the Hereafter, that is life
if they but knew* (29:64).

Spirits in the intermediate world will see and hear us, provided God allows this. If He does, He may permit some saintly
people to see, and hear, and communicate with us.

Our account is not closed after we die. If we leave behind
good, virtuous children, books, or institutions from which people
continue to benefit, or if we have raised or contributed to raising those who benefit others, our reward increases. If we leave
evil behind, our sins increase as long as our evil harms others.
Therefore, if we want to help our beloved ones who have died, we
should do good deeds. If we help the poor, take part in Islamic
services, lead a good and virtuous life, and especially spend to promote Islam and the good of Muslims and humanity at large, we
will cause their reward to increase.

SUPERNORMAL PHENOMENA

The spirit issues forth from the world of unconditioned existence,
where Divine commands are carried out instantly and directly.

However, like energy requiring cords or bulbs to function, the spirit needs matter to function in this world although matter restricts its activity. So, to make the spirit more active and less confined within time and space, we can follow one of three ways:

Supernormal Phenomena, the Prophets, and Saints

Every person can give the spirit more room in which to act. This goal is accomplished by firm religious belief and spiritual development through regular worship and asceticism. The more refined matter is, the freer and more active the spirit. Eating less food, fasting frequently, sleeping less, refraining from sin, and regular and more frequent worship help you reach this goal. If you use your innate ability to develop your spiritual faculties, you can transcend the limits of this world, travel in the spirit in other dimensions of existence, and, to some degree, establish contact with the past and future.

Consider the following analogy: When you are in a room, you see that which is confined by the four walls. When you go outside, you can see all of your immediate surroundings. You can see even more from the top of a hill. The higher you ascend, the more you see. It is the same with time. The freer the spirit is from the prison of matter and the body, the broader the realm of its activity with respect to time and space.

This way is usually the way of the Prophets and saints. Either through traveling in spirit in time and space or being taught by God, the Knower of the Seen and Unseen, they penetrate into the depths of time and space. Just as sunlight is in innumerable places simultaneously, although it is a material body, so a Prophet's or a saint's spirit, especially that of a "substitute" (*abdal*), can be present in many places at the same time in his or her body's immaterial or energetic form. The Qur'an points to this: *She (Mary, the mother of Jesus) placed a screen to seclude herself from them. Then We sent to her Our spirit, and he appeared before her as a man without fault* (19:17). Many interpreters of the Qur'an say this spirit was Archangel Gabriel. Such accounts also are reported in many authentic narrations.

A saint's spirit, if it has acquired sufficient enlightenment or luminosity, encounters symbols or signs of past or future events while traveling in time. Saints interpret these visions and relate certain past or future events. This is comparable to dream interpretation. They may err in their interpretation.

However, Prophets do not err in their interpretations and predictions, since they receive Revelation and are taught directly by God Almighty, the Knower of the Unseen. Whatever they predicted always came true. For example, Prophet Muhammad predicted numerous future events (e.g., the martyrdom of 'Uthman and 'Ali, the Battle of Jamal (Camel) between 'Ali and such leading Companions as Talha and Zubayr, and the Muslims' conquest of Damascus, Iran, and Istanbul). Most of his predictions have already come true; others are waiting for their time to come true.[5]

Muhyi al-Din ibn al-'Arabi (d. 1240 CE), a Muslim saint who died about 50 years before the founding of the Ottoman State, predicted many important events of Ottoman history. His *Shajarat al-Nu'maniya*, manuscripts of which are available in libraries in Edirne and Istanbul, is like a symbolic history of the Ottoman State. For example, he predicted that his grave would be discovered when Selim entered Damascus (it was), that despite 9 months of siege Hafiz Ahmad Pasha would not capture Baghdad (he did not), that Sultan Murad would conquer it in 40 days (he did), and that Sultan 'Abd al-'Aziz would be dethroned and killed (he was).

Similarly, Mushtaq Dada of Bitlis, who lived in the first half of the eighteenth century, predicted that after a war someone named Kemal would make Ankara the capital of Turkey (all of which happened). His *Diwan*, a book of his poems that contains this prediction, is still available.

Such beloved servants of God, whether Prophets or saints, make predictions only if He allows them to do so through His permission and power. The Messenger reports from God:

> My servant can draw near unto Me in no safer and better way than performing his obligatory religious duties. He becomes nearer to me through supererogatory prayers. Once he becomes near to Me, I become his eyes with which he sees, his ears with which he hears, and his hands with which he holds.

Supernormal Phenomena and the Divine Names

The second way to travel in spirit in time and space or to penetrate into further and deeper dimensions of time and space is to follow the guidance of the relevant Divine Name or Names. All existence depends on the Divine Names' manifestations. We can see only because the manifestation of His Name the All-Seeing enables us to see. We continue to exist because of the manifestation of His Names the Self-Subsistent and the One-Causing-to-Subsist allows us to do so. If He no longer manifested His Name the One-Causing-to-Subsist in connection with existence, the universe would cease to exist instantly.

Similarly, this practice allows angels and jinn to assume animal and human forms, provided that God allows them to do so. Especially jinn can enter an animal's body and govern its actions. They can also control people. So, by discovering the Divine Name that allows one to penetrate such dimensions and then following Its guidance in a particular affair, we can travel in time and space, and see and hear certain things that others cannot.

Various supernormal phenomena

Such supernormal phenomena as telepathy and spiritualism are widespread. Millions of people who seek peace and happiness to counteract the domination of their worldview, mind, and spirit by technology and materialism, attend séances for so-called transcendental experiences. Some people are more inclined to and can perform supernormal phenomena. For example, Madame Gibson predicted the partition of India in 1947 and the murder of John Kennedy. Likewise, Fenni Bey from Ordu, Turkey, who fought at the front of Madina during World War I, relates:

> We were under siege in Madina. I was unable to communicate with my family in Istanbul. One night in a dream I saw fire and smoke in my house. In the morning I sent for a private of mine, who was a medium. I told him to go into a trance and, travelling to my house—I told him where it was situated—describe to me what he saw. He did what I told him and began to describe: "I have reached the house, I have knocked on the door and an old

woman in a headscarf has come out with a child in her arms." I
told the private to ask the woman if there was anything wrong in
the house? He related to me: "She says your wife died yesterday."

Spiritualism is now widespread. Before further explanation,
I should point out that I discuss such things only to emphasize
that existence is not restricted to matter. Rather, as a book's main
existence lies in its meaning, that which is metaphysical, spiritual, or immaterial is the essential part of existence. Matter, on the
other hand, is accidental and a changing means for manifesting
what is immaterial. Great saints like Ibn al-'Arabi communicat-
ed with the spirits of the dead and even of those who had not
yet been born.[6] Contemporary spiritualists and mediums communicate with unbelieving jinn or devils who appear as the dead
person with whose soul they wish to communicate. Also, mediums predicting future events usually make contact with jinn and
then report what they are told.

Jinn live longer than us, are active in broader dimensions
(realms) of time and space, are much quicker than us, and can see
things that we cannot. But they cannot see the future, and so we
should not believe their predictions, even though a very few of
them do come true. In the past, American and Soviet intelligence
services competed with each other in studying telepathy and
other supernormal ways of communication. As will be explained
later, in a not-too-distant future, world powers will use jinn to
communicate with each other, especially in intelligence matters.
However, it is dangerous to seek to contact and communicate
with jinn or devils, for such beings can easily assert their influence and control the seekers.

A psychiatrist friend relates the following account:

> I was invited to a necromantic event in a house in Samsun (a
> province in northern Turkey). The youngest daughter arranged
> cups and letters on a table. One of the participants invited the
> soul of his late grandfather. After several calls, a man appeared.
> When we asked him insistently who he was, he answered:
> "Satan." We were greatly astonished. A while later, I asked him
> why he had come although we had not called him. He wrote

on the table with the cups: "So I come!" I asked him whether he believed in God. He wrote "No!" When I asked whether he believed in the Prophet, again he wrote, "No!" I began reading to him some passages from a book concerning the existence of God. When I read: "A factory with such and such features points to the engineer who planned and built it," he wrote: "True"; but when I read: "So too the universe with all the planets and particularly the world with all plants and animals in it indicate God," he wrote, "No!" This continued for some time, and I began reciting to him from Jawshan al-Kabir (The Great Armor), a collection of supplications to God. While I was reciting, the cups were moving on the table. Meantime he wrote: "Give up that nonsense!" When I continued to recite, he could not endure listening and disappeared.

Like such supernormal experiences, observations of some doctors at the time of death also prove the existence of the spirit and spirit beings. What Bedri Ruhselman reports in *Ruh ve Kainat* (The Spirit and the Universe) from a doctor agrees fully with the observations of a group of doctors from Holland, which were published in the newspapers. A doctor narrates:

My wife was ill. When she went into the pangs of death, two things resembling two clouds descended into the room and hovered above her head. Meanwhile a form appeared, which was connected to my wife on the nape of the neck with a cord and was fluttering. This continued for five hours. In the end, the cord broke off and the form, the spirit, rose away. This was the end of my wife's life.

DREAMS

While you sleep with your eyes closed, your ears deaf, your tongue mute, and your arms and legs motionless, how do you travel, meet people, and do many things in a few minutes or even seconds? When you get up in the morning, you feel deeply influenced by that adventure of few seconds. Although Freud and his followers attribute dreams to the subconscious self, to thoughts and desires, impulses and past experiences, how can you explain dreams that inform you of a future event with which you have no contact or have never thought about? How do we dream? With what part of our body or being do we dream? Why do dreams last only a few seconds? How (and why) do we remember what we dreamed? All of these and many similar questions are like puzzles awaiting to be solved by science.

Sometimes while we are asleep, our subconscious (namely, our thoughts and desires, impulses and past experiences) are revealed unconsciously. We may be sick or hungry, or be facing an unsolvable problem. The imagination gives form to the deviations of a bad temper, or the mind remembers a past exciting event and gives it a new, different form. All such dreams are jumbled; they have some meaning, but are not worth interpreting. For example, if we eat salty things before sleep, we may dream that we are lying by a pool; if we go to bed angry, we may dream that we are fighting with others.

If we do not know how to interpret dreams, true dreams may be confused with or taken for such jumbled dreams. For example, although the dream Pharaoh told to Prophet Joseph was true, his men described it as jumbled.[7]

True Dreams

One type of dream has nothing to do with the subconscious self. Such dreams carry important messages: either good tidings from God, which encourage us to do good things and guide us, or warnings concerning the evil we have done. Those dreams, which we call true dreams, are very clear and unforgettable.

Some true dreams contain news of the future. To understand their nature and mechanism, consider the following:

Just as a book's essence—its meaning—exists before it assumes a written, visible form, everything has an essential form of existence in God's Knowledge before it appears in the world. Islamic philosophers call these essential forms archetypes. When God wills to send them to this world, through the manifestation of His Wisdom and Power and the appropriate Divine Names, He clothes them in material bodies. There is another world between the world of archetypes (where God's Knowledge has primary manifestation) and this world —the world of immaterial forms or symbols. There, things exist in ideal forms or as symbols, and the concept and measure of time are completely different from their counterparts here. Dreamers find or receive these symbols differently, based on such factors as time and place, culture, and even national and individual characteristics.

When we sleep, our spirit ascends to this world of ideal forms without completely breaking its connection with the body.[8] It enters a different dimension of existence, where past, present, and future are combined. As a result, we may experience a past event or witness a future one. However, since things in that world exist in ideal forms or symbols, the spirit usually receives symbols that require interpretation.

For example, clear water there might correspond to knowledge here. If you see your own waste matter, it may be interpreted to mean that you will earn money in lawful ways. If the waste matter belongs to others, it may mean that money will come to you in unlawful ways. As mentioned in *Sura Yusuf*, a fat cow may mean a year of abundant crops, while a lean one means a year of severity. The metaphors, similes, and parables found in the Qur'an and the Prophetic sayings, and sometimes among people, may provide significant keys to dream interpretation. Some true dreams are so clear that no interpretation is needed.

As time is measured differently in these two worlds, and as the spirit is far more active while we are dreaming, great saints who free their spirits, to a certain degree, can travel long distances in a much shorter time than normal people.

Many people have had true dreams. For example:

- Abraham Lincoln's dream the night before his assassination is famous. He dreamed of White House servants running to and fro, telling each other that Mr. Lincoln had been killed. He woke up in great excitement and spent an uneasy day. Despite warnings, he went to the theater that evening and was killed.
- Eisenhower's dream just before he landed on Normandy in June 1944 changed the course of World War II. A few days

before the date on which he had decided to land, he dreamed that a big storm broke out and overturned the landing crafts. This caused him to move up the date. History records that his dream was accurate.

- The mother of Anne Ostrovosky, a Russian writer, saw many scenes of the German–Russian battles 5 years before World War II broke out. Her dream was published in several newspapers.

- Several scientific or technological discoveries were first seen in dreams. Elias Howe, while trying to figure out how to thread a sewing machine, dreamed he was a prisoner of an African tribe that wanted him to thread a sewing machine. In mortal fear and puzzled, he suddenly saw holes at the ends of his captors' spears. He woke up and made a little "spear" with a hole at one end. Niels Bohr, who was studying atomic structures, dreamed of planets connected to the sun with threads and turning around it. When he woke up, he conceived of a resemblance between what he had dreamed and atomic structures.

Many other true dreams have predicted future events or resulted in scientific or technological discoveries. But these examples are sufficient to show that dreams are the result of the sprit's journey in inner dimensions of existence (the world of immaterial forms or symbols) and of receiving signals therein.

Finally, dreams provide a strong proof for the existence of immaterial worlds as well as for Divine Knowledge and Destiny. If God Almighty had not predetermined and recorded all events in "the Supreme Guarded Tablet," how could we be informed of future events? Also, dreams show that the measure of time differs according to each world's features.

ANGELS AND THEIR FUNCTIONS

Angels are created from light. The Arabic word for angel is *malak*. According to its root form, *malak* means messenger, deputy, envoy, superintendent, and a powerful being. The root meaning also implies descent from a high place. Angels build relations between the macrocosmic world and the material one, convey God's commands of creation and operation of the universe, direct the acts and lives of beings (with God's permission), and represent their worship in their own realms. Having refined or subtle bodies of light, angels move very rapidly and can be found in all realms of existence. They place themselves in our eye pupils or in the bodies of other beings to observe the works of God; they also make us percieve the inspirational beauty around us by turning our attention to the works of God. They also descend into the hearts of Prophets and saints to bring them inspiration. Such inspirations are usually from God, but sometimes they come from angels.

Some animals, like honeybees, act according to Divine inspiration. Science asserts that all animals are directed by impulses, but cannot explain what an impulse is and how it occurs. Scientists are trying to discover how migrating birds find their way, how young eels hatched in the waters of Europe find their way to their ancestral waters in the Pacific. Even if such information is encoded in their DNA, this information is assuredly from God, Who knows everything, controls the universe, and assigns angels to direct these creatures' lives. If science says we cannot question the existence of such invisible forces as the law of growth in living creatures, it is even more scientific to attribute such forces to angels, God's special servants.

Everything that exists, whether an individual or a species, has a collective identity and performs a unique, universal function. Each flower displays a superlative design and symmetry and recites, in the tongue of its being, the Names of the Creator manifested on it. The entire Earth performs a universal glorification as though it were a single flower. The vast "ocean" of the heavens praises and glorifies the Majestic Maker of the universe through its suns, moons, and stars. Even inert material bodies, although outwardly inanimate and unconscious, perform a vital function in praising God. Angels represent these immaterial bodies in the world of the inner dimensions of things, and express their praise. In return, these immaterial bodies are the angels' representatives, dwellings, and mosques in this world.

There are classes of angels. One class is engaged in constant worship; another worships by working. These working angels have functions that resemble human occupations, like shepherds or farmers. The face of the Earth resembles a farm, and an appointed angel oversees all animal species by the command of the All-Majestic Creator, by His permission and power and strength, and for His sake. Each animal species is overseen by a lesser angel appointed to act as its shepherd.

The face of the Earth is also an arable field in which all plants are sown. Another angel is appointed to oversee all of them in the Name of Almighty God and by His power. Lower ranking angels worship and glorify Almighty God by supervising particular plant species. Archangel Michael, one of the bearers of God's Throne of Sustenance,[9] oversees the angels of the highest rank.

Angels who function as shepherds or farmers bear no resemblance to human shepherds or farmers, for their supervision is purely for God's sake, in His Name, and by His power and command. They observe the manifestations of God's Lordship in the species they are assigned to supervise, study the manifestations of Divine Power and Mercy in it, communicate Divine commands to it through inspiration, and arrange its voluntary actions.

Their supervision of plants, in particular, consists of representing, in the angelic tongue, the plants' glorification in the tongue of their being. In other words, these angels proclaim the praises and exaltations that all plants offer to the Majestic Creator through their lives. These angels also regulate and employ the plants' faculties correctly and direct them toward certain ends. Angels perform such services through their partial willpower and a kind of worship and adoration.[10] They do not originate or create their acts, for everything bears a stamp particular to the Creator of all things. Only God creates. In short, whatever angels do is worship, and it is therefore not like the ordinary acts of human beings.

Since there is one angel to represent every kind of creature and present its service and worship to the Divine Court, the Prophet's description of angels is entirely reasonable and true. According to him, there are angels with 40,000 heads, each with 40,000 mouths, and 40,000 praises sung by 40,000 tongues in each mouth.

This Prophetic tradition means that angels serve universal purposes, and that some natural creatures worship God with 40,000 heads in 40,000 ways. The firmament, for example, praises the Majestic Creator through its suns and stars; the Earth, although a single body, worships with many thousands of "heads," each with many thousands of "mouths," and each with many thousands of "tongues." Thus this tradition is considered to refer to the angel who represents the Earth in the world of the inner dimensions of things (the world of immaterial bodies).

The Majestic Maker of this huge palace of creation employs four classes of laborers: angels and other spirit beings; inanimate things and vegetable creations, which are quite important servants working without wages; animals, which serve unconsciously in return for a small wage of food and pleasure; and humanity, which works in awareness of the Majestic Creator's purposes. Men and women learn from everything, and supervise lower-ranking servants in return for wages (reward) here and in the Hereafter.

The first class consists of angels. These beings are never promoted for what they do, for each has a fixed, determined rank and receives a particular pleasure from the work itself as well as a radiance from worship. Their reward is found in their service. Just as we are nourished by and derive pleasure from air and water, light and food, angels are nourished by and receive pleasure from the lights of remembrance and glorification, worship and knowledge, and love of God. Since they are created of light, light sustains them. Fragrant scents are enjoyable nourishment for them as they love fragrant smell. Indeed, pure spirits take pleasure in sweet scents.

Angels receive their own reward (elevated bliss) for carrying out the commands of the One Whom they worship, working for His sake, rendering service in His Name, and supervising through His view. They gain honor through their connection with Him, are refreshed by studying His Kingdom's material and immaterial dimensions, and are satisfied by observing His Grace and Majesty's manifestations. The resulting bliss is so elevated that we cannot even begin to comprehend it.

Angels do not sin or disobey, for they do not have an evil-commanding soul that must be resisted. They have fixed ranks, and so are neither promoted nor abased. They have no experience with such negative qualities as envy, rancor, enmity, and all the lusts and animal appetites found in human beings and jinn. They have no gender, do not eat or drink, and do not feel hunger, thirst, or tiredness. Although they receive no wages for their worship, they derive special pleasure from carrying out God's commands, delight in being near to Him, and receive spiritual pleasure from their worship. Praise, worship, recitation of God's Names, and glorification of Him are their nourishment, as are light and sweet fragrances.

On the other hand, we struggle with our evil-commanding soul and Satan. While angels invite us to true guidance, inspire us with belief, good conduct and virtue, and call us to resist the temptations of Satan and our evil-commanding selves, Satan and our evil-commanding selves try to seduce us. A person's life is the history of his or her continuous struggle between angelic inspiration and satanic temptation. This is why we can be elevated to the highest rank or abased to the lowest rank. Also, this is why the elect of humanity, the Prophets and great saints, are higher in rank than the greatest angels, and why ordinary believers are higher than common angels. Also, although angels have more knowledge of God and His Names and Attributes than we do, we are more comprehensive mirrors of God's Names and Attributes due to our developed human senses, our ability to reflect, and our complex nature.

There are different kinds of angels. Besides those deputed to represent and supervise various species and present their worship to God, there are four Archangels and angels who carry God's Throne.[11] Other groups of angels are known as *Mala'-i A'la* (the Highest Council), *Nadiyy-i A'la* (the Highest Assembly), and *Rafiq-i A'la* (the Highest Company).

Specific angels have been appointed to Paradise and Hell. Angels who record a person's deeds are called *Kiramun Katibun* (the Noble Recorders), and, as stated in a *hadith*, 360 of them are responsible for each believer's life. They guard their charges, especially during infancy and old age, pray for them, and ask God to forgive them. Other angels help believers during times of war and attend assemblies that praise and glorify God, as well as study meetings held for God's sake and to benefit people.

Angels, particularly angels of mercy, refrain from close contact with ritually impure people. They also avoid those with bad breath (derived from eating onions or garlic or from smoking), and do not visit those who sever relations with their parents and relatives.

Although God is All-Powerful and can guard everyone by Himself, He may appoint angels to guard His servants. To earn such a guardianship, believers have to do willingly that which is good and establish a close relation with God Almighty. They must have strong belief in God and all other pillars of faith, never abandon regular worship and prayer, lead a disciplined life, and refrain from forbidden things or sinful acts.

Angels helped the believers during the battles of Badr and Uhud, and also during the conquest of Makka. They always help believers who sincerely struggle in the way of God, regardless of time and place.

Belief in angels has many benefits. For example, it gives us peace and removes our loneliness. The inspiration breathed by angels exhilarates us, enlightens us intellectually, and opens new horizons of knowledge and thought. Awareness of their continuous company also helps us abstain from sin and improper behavior.

We may cite some Qur'anic verses to comprehend angels:

> By the loosed ones successively, storming tempestuously; by the scatterers scattering, and the severally severing and those hurling a reminder, excusing or warning. (77:1-6)

> By those that pluck out violently; and those that draw out gently; by those that float serenely, and those that outstrip suddenly; by those that direct an affair. (79:1-5)

> ... in (the Night of Power) the angels and the spirit descend, by the leave of their Lord, upon every command. (97:4)

> ... a Fire whose fuel is men and stones, and over which are harsh, terrible angels who disobey not God in what He commands them and do what they are commanded. (66:6)

Glory be to Him! Nay, but they are honored servants that outstrip Him not in speech, and perform as He commands. (21:26-27)

JINN AND THEIR FUNCTIONS

Jinn literally means "something hidden or veiled from sight." Jinn are a species of invisible beings. A short Qur'anic chapter is named for them. In that chapter we learn that some jinn listened to Prophet Muhammad and became believers:

> Say: "It has been revealed to me that a company of the jinn gave ear, and they said: 'We have heard a wonderful Qur'an, which guides to righteousness, so we believe in it and we shall not join (in belief and worship) any (gods) with our Lord. And (we believe) that He—exalted be the glory of our Lord—has taken neither wife nor son .... Among us there are righteous folk and among us there are far from that. We are sects having different rules." (72:1-3, 11)

Given this, we can understand that jinn are conscious beings charged with Divine obligations. Recent discoveries in biology make it clear that God created beings particular to each realm. Jinn might have been created while the Earth was still a body of fire. They were created before Adam and Eve, and were responsible for cultivating and improving the world. Although God later superseded them with us, He did not exempt them from religious obligations.

The Qur'an states that jinn are created from *smokeless fire* (55:15). In another verse, it clarifies that this fire is of a *scorching wind* (15:27) and penetrates as deep as the inner part of the body.[12]

Like angels, jinn move extremely fast and are not bound by our time and space. However, since the spirit is more active and faster than jinn, those who live at the level of the spirit's life and can transcend the limits of matter and the confines of time and space, can be quicker and more active than them. For example, the Qur'an relates that when Prophet Solomon asked who could bring the throne of the Queen of Sheba (Yemen), one jinn answered he could bring it before the meeting ended and Prophet Solomon stood up. However, a man with a special knowledge from God replied: *"I can bring it to you quicker than the blink of an eye,"* and he did so (27:38-40).

As nothing is difficult for God Almighty, He has provided human beings, jinn, and angels with the power and strength appropriate for their functions or duties. As He uses angels to supervise the movements of celestial bodies, He allows humanity to rule the Earth, dominate matter, build civilizations, and produce technology.

Power and strength are not limited to the physical world, nor are they proportional to bodily size. We see that immaterial things are far more powerful than huge physical entities. For example, our memory is far more spacious and comprehensive than a large room. Our hands can touch a near-by object, but our eyes can travel long distances in an instant. Our imagination can transcend time and space all at once. Winds can uproot trees and demolish large buildings. A young, thin plant shoot can split rocks and reach the sunlight. The power of energy, whose existence is known through its effect, is apparent to everybody. All of this shows that something's power is not proportional to its physical size; rather the immaterial world dominates the physical world, and immaterial entities are far more powerful than material ones.

ANGELS AND JINN IN THIS WORLD

Angels and jinn can assume any form or shape and appear in this world. Here, we observe movement from the visible to the invisible: water evaporates and disappears into the atmosphere, solid matter becomes a liquid or a gas (steam), and matter becomes energy (nuclear fission). Likewise, we observe movement from the invisible to the visible: gases become fluids, evaporated water becomes rain (as well as snow or hail), and energy becomes matter. Similarly, intangible thoughts and meanings in our minds can appear in the tangible form of letters and words in essays and books.

In an analogous way, such invisible beings as angels, jinn, and other spirit entities are clothed in some material substance, such as air or ether, and then become visible. According to Imam Shibli, God may allow them to assume a form when they utter any of His Names, for this functions like a key or a visa enabling them to assume a form and become visible in this world. If they try to do so without God's permission, by relying on their own abilities, they are torn into pieces and perish.

We read in the Qur'an (19:17) that the spirit God sent to Mary (the mother of Jesus), and whom Muslim scholars say is Archangel Gabriel, appeared before her as a man. When Gabriel came to Prophet Muhammad with Revelation or God's Messages, he usually came as a warrior, a traveler, or a Companion named Dihya. For example, he came as a warrior on horseback following the end of the Battle of the Trench and told the Prophet: "O Messenger of God, you have taken off your armor but we, the angels, have not yet done so. God orders you to march upon the Banu Qurayza." Once he came as a traveler dressed in white and, in order to instruct the Companions in religion, asked the Prophet such questions as: What is belief? What is Islam? What is *ihsan* (excellence or perfection of virtue)? When is the Day of Judgment?

Like angels and jinn, Satan (who is a jinn) can appear in different forms. It is narrated that before the Battle of Badr, he appeared to the Qurayshi leaders as an old man from Najd and advised them. Likewise, a Companion guarding the spoils of war caught Satan in disguise trying to steal some items.[13] Satan entreated the Companion to release him, which he did—twice. On the third time, the Companion tried to take him to God's Messenger. But Satan appealed: "Release me, and I'll tell you how you can secure yourself against me." The Companion asked what that was, and Satan replied that it was the Verse of the Throne (2:255). When informed of this, God's Messenger commented: "That wicked one is a liar, but on that occasion he told the truth."

The Qur'an relates that a group of jinn listened to God's Messenger recite the Qur'an and, when they returned to their people, said: *"O people! Surely we listened to a Book that has been revealed after Moses, affirms what precedes it, and guides to right and the Straight Path"* (46:30). The *sura* continues with what they thought about what they had heard. Some Traditions tell us that the Messenger recited parts of the Qur'an and preached his Message to the jinn.

Jinn can also appear as snakes, scorpions, cattle, donkeys, birds, and other animals. When our Prophet accepted the jinn's oath of allegiance in the valley of Batn al-Nakhla, he wanted them to appear to his community either in their own form or in other agreeable forms, not as such harmful animals as dogs and scorpions. He warned his community: "When you see any vermin in your house, tell it three times: 'For God's sake, leave this place,' for it may be a friendly jinn. If it does not leave, it is not a jinn. If it is harmful, you may kill it."

The jinn who gave allegiance to God's Messenger promised him: "If your community recites the *basmala* (In the Name of God, the All-Merciful, the All-Compassionate) just when they begin to do something (good and lawful), and cover their dishes, we will not touch their food or their drink."[14] Another Tradition says: [When you have relieved yourselves] do not clean yourselves with bones and dried pieces of dung, for they are among the foods of your jinn brothers.

JINN AND HUMAN BEINGS

Some people can go into a trance and contact beings from the invisible realms. However, we should remember that whether these are angels or jinn, invisible beings have their own conditions of life and are bound to certain limits and principles. For this reason, one who communicates with jinn should be careful not to fall under their influence and become their plaything.

Some assert that Mirza Ghulam Ahmad (1839-1908) of Qadiyan (India),[15] fell victim to such tricks. He attempted to serve Islam by struggling against Hindu Yogism through Fakirism, but evil spirits got control of him. First they whispered to him that he was a reviver (of religion), then that he was the Mahdi (Messiah), and when he was finally under their influence and control, told him to proclaim that he was an incarnation of God.

Sins and uncleanliness invite the influence of evil spirits and unbelieving jinn. People of a susceptible nature, those who tend to be easily melancholical and those who lead dissipated and undisciplined lives, are their primary targets. Evil spirits usually reside in places for dumping garbage or other dirty places, public baths, and bathrooms.

Jinn can penetrate a body even deeper than X-rays. They can reach into a being's veins and the central points of the brain. They seem to be like lasers, which are used in everything from computers to nuclear weaponry, from medicine to communication and police investigations, and to removing obstructions in our veins and arteries. So, when we consider that Satan and jinn are created from smokeless fire that penetrates deep into the body, like radiation or radioactive energy, we can understand the meaning of the Prophetic Tradition: "Satan moves where blood moves."

Jinn can harm the body and cause physical and psychological illnesses. It might be a good idea for medical authorities to consider whether jinn cause certain types of cancer, since cancer is an unordered and diseased growth in the body that we can describe as cellular anarchy. Maybe some jinn have settled in that part of the body and are destroying its cellular structure.

Although science does not yet accept the existence of invisible beings and restricts itself to the material world, we think it is worth considering the possibility that evil spirits play some part in such mental illnesses as schizophrenia. We constantly hear of cases that those who suffer from mental illness, epilepsy, or even cancer recover by reciting certain prayers. Such cases are serious and significant, and should not be denied or dismissed by attributing them to suggestion or auto-suggestion. When science finally accepts the existence of the metaphysical realm and the influence of metaphysical forces, its practitioners will be able to remove many obstructions and make far greater advances and fewer mistakes.

Today, the doors to the metaphysical worlds are only slightly ajar. We are barely at the beginning of contact with jinn and devils. However, one day we will feel obliged to enter these worlds to solve many of their problems pertaining to this world.

The Qur'an states that God bestowed upon the House of Abraham the *Scripture, Wisdom, and a mighty kingdom* (4:54).

This mighty kingdom manifested itself most brilliantly through Prophets David and Solomon. Prophet Solomon ruled not only a part of humanity, but also jinn and devils, birds and winds: *God subdued unto him devils, some of whom dived for pearls and did other work* (21:82). Solomon had armies of jinn and birds, and he employed jinn in many jobs: They made for him what he willed: *synagogues, fortresses, basins like wells and boilers built into the ground* (34:13); and *Wind was also subdued to him; its morning course was a month's journey and the evening course also a month's journey* (34:12). As pointed out earlier, a jinn offered to bring the throne of the Queen of Sheba from Yemen to Jerusalem before Solomon rose from his council (27:39).

The verses relating to Solomon's kingdom point to the final limit of humanity's use of jinn and devils. They also suggest that one day we will use them in many jobs, especially in communication. It is quite probable that they will also be employed in security affairs, mining and metal-work, even in space studies and historical research. Since jinn can live about 1,000 years, they may be useful in establishing historical facts.

SATAN AND HUMANITY

Satan as one of the jinn was created from fire. Before his obedience and sincerity were tested through Adam, he had been in the company of angels, acting and worshipping as they did. Unlike angels, however, who cannot rebel against God (66:6), Satan (called *Iblis* prior to his test) was free to choose his own path of conduct. When God tested him and the angels by commanding them to prostrate before Adam, the seeds of his self-conceit and disobedience blossomed and swallowed him. He replied in his vanity: *"I am better than him. You created me from fire, whilst him You did create of clay"* (38:76).

Why Was Satan Created?

Satan was created for important purposes. If Satan, who continually tries to seduce us, did not exist, our creation would be meaningless and futile. God has innumerable servants who cannot rebel and thus do whatever they are told. In fact, the existence of an absolute Divine Being Who has many beautiful Names and Attributes requires, not because of some external necessity but because of the essential nature of His Names, that His Names be manifest. He manifests all of these Names through humanity.

Since God has free will, He also gave us free will. We feel a constant battle taking place in our inner world to choose between good and evil. In addition, God gave us great potentials. So, by knowing good from evil and choosing good, or by using our free will in the right way, we can spiritually evolve. Just as God sends hawks upon sparrows so that the latter will develop their potential to escape, He created Satan and allowed him to tempt us so that our resistance to temptation will raise us spiritually and strengthen our willpower. Just as hunger stimulates human beings and animals to further exertion and discovery of new ways to be satisfied, and fear inspires new defenses, so Satan's temptations cause us to develop our potentials and guard against sin.

Angels do not rise to higher spiritual ranks because Satan cannot tempt them and cause them to deviate. Animals have fixed stations, and so cannot attain a higher or a lower station. Only human beings can change their station.

There is an infinitely long line of spiritual evolution between the ranks of the greatest Prophets and saints down to people such as Pharaoh and Nimrod. Therefore, it cannot be claimed that the creation of Satan is evil. Although Satan is evil and serves various important purposes, God's creation involves the whole universe and should be understood in relation to the results, not only with respect to the acts themselves. Whatever God does or creates is good and beautiful in itself or in its effects. For example, rain and fire are very useful but can cause great harm when abused. Therefore, one cannot claim that the creation of water and fire is not totally good. It is the same with the creation of Satan. His main purpose is to cause us to develop our potential, strengthen our willpower by resisting his temptations, and then rise to higher spiritual ranks.

To the argument made by some that Satan leads many people to unbelief and subsequent punishment in Hell, I reply:

First, although Satan was created for many good, universal purposes, many people may be deceived by him. But Satan only whispers and suggests; he cannot force you to indulge in evil and sin. If you are so weak that his false promises deceive you, and you allow yourself to be dragged down, you earn the punishment of Hell by misusing an important God-given faculty that enables you to develop your potential and raise to the highest rank. You must use your free will, which makes you human and gives you the highest position in creation, properly to further your intellectual and spiritual evolution. Otherwise, you must complain about being honored with free will and therefore about being human.

Second, as quality is much more important than quantity, we should consider qualitative, as opposed to quantitative, values when making our judgment. For example, 100 date seeds are worth only 100 cents if they are not planted. If only 20 out of 100 seeds grow into trees due to the other 80 being destroyed by too much water, can we argue that it is an evil to plant and water seeds? I think all of us can agree that it is wholly good to have 20 trees in exchange for 100 seeds, since 20 trees will produce 20,000 seeds.

Again, 100 peacock eggs may be worth a couple of dollars. But if only 20 eggs hatch and the rest do not, who will say that it is wrong to risk 80 eggs being spoiled in return for 20 peacocks? On the contrary, it is wholly good to have 20 peacocks at the expense of 80 eggs, for those 20 peacocks will lay even more eggs.

It is the same with humanity. By fighting Satan and their evil-commanding selves, many "worthless" people have been lost in exchange for hundreds of thousands of Prophets, millions of saints, and billions of men and women of wisdom and knowledge, sincerity and good morals. All of these people are the sun, moon, and stars of the human world.

How Does Satan Try to Seduce Humanity?

We read in Qur'an 7:17 that when God cursed Satan because of his haughty disobedience, Satan asked for a respite until the Day of Judgment so he could seduce human beings. God allowed him to do so, as was discussed above, and Satan retorted: *"Then I shall come upon them from before and behind, from their right and their left, and You will not find most of them grateful."*

The verse means that Satan does everything he can to seduce us. We are very complex beings, for God has manifested all of His Names on us. This world is an arena of testing, where we are trained so that we can serve as a mirror to God and earn eternal happiness. God has endowed us with innumerable feelings, faculties, and potentials to be trained and developed. If certain feelings and faculties (e.g., intellect, anger, greed, obstinacy, and lust) are not trained and directed to lofty goals but rather are misused, and if our natural desires and animal appetites are not restricted and satisfied in lawful ways, they can cause us great harm here and in the Hereafter.

Satan approaches us from the left and, working on our animal aspect, our feelings and faculties, tries to lead us into sin and evil. When he approaches us from the front, he causes us to despair about the future, whispers that the Day of Judgment will never come, and that whatever religions say about the Hereafter is mere fiction. He also suggests that religion is outdated and obsolete, and thus of no use for anyone living now or in the future. When he comes upon us from behind, he tries to make us deny Prophethood and other essentials of belief like God's Existence and Unity, Divine Scriptures, and angels. Through his whispers and suggestions, Satan tries to sever our contact with religion completely and lead us into sin.

Satan can only seduce devout, practicing believers by coming upon them from their right and tempting them to ego and pride. He whispers that they are wonderful believers, and gradually causes them to fall through self-conceit and the desire to be praised for their good deeds. For example, if believers perform supererogatory late-night prayer (*tahajjud*) and then proclaim it so that others will praise them, and if they attribute their accomplishments and good deeds to themselves and criticize others in secret, they have fallen under Satan's influence. This is a perilous temptation for believers, so they must be incessantly alert to this tactic.

Another trick of Satan is to cause unimportant things to appear important, and vice versa. If believers dispute in the mosque over a secondary matter, such as whether one can use a rosary when glorifying God after the daily prescribed prayers, while their children are being dragged into unbelief and materialism or are drowning in the swamp of immorality, Satan has seduced them.

Satan incessantly whispers new, original ideas to sinful unbelievers, in the name of unbelief, and teaches them how to struggle against true religion and its followers.

Involuntary thoughts and fancies. If Satan cannot seduce devout believers, he whispers disagreeable thoughts and fancies to them. For example, by associating some ideas with others, he makes believers have some unpleasant conceptions of the Divine Being, or conceive of unbelief or disobedience. If they dwell on such ideas, Satan pesters them until they fall into doubt about their belief or despair of ever leading a virtuous life.

Such involuntary evil thoughts, fancies, and ideas are usually the result of Satan's whispering. Like a battery's two poles, the human heart (by "heart" we mean the seat or center of spiritual intellect) has two central points or poles. One receives angelic inspiration, and the other is vulnerable to Satan's whispering.

When believers deepen their belief and devotion, and if they are scrupulous and delicate in feeling, Satan attacks them from different directions. He does not tempt those who follow him voluntarily and indulge in all that is transitory, but usually seeks out sincere, devout believers trying to rise to higher spiritual ranks.

Another trick is to cause good, devout believers to suspect the correctness or validity of their religious acts. For example: Did I perform my prayer correctly? Did I wash hands or face completely while performing the ritual ablution? How many times did I wash the parts of my body that must be washed?

Believers who are pestered with such involuntary thoughts, fancies, and doubts should know that they are involuntary and that their hearts have no part in them. Just as pirates attack treasure ships, thieves rob rich people, and strong countries try to control rich countries, Satan uses his evil suggestions to harm them. Believers' hearts become troubled. This resembles a fever, for when the body's temperature rises, antibodies are formed in the patient's blood to inhibit or destroy harmful bacteria or germs. Similarly, those with troubled hearts begin to fight.

This shows that such thoughts and suggestions do not come from, and are not approved of or adopted by, the heart. So, just as the reflection of something foul is not foul and does not make you dirty, and just as a snake's reflection does not bite, conceiving of unbelief is not the same as unbelief, and imagining yourself in unbelief does not make you an unbeliever. It might even be said that Satan's evil suggestions are beneficial, for they keep believers always on guard ready to resist temptation and to continue their struggle against the carnal self and Satan. This causes them to make spiritual progress.

How to Resist Satan

In fact, Qur'an 4:76 tells us that *the guile of Satan is ever feeble.* It resembles a cobweb that appears while you are walking between two walls. It does not cause you to stop, and you should not give it any importance. He suggests or whispers and presents sinful acts in a "falsely ornamented wrapper," thus believers must never accept his "gifts." When he whispers evil thoughts, believers should know that this is his last and weakest strategy and treat it accordingly. If they pay attention to such whispering, they might be defeated. Like a commander who, deceived by his own fear, dispatches his army to the two wings and leaves the center exposed, believers exhaust their powers of perseverance and resolve by fighting Satan and their own carnal selves when they concentrate on such whispering. In the end, they cannot withstand the real fight.

To free yourself from such evil suggestions, remove yourself from the attractive fields of Satan and sin. Heedlessness and neglect of worship are invitations to Satan's "arrows." The Qur'an declares: *Whose sight is dim to the remembrance of the All-Merciful, We assign unto him a devil who becomes his comrade* (43:36). Remembrance of the All-Merciful, noble or sacred phenomena, and a devout religious life protect us from Satan's attacks. Again, the Qur'an advises: *If a suggestion from Satan occurs to you, then seek refuge in God. He is All-Healing, All-Knowing. Those who fear God and ward off (evil), when a passing notion from Satan troubles them, they remember, and behold, they see* (7:200-1).

God's Messenger advised: "When you are angry, sit; if you are standing, sit down; lie down or stand up if you are sitting and perform the ritual ablution." On the way back from a military expedition, the Prophet called a halt at a certain place. They were so tired that they slept through the time for the dawn prayer. When they woke up, the Prophet commanded: "Leave here at once, for Satan rules this place." The Prophet also says that Satan flees the call to prayer.

Satan sometimes tries to tempt us through obscene scenes. He causes us to obsess over illicit pleasures. On such occasions, try to persuade yourself that any illicit pleasure will result in fits of remorse and may endanger your afterlife or even your mortal life. Know that the life of this world is but a passing plaything, a comforting illusion, and that the true life is that of the Hereafter. When some of his men hesitated to join the expedition to Tabuk because of the scorching summer heat, God warned them: *The heat of Hell is much more intense, if they would but understood* (9:81).

SPELLS AND SORCERY

Those who deny spells and sorcery do so either because they do not believe in anything related to metaphysics or what they suppose to be connected with religion, or because they are unaware of realities beyond the physical realm. A man in his fifties once told me:

> Until last year I did not believe in spells and sorcery. However, last year one of my relatives went mad. When he had a fit, he became rigid with his eyes fixed on a certain point. We sought the help of every doctor, but in vain. Finally, we went to someone who could break spells. He recited incantations and did some other things. On the way back, the patient asked in a normal tone: "Where am I? What happened to me?" He had recovered. I now believe that sorcery is real.

Most of us have heard of or even seen such cases. As the Prophet declared that the evil eye is an undeniable fact, sorcery is also an undeniable reality. The Qur'an speaks about (and severely condemns) the sorcery practiced to cause a rift between spouses. According to the Qur'an and Islam, sorcery and casting spells are as sinful as unbelief.

While breaking a spell is a good, meritorious deed, it must not be adopted and practiced as a profession. Although our Prophet met with jinn, preached Islam to them, and took their allegiance, he never explained how to contact them or how to cast or break a spell. However, he taught how jinn approach us and seek to control us, how to protect ourselves against their evil, and how to protect ourselves against the evil eye.

The safest way to protect ourselves against evil spirits is to have a strong loyalty to God and His Messenger. This requires following the principles of Islam strictly. In addition, we should never give up praying, for prayer is a weapon against hostility, protects us from harm, and helps us to attain our goals.

Praying

Prayer does not mean to ignore and neglect material means in attaining goals. Rather, prayer can be divided into four types. First is that which reaches to the Court of God from the whole universe. For example, plants and animals pray through the tongue of their potential to achieve a full form and to manifest certain Divine Names. Second is that which is expressed in the tongue of natural needs. All living beings pray to God, the Absolutely Generous One, to satisfy their vital needs, for they cannot do so themselves. Third is that which is done in the tongue of complete helplessness. A living creature in straitened circumstances takes refuge in its Unseen Protector with a genuine supplication, and turns to its All-Merciful Lord. These three kinds of prayer are always acceptable unless somehow impeded.

The fourth type of prayer is the one we do. This also falls into two categories: active and by disposition, and verbal and with the heart. For example, acting in accordance with causes is active prayer. By complying with causes, we try to gain God's approval for our requests, for only God can produce the result. For example, plowing the soil is an active prayer, for it involves actually knocking at the door of the treasury of God's Mercy. Similarly, going to a doctor is an active prayer for recovery from illness. For this reason, believers must seek medical help when ill. Believing psychiatrists should be preferred in cases of mental illnesses, for innumerable cases show that most mental illnesses are not due to material causes and that (physical) therapy cannot cure them. Most of them require spiritual therapy. This active type of prayer is usually acceptable, for it is a direct application to the Divine Name the All-Generous.

The second type of prayer, which is done with the tongue and the heart, is the real one. It is to ask God from the heart for something that we cannot obtain on our own. Its most important aspect and finest and sweetest fruit is that the supplicants know that He hears them, is aware of whatever occurs to their hearts, has power that extends everywhere, can satisfy all their desires, and helps them because He is merciful to the weak and helpless.

Prayer is a form of worship rewarded primarily in the Hereafter. For this reason, we must not say that our prayers are not answered when we do not receive that for which we prayed. Just because a prayer is "answered" does not mean that it is "accepted" in all circumstances. There is an answer for every prayer, but its acceptance and answer depend on God's Wisdom. Suppose a sick child asks a doctor for a certain kind of medicine. The doctor either will give that medicine or something better, or will give no medicine at all, especially if there is some reason to think that it will harm the child.

Similarly, God Almighty, the All-Hearing and All-Seeing, answers His servants' prayers and changes the depression of loneliness into the pleasure of His Company. But His Divine answer does not depend on our fancies; rather, it depends on Divine Wisdom, according to which He either gives what is requested or what is better, or He gives nothing at all. However He answers, we must pray.

As we pray for ourselves, we also must request those who we believe to be near to God to pray for us. The Companions frequently asked the Prophet to pray for them. As recorded by Ibn Hanbal, Abu Dawud, al-Tabarani, and Umm Hani: An insane child was brought to God's Messenger, who touched him and said: "Come out, O enemy of God." Then, he washed the child's face and prayed. The child recovered. Many similar cases are narrated in the Bible. The Prophet Jesus was famous for healing the insane by God's permission and power.

Avoiding Exorcists

Some people go to exorcists. Although a few people might know how to drive out evil spirits, such activity is usually quite dangerous, for most exorcists deceive people. In addition, an exorcist must be very careful about his or her religious obligations, refrain from sin, and be an upright person who really knows what he or she is doing. Patients usually rely on exorcists and attribute their recovery to them, and also rely on the written charm or amulets they are advised to carry. However, our Prophet declared that God would admit into Paradise 70,000 people without calling them to account for their deeds. These people would be those who do not wear armlets or amulets, who do not consider things auspicious or inauspicious, and who trust completely in God.

Consulting Believing Psychiatrists

Believers should not go to psychiatrists or doctors who restrict themselves to a materialist view of existence. Such psychiatrists, who do not believe in the spirit and spirit beings, may advise patients suffering from spiritual dissatisfaction or being possessed to indulge themselves in pleasure and amusement. This is like advising thirsty people to quench their thirst with salt water.

Reciting Specific Prayers

God's Messenger mentioned that special prayers should be recited to protect oneself against the evils of Satan and other unbelieving jinn. The Verse of Throne (2:255) is one of them. We also read that: *If a stimulus from Satan occurs to you, seek refuge in God immediately* (41:36) by saying: "I seek refuge in God from Satan, the accursed."

As reported by 'A'isha, the Mother of Believers and one of the Prophet's wives, God's Messenger recited *Surat al-Falaq* and *Surat al-Nas* three times every morning and evening, and then breathed into his joined palms and rubbed them against the parts of his body he could reach. He also recited three times every morning and evening: "In the Name of God, whom nothing on the earth and in the heaven can give harm despite His Name, and He is the All-Hearing, the All-Knowing." This recitation and the following one are among the prayers advised for protection against paralysis: "I seek refuge in all of God's words from all devils and vermin and from all evil eyes."

Imam Ghazali advises us to protect ourselves against spells, charms, and evil spirits by reciting: "In the Name of God, the All-Merciful, the All-Compassionate" once, "God is the Greatest" ten times, and: *The magician will not be successful wherever he appears* (20:69), and *from the evil of blowers upon knots* (113:4). Another imam advises us to recite these two verses 19 times after each sip of any liquid. We should remind that these are to be recited in their original, Arabic form.

ENDNOTE: Further views on the invisible realm of existence

Scientists restrict the concept of life to the conditions that obtain on or beneath Earth's outer surface. Therefore, when they look for extraterrestrial life, they look for conditions that are the same as or closely correspond to the conditions for life on Earth. If they had retained a sufficient sense of the absolute wonder of life (an aspect of life's being a direct manifestation of the Ever-Living), they should not have ruled out forms and conditions of life currently beyond their understanding. In their view, the arguments put forward by Said Nursi for the existence of angels and other spirit beings may not be worthy of consideration. However, the latest discoveries in deep-sea biology may persuade them to review his arguments. Writing at the beginning of the 1930s, Said Nursi stated:

> Reality and wisdom in the existence of the universe require that the heavens should have conscious inhabitants of their own, as

does the Earth. These inhabitants of many different kinds are called *angels* and *spirit beings* in the language of religion.

It is true that reality requires the existence of angels and other spirit beings because the Earth, although insignificant in size compared with the heavens, is continually being filled with and emptied of conscious beings. This clearly indicates that the heavens are filled with living beings who are the perfect class of living creatures. These beings are conscious and have perception, and they are light of existence; they are the angels, who, like the jinn and mankind, are the observers of the universal palace of creation and students of this book of the universe and heralds of their Lord's Kingdom.

The perfection of existence is through life. Moreover, life is the real basis and the light of existence; consciousness, in turn, is the light of life. Since life and consciousness are so important, and a perfect harmony evidently prevails over the whole creation, and again since the universe displays a firm cohesion, and as this small ever-rotating sphere of ours is full of countless living and intelligent beings, so it is equally certain that those heavenly [realms] should have conscious, living beings particular to themselves. Just as the fish live in water, so those spirit beings may exist in the heat of the sun. Fire does not consume light; rather, light becomes brighter because of fire. We observe that the Eternal Power creates countless living beings from inert, solid substances and transforms the densest matter into subtle living compounds by life. Thus It radiates the light of life everywhere in great abundance and furnishes most things with the light of consciousness.

From this we can conclude that the All-Powerful, All-Wise One would certainly not leave without life and consciousness more refined, subtle forms of matter like light and ether, which are close to and fitting for the spirit. Indeed He creates animate and conscious beings in great numbers from light, darkness, ether, air and even from meanings and words. As He creates numerous species of animals, He also creates from such subtle and higher forms of matter numerous different spirit creatures. One kind ... are the angels, others are the varieties of spirit beings and jinn. [Nursi, S., *The Words*, Twenty-ninth Word]

Half a century after Said Nursi wrote this, nearly 300 animal species, almost all of them previously unknown, were discovered living around hydrothermal vents that form when sea-water leaking through the ocean floor at spreading ridges is heated by the underlying magma and rushes into the cold ocean.

V. Tunniclife writes:

> All life requires energy, and nearly all life on Earth looks to the sun as the source. But solar energy is not the only kind of energy available on the Earth. Consider the energy that drives the movement and eruption of the planet's crust. When you look at an active volcano, you are witnessing the escape of heat that has been produced by radioactive decay in the Earth's interior and is finally reaching the surface. Why should there not be biological communities associated with the same nuclear energy that moves continents and makes mountains? And why could not whole communities be fuelled by chemical, rather than, solar energy?
>
> ... Most of us associate the escape of heat from the interior of the Earth with violent events and unstable physical conditions, with extremely high temperatures and the release of toxic gasses—circumstances that are hardly conducive to life. The notion that biologic communities might spring up in a geologically active environment once seemed fantastic. And until recently, few organisms were known to survive without a direct or indirect way to tap the sun's energy. But such communities do exist, and they represent one of the most startling discoveries of 20th century biology. They live in the deep ocean, under conditions that are both severe and variable. (American Scientist, 1995)

This startling discovery contains clues to other realities, which science should consider. Prophet Muhammad states that angels are created from light. We read in the Qur'an that God created humanity from dried soil, wet clay, and an extract of clay, and then made humanity His *khalifa* [one who comes after (to rule according to God's commandments)] for this planet. Many interpreters of the Qur'an have concluded from this that jinn once ruled the Earth and were succeeded by humanity.

Starting from the clues above, it should be possible to do formal studies to determine the worth of such propositions as the following:

God first created "pure light" (*nur*) and then light. The process of creation followed a gradual, regular accumulation of identities and/or an evolutionary sequence of abrupt leaps. Fire followed light, and then came water and soil. God spread one existence through another, compounding and interweaving, and created living beings appropriate for each phase of creation. When the universe was in a state of pure fire or some other high energy, He created appropriate life forms. When the Earth became suitable for life, He created plants, animals, and humanity. He adorned every part and phase of the universe with creatures, including living ones, appropriate for that part and phase.

Finally, just as He created innumerable beings from light, ether, air, fire, water, and soil, so does He create Paradise or Hell from each of our words and deeds. In other words, just as He grows a tree from a tiny seed through particles of soil, air and water, so will He build the other world, including Paradise and Hell, from the material of this world by adapting it for the other world during the convulsions of the Day of Judgment. [*The Fountain*, Issue 13 (Jan.-Mar. 1996), pp. 36-37.]

CHAPTER 3

Divine Decree and Destiny, and Human Free Will

DIVINE DECREE AND DESTINY, AND HUMAN FREE WILL

INTRODUCTION

The Arabic word translated as destiny is qadar. In its derivations, this word also means determination, giving a certain measure and shape, dividing, and judging. Muslim scholars of Islam define it as Divine measure, determination, and judgment in the creation of things.

Before discussing Divine Decree and Destiny further, consider the following relevant verses:

> With Him are the keys of the Unseen. None but He knows them. He knows what is in the land and the sea. Not a leaf falls but He knows it, not a grain amid the darkness of the soil, naught of wet or dry but it is in a Manifest Book (*Kitabun Mubin*). (6:59)

> There is nothing hidden in the heaven or the Earth but it is in a Manifest Book. (27:75)

> It is We Who bring the dead to life. We record what they send (of their lives and conduct to the Hereafter) and what is left of them. All things we have kept in a Manifest Record (*Imamun Mubin*). (36:12)

> They ask: "When (will) this promise (be fulfilled), if you are truthful?" Say: "The knowledge is with God only, and I am but a plain warner." (67:25-26)

> Nay, but it is a glorious Qur'an. On a Preserved Tablet (*Lawhun Mahfuz*). (85:21-22)

In one sense, Decree and Destiny mean the same thing. In another sense, however, Destiny means to predetermine or preordain, while Decree means to implement or put into effect. To be more precise, Destiny means that everything that exists, from subatomic particles to the universe as a whole, is known by God Almighty. His Knowledge includes all space and time, while He Himself is absolutely free from both. Everything exists in His Knowledge, and He assigns certain shape, life span, function or mission, and certain characteristics to each and every thing.

Consider the following analogy: Authors have full and exact knowledge of the books they will write, and arrange its contents before writing it. In this sense, Destiny is almost identical with Divine Knowledge, or is a title of Divine Knowledge. Therefore it is also called the "Supreme Preserved or Guarded Tablet" (or the "Manifest Record"). Destiny also means that God makes everything according to a certain, particular measure and in exact balance:

> God knows what every female bears and what the wombs absorb and what they grow. And everything with Him is measured. (13:8)

> The sun and the moon are made punctual according to a calculation. The stars and the trees adore, in subservience to Him. And the sky He has uplifted; and He has set the balance, that you exceed not the balance, but observe the balance strictly, nor fall short thereof. (55:5-9)

The exact measure and balance, order and harmony in the universe clearly show that everything is determined and measured, created and governed by God Almighty. Therefore, Divine Destiny exists. The acceptance of determinism by many people, including even some Marxists, to explain this obvious universal order, is a tacit acceptance of Destiny. But we have to clarify one point here: According to Islam, absolute determinism cannot be used in the context of human action.

All seeds, measured and proportioned forms, and the universe's extraordinary order and harmony (which has continued for billions of years without interruption or deviation) demonstrate that everything occurs according to God Almighty's absolute determination. Each seed or ovum is like a case formed by Divine Power into which Divine Destiny inserts the future life-history of a plant or a living being. Divine Power employs atoms or particles, according to the measure established by Divine Destiny, to transform each seed into a specific plant, and each fertilized ovum into a specific living being. This means that the future life-history of these entities, as well as the principles governing their lives, are prerecorded in the seed or the fertilized ovum as determining factors and processes.

Plants and living beings are formed from the same basic materials. However, there is an almost infinite variety between species and individuals. Plants and living beings grow from the same constituent basic elements, and display great harmony and proportion. Yet, there is such abundant diversity that we are forced to conclude that each entity receives a specific form and measure. This specific form and measure is established by Divine Destiny.

THE MANIFEST RECORD AND THE MANIFEST BOOK

In order to better understand these two terms, let's take the lucid example of a seed exhibiting Destiny in two ways: demonstrating the Manifest Record (*Imamun Mubin*) and displaying the Manifest Book (*Kitabun Mubin*).

The Manifest Record, another title for Divine Knowledge and Command, includes all things and events in the universe. That is, every thing and event has a pre-existence in Divine Knowledge. When it is time for them to come into the world or when God wills to bring them into the world, He clothes them in material existence.

The Manifest Record refers to this phenomenon. A seed contains the future life of the plant that will grow from it. The plant's life also ends in seeds, each of which may be regarded as the plant's memory. The new plants that will grow from those seeds will be almost identical with the original plant, because none of them has a conscious spirit endowed with free will. Thus, besides serving as an analogy for the Manifest Record and therefore Divine Destiny and Knowledge, a seed also indicates the

Supreme Preserved Tablet (*Lawhun Mahfuz*) and corresponds to human memory in the human kingdom. In addition, because a seed indicates that the life-histories of creatures are recorded, it also points to afterlife.

The Manifest Book is another title for Divine Will and God's creational and operational laws of the universe. If we refer to the Manifest Record as Formal or Theoretical Destiny, the Manifest Book can be referred to as Actual Destiny. The future full-grown form of a plant or a living being, which displays all the content of the seed or fertilized ovum, can be understood as its Actual Destiny.

In short, like seeds or plants or fertilized ovums and living beings, everything that exists clearly points to Divine Destiny, determining and judging, as well as measuring, particularizing, and individualizing.

True dreams that inform us of certain future events are another, undeniable indication of Destiny or Divine predetermination.

Question: Why is belief in Destiny one of the essentials of faith?

Answer: Our self-conceit and weak devotion leads us to attribute our accomplishments and good deeds to ourselves and to feel proud of ourselves. But the Qur'an explicitly states: *God creates you and what you do* (37:96), meaning that Divine Compassion demands good deeds and the Power of the Lord creates them. If we analyze our lives, eventually we realize and admit that God directs us to good acts and usually prevents us from doing what is wrong.

In addition, by endowing us with sufficient capacity, power, and means to accomplish many things, He enables us to realize many accomplishments and good deeds. As God guides us to good deeds and causes us to will and then do them, the real cause of our good deeds is Divine Will. We can "own" our good deeds only through faith, sincere devotion, praying to be deserving of them, consciously believing in the need to do them, and being pleased with what God has ordained. Given this, there is no reason for us to boast or be proud; rather, we should remain humble and thankful to God.

On the other hand, we like to deny responsibility for our sins and misdeeds by ascribing them to Destiny. But since God neither likes nor approves of such acts, all of them belong to us and are committed by acting upon our free will. God allows sins and gives them external forms, for if He did not, our free will would be pointless. Sins are the result of our decision, through our free will, to sin. God calls and guides us to good deeds, even inspires them within us, but free will enables us to disobey our Creator. Therefore, we "own" our sins and misdeeds. To protect ourselves against sin and the temptations of Satan and our carnal, evil-commanding self, we must struggle to remove or discipline our inclinations toward sin through repentance and asking forgiveness for them. In addition, we must direct and exhort ourselves to do good deeds through prayer, devotion, and trust in God.

In short, because we have free will and are enjoined to follow religious obligations and refrain from sin and wrong deeds, we cannot ascribe our sins to God. Divine Destiny exists so that believers do not take pride in their "own" good deeds but rather thank God for them. We have free will so that the rebellious carnal self does not escape the consequences of its sins.

A second, important point is that we usually complain about past events and misfortune. Even worse, we sometimes despair and abandon ourselves to a dissolute lifestyle, and might even begin to complain against God. However, we relate past events and misfortunes to Destiny and feel relief, security, and consolation.

So, whatever happened in the past should be considered in the light of Destiny; what is to come, as well as sins and questions of responsibility, should be referred to human free will. In this way, the extremes of fatalism and denying Destiny's role in human actions (the view of the Mu'tazila) is reconciled.

DIVINE DECREE AND DESTINY

Divine Knowledge

God is completely beyond our abilities of comparison and conception, and so we can acquire only some knowledge of His

Attributes and Names, not of His Divine Essence, by meditating on and studying His acts and creatures. To understand His acts, sometimes we have to resort to comparisons, as allowed in the Qur'anic verse: *God's is the highest comparison* (30:27). We may get a glimpse of the relationship between Divine Decree and Destiny and Divine Knowledge by pondering the following comparisons:

Suppose an extremely skilful man, who is an engineer as well as an architect and a builder, wants to build a magnificent house. First, he must determine what type of house he wants (the house exists in his mind). Then, he draws the blueprints (the house exists as an actual design or plan). After this, he builds the house according to the blueprints (the house acquires a material existence). As people can see the house, its image is recorded in numerous memories. Even if it is completely destroyed, it lives on in these memories and in the builder's mind and plan (the final form of the house's existence, which has acquired some kind of perpetuity).

Before writing a book, an author must have its full content or knowledge of its full meaning in his/her mind (the book exists as knowledge or meaning). To make this knowledge or meaning visible and known, he/she must express it in words. Before doing this he/she must arrange it (a "blueprint"), and then write it down (material existence). Even if the book is destroyed and vanishes, it continues to live in the memories of those who read or heard of it, and in the author's own mind.

Such existence—existence in mind—is the thing's essential existence. Even if the thing in question is not put into words or practice, its knowledge or meaning exists in the mind. Therefore, although knowledge or meaning needs matter to be seen and known in this world, they are the essence of existence, upon which material existence depends.

Likewise, God has full and exact knowledge of the universe and all its contents. This is stated in the Qur'an many times. For example:

> It may be that you dislike a thing although it is good for you, and love a thing although it is bad for you. God knows, but you know not. (2:216)

Say: "Whether you hide what is in your breasts or reveal it, God knows it. He knows all that the heavens and the Earth contain; and He has power over all things." (3:29)

With Him are the keys of the Unseen. None but He knows them. And He knows what is in the land and the sea. Not a leaf falls but He knows it; not a grain amid the darkness of the soil, nothing of wet or dry, but (it is) in a Manifest Book. (6:59)

Say: "If the ocean were ink for the words of my Lord, assuredly the ocean would be used up before the words of my Lord were finished, even if We brought another (ocean) like it, for its aid." (18:109)

Even if He had not created the universe, it still would exist in His Knowledge. Since God is beyond all time and space, both of which are united in His Knowledge as a single point, and since His eternal, all-encompassing Knowledge does not depend on them, time is a unified whole. Given this, precedence or posteriority, sequence or division of time, and all other time-related concepts do not exist for Him. We should always remember that our categories of past, present, and future time are only artificial categories designed to make our lives more manageable. Time and space are two dimensions of creation.

Everything eternally exists in God's Knowledge, and He literally knows everything about everything. Divine Power clothes a thing in material existence according to Divine Will, and this transference from Knowledge into our own world takes place within the limits of time and space. Knowledge and Will are two essential Attributes of Divine Being: God knows things, things exist in His Knowledge, His Will determines all of their specific and general characteristics, and His Power gives them material existence. The overall relationship between Divine Knowledge and Destiny is best expressed as: *There is not a thing but with us are the stores thereof. We send it not down save in appointed measure* (15:21).

Registry and Duplication

Everything that exists in Divine Knowledge has an individualized form and a certain measure, or, if we may say so, as a plan or project, is in a Record. This record is called, in one respect, the *Supreme Preserved Tablet* (85:22) and, in another, the *Manifest Record* (36:12). The Qur'an states that *nothing befalls us save that which God has decreed or preordained for us* (9:51) and *there is not a moving creature on the earth, nor a flying creature flying on two wings, but they are communities like humanity, and that God has neglected nothing in the Record* (6:38).

This Record (or original Register) is a title for Divine Knowledge in relation to creation. During the "process" of creation, this Register is duplicated. Its first, most comprehensive duplication—all of creation—is the *Tablet of Effacement and Confirmation* (or the Manifest Book). While the Supreme Preserved Tablet (or the Manifest Record) contains the originals of everything in Divine Knowledge, as well as the principles and laws of creation, the Tablet of Effacement and Confirmation is the reality and, metaphorically, a page of the stream of time. Divine Power transfers things from the Supreme Preserved Tablet onto the Tablet of Effacement and Confirmation, arranges them on the page of time and, in turn, attaches them to the string of time. Nothing changes on the Supreme Preserved Tablet, for everything there is fixed. But during the process of creation, *God effaces what He wills, and confirms and establishes what He wills* (13:39).

After birth, everyone is registered in a Registry of Births. Then, based on this information, everyone receives an identity document. Similarly, everyone's complete personal characteristics, particularities, and future life-history are registered on the Supreme Preserved Tablet, which then is copied by angels. They record all the information related to one's body, and encode it in cells as information or laws. For this information to work and come to life, however, the spirit must be breathed into the body.

The other part of this copy is fastened around our neck as an invisible book (17:13). We enact whatever is in that book as long as we are alive. This does not mean that Destiny or predetermination compels us to act in a certain way, for Destiny is no more than a sort of knowledge. For example, you send someone somewhere to do a job. Having procured the necessary supplies, you brief the man and send him on his way. Since you know in advance how he will behave, you record the journey's details in a notebook and hide it in a secret pocket in his jacket. Unaware of the notebook, this fellow behaves as he wishes while traveling. You also dispatch two of your most reliable men to follow him in order to observe and videotape secretly whatever he says and does. When he returns, you compare the videotapes with the notebook and see that they are exactly the same. Afterwards, you interview him to see if he followed your instructions, and then either reward, punish, or forgive him accordingly.

As in the example above, God, Who is beyond all time and space, and therefore has comprehensive knowledge, records our life-history in the original Register. Angels copy this information and fasten a personal register, which we call destiny or fate, around each person's neck. God's apparent foreknowledge and recording of our deeds and words do not compel us to perform them, for whatever we say or do is the result of using our free will.[1] Our complete life is recorded by two angels, called Kiramun Katibun (the Noble Recorders). On the Day of Judgment, our record will be presented to us, and we will be told to read it:

> Every man's book of life-history (fate) have We fastened around his neck, and We shall bring forth for him on the Day of Resurrection a book which he will find wide open. (It will be said unto him): "Read your book. Your own self suffices as a reckoner against you this day." (17:13-14)

Divine Will

God registers everything in His Knowledge in a record containing each thing's unique characteristics, life span, provision, time and place of birth and death, and all of its words and actions. All of this takes place by Divine Will, for it is through Divine Will that every thing and event, whether in the realm of Divine Knowledge or in this world, is known and given a certain course or direction. Nothing exists beyond the scope of the Divine Will.

For example, an embryo faces innumerable alternatives: whether it will be a live being, whether it will exist or not, when and where it will be born and die, and how long it will live, to mention just a few. All beings are completely unique in complexion and countenance, character, likes and dislikes, and so on, although they are formed from the same basic elements. A particle of food entering a body, whether an embryo or fully developed, also faces countless alternatives as to its final destination. If a single particle destined for the right eye's pupil were to go to the right ear, this would result in an anomaly.

Thus, the all-encompassing Divine Will orders everything according to a miraculously calculated plan, and is responsible for the universe's miraculous order and harmony. No leaf falls and no seed germinates unless God wills it to do so.

Our free will is included in Divine Will. However, our relation with Divine Will differs from that of other beings, for only we (and the jinn) can choose as a consequence of having free will. Based on His knowledge of how we will act and speak, God Almighty has recorded all details of our life. As He is not bound by the artificial division of time into past, present, and future, what we consider predetermination exists in relation to us, not to God Himself. For Him, predetermination means His eternal knowledge of our acts.[2]

In sum: Divine Will dominates creation, and nothing can exist or happen beyond Its scope. It is also responsible for the universe's miraculous order and harmony, and gives every thing and event a specific direction and characteristics. The existence of Divine Will does not negate human free will.

Creation

There are two aspects of the relation between Divine Decree and Destiny and creation. First, as a determining and compelling factor, Destiny is absolutely dominant everywhere, except where our free will has a part. Everything occurs according to Its measure and determination, judgment and direction. God is the absolute owner of sovereignty, and thus does what He wills. No one can call Him to account for His acts. Being absolutely Just and Wise, and absolutely Merciful and Compassionate, He does only good and never wrongs His creatures.

We cannot interfere with the universe's operation. The sun always sends heat and light independent of us, the Earth rotates on its axis and around the sun, days and months pass, the seasons and years come and go, and we have no control over nature. There are innumerable instances of wisdom in all of God's acts, all of which benefit us. So, we must study and reflect on His acts to discover their wisdom:

> In the creation of the heavens and the Earth, and in the alter-
> nation of night and day, there are signs for men of understand-
> ing. Those that remember and mention God standing, sitting,
> and lying down, and reflect upon the creation of the heavens
> and the Earth: "Our Lord! You have not created this in vain.
> Glory be to You! Protect us from the punishment of the Fire."
> (3:190-91)

We should reflect on what happens to us. God never wills evil for His creatures, for *whatever evil befalls you is from yourself* (4:79). In other words, our sins are the source of our misfortunes. God allows misfortunes to strike us so that our sins will be forgiven or so that we will be promoted to higher ranks. But this does not mean that God, for a reason known only to Him, sometimes overlooks our sins and does not punish us.

The second aspect of this relationship concerns the religious injunctions and prohibitions, which relate to human free will. While Divine Destiny is absolutely dominant in those areas in which our free will has no part (e.g., creating and controlling all things and beings, as well as animate and inanimate bodies, planetary movements, and all natural events or phenomena), It takes our free will into consideration. God creates all things and events, including all our deeds, because He has honored us with free will and prepared an eternal abode for us. Although He desires that we always do what is good and insistently invites us to it, He does not refrain from giving eternal, physical existence to our bad choices and evil acts even though He is displeased with them.

DESTINY AND HUMAN FREE WILL

Human free will exists because:

- We feel remorse when we do something wrong. We beg God's forgiveness for our sins. If we trouble or harm someone, we ask that person to excuse us. These actions show that we choose to act in a particular way. If we could not choose our actions and were compelled to do them by a superior power, why should we feel remorse and seek forgiveness for anything?

- We choose to move our hands, speak, or stand up to go somewhere. We decide to read a book, watch television, or pray to God. We are not forced to do anything, nor are we somehow remotely controlled by an invisible, superior power.

- We hesitate, reason, compare, assess, choose, and then decide to do something. For example, if our friends invite us to go somewhere or do something, we first go through a mental process and then decide whether we will accompany them or not. We repeat this very process maybe 100 times a day.

- When we are wronged, we sometimes sue the one who wronged us. The court does not ascribe the crime to a compelling superior power like Destiny, and neither do we. The accused does not excuse himself or herself by blaming that power. Virtuous and wicked people, those who are promoted to high social ranks and those who waste their time, those who are rewarded for their good acts or success and those who are punished for their crimes—all of this proves that each of us has free will.

- Only the insane are not held responsible for their acts. Human reason and other mental faculties require us to decide and act freely; the results seen in our lives prove the truth of this assertion. Without free will, human reason and other faculties have no meaning.

- Animals have no will power, and so act under God's guidance ("instinct," according to materialistic science). For example, bees always build hexagonal hives. Since they have no will power, they never even try to build triangular hives or a nest. But we consider many alternatives before acting or speaking.

We also are free to change our minds, which we do when confronted with emergencies or new, better proposals. This also indicates our free will.

The Nature of Our Free Will

Our free will is not visible and has no material existence. However, such factors do not render its existence impossible. Everyone has two (physical) eyes, but we also can see with our third (spiritual) eye. We use the former to see things in this world; we use the latter to see things beyond events and this world. Our free will is like our third eye, which you may call insight. It is an inclination or inner force by which we prefer and decide.

We will and God creates. A project or a building's plan has no value or use unless you start to construct the building according to it, so that it becomes visible and serves many purposes. Our free will resembles that plan, for we decide and act according to it, and God creates our actions as a result of our decisions. Creation and acting are different things. God's creation means that He gives actual existence to our choices and actions in this world. Without God's creation, we cannot act.

To illuminate a magnificent palace, we must install a lighting system. However, the palace cannot be illuminated until we flick the switch that turns on the lights. Until we do so, the palace will remain dark. Similarly, each man and woman is a magnificent palace of God. We are illuminated by belief in God, Who has supplied us with the necessary lighting system: intellect, reason, sense, and the abilities to learn, compare, and prefer.

Nature and events, as well as Divinely revealed religions, are like the source of electricity that illuminates this Divine palace of the human individual. If we do not use our free will to flick the switch, however, we will remain in darkness. Turning on the light means petitioning God to illuminate us with belief. In a manner befitting a servant at the master's door, we must petition the Lord of the Universe to illuminate us and so make us a "king" or a "queen" in the universe. When we do this, the Lord of the Universe treats us in a way befitting Himself, and promotes us to the rank of kingship over other realms of creation.

God takes our free will into account when dealing with us and our acts, and then uses it to create our deeds. Thus we are never victims of Destiny or wronged by Fate. However insignificant our free will is when compared with God's creative acts, it is still the cause of our deeds. God makes large things out of minute particles, and creates many important results from simple means. For example, He makes a huge pine tree from a tiny seed, and uses our inclinations or free choice to prepare our eternal happiness or punishment.

To better understand our part, and that of our willpower, in our acts and accomplishments, consider the food we consume. Without soil and water, air and the sun's heat, none of which we can produce or create despite our advanced technology, we would have no food. We cannot produce even a corn seed. We did not create our body, one single part of which cannot control, or establish its relationship with food. For example, if we had to wind our heart like a clock at a fixed time every morning, how long would we survive?

Obviously, almost all parts of the whole complex and harmonious universe, which is a most developed organism, work together according to the most delicate measures to produce a morsel of food. Thus, the price of that morsel is almost as much as the price of the whole universe. How can we possibly pay such a price, when our part in producing that morsel is utterly negligible, consisting of no more than our own effort?

Can we ever thank God enough for even a morsel of food? If only a picture of grapes were shown to us, could all of us work together and produce it? No. God nourishes us with His bounty, asking in return very little. If He told us to perform 1,000 *rak'as* (units) of prayer for a bushel of wheat, we would have to do so. If He sent a raindrop in return for one rak'a, we would have to spend our whole lives praying. If you were left in the scorching heat of a desert, would you not give anything for a single glass of water?

How can we thank Him enough for each bodily limb? When we see sick and crippled people in hospitals, or when we ourselves are ill, we understand how valuable good health is. But can we ever thank Him enough for this blessing? The worship God Almighty orders us to perform is, in fact, for our personal benefit and spiritual refinement, as well as for a good personal and collective life. Furthermore, if we believe in and worship God, He rewards us with infinite happiness and bounties in Paradise.

In sum: Almost everything we have is given to us for practically nothing, and our part in the bounty we enjoy here is therefore quite negligible. Similarly, our free will is equally negligible when compared with what God Almighty creates from our use of it. Despite our free will's weakness and our own inability to really understand its true nature, God creates our actions according to the choices and decisions we make through it.

Divine Destiny is Compatible With Human Free Will

Throughout history, people have tried to distinguish or reconcile Divine Will and human free will. Some have denied free will, while others have claimed that we create our own deeds and thereby ignore Destiny. However, as Islam is the middle way in everything, it proclaims that Divine Destiny dominates existence, including the human realm, but that we can use our free will to direct our lives.

The Qur'an expresses the true nature of this relation as follows: *This [Qur'an] is a reminder unto the worlds, unto whoever among you wills to walk straight. You do not will, unless God wills, the Lord of the Worlds* (81:27-29). These verses attribute absolute will to God Almighty, but do not deny human free will. In another verse, we read that *God creates you and whatever you do* (37:96).

Other verses speak of a covenant between us and God, and openly declare that we direct history: *Fulfill [your part of] the covenant so that I fulfill [My part of] the covenant* (2:40); *If you help God['s religion], He will help you and will make your foothold firm* (47:7); and *God changes not the condition of a people unless they change what is in their hearts* (13:11).

Except for humanity and jinn, both of whom have free will and must account for their acts, Divine Destiny is the only absolutely dominant factor in existence. To reconcile Destiny and human free will, consider the following:

- Destiny is a title for Divine Knowledge. God's Knowledge comprehends everything within and beyond time and space. If your knowledge allows you to know beforehand that a certain thing will happen at a certain future time, your "prediction" will come true. But this does not mean that your foreknowledge caused it to happen. Since every thing and event are comprehended in God's Knowledge, He writes what will happen at a given time and place, and it does so. What God writes and what we do are exactly the same; not because God writes it and then forces us to do it, but because we will it and then do it.

  For example: A train travels between two cities. Considering its speed and characteristics, the railway's condition, the distance between the two cities, as well as the number of stations along the way and how much time must be spent in each, a timetable can be prepared. Does this timetable cause the train to travel?

  The time and duration of solar and lunar eclipses are known and written beforehand based on astronomical calculations. Does such foreknowledge and recording cause them? Of course not. Since astronomers knew beforehand when the eclipse would occur, they recorded it. The same relationship exists between Destiny and human free will.

- Our free will is included in Destiny. For example, someone asks you whether the clock in the next room is working. You hear it and answer in the affirmative. The questioner does not need to ask whether its hands are moving, for if the clock is working, its gears are working and its hands are moving. In an analogous way, Destiny and human free will are not mutually exclusive. We are neither dried leaves blown by the wind of Destiny nor completely independent of it. As Islam always follows the middle way, it explains the true relationship between Destiny and our free will: we will and do something, and God creates it.

- In the view of Destiny, cause and effect cannot be separated. It is destined that this cause will produce that effect. But we cannot argue that killing someone is alright because the victim was destined to die at that time or place, and would have died anyway even if he or she had not been shot. Such an argument is baseless, since the victim is actually destined to die as a result of being shot. The argument that the victim would have died even without being shot would mean that this death was senseless. How would we explain such a death? Remember that there are not two kinds of Destiny, one for the cause and the other for the effect. Destiny is one.

- People tend to imagine, excluding themselves from the passage of time, a limit for past time extending through a certain chain of things. They call this *azal* (past eternity). But to reason according to such an idea is unacceptable. To understand this subtle point better, consider the following:

    Imagine you are holding a mirror in your hand. Everything reflected on the right represents the past, while everything reflected on the left represents the future. The mirror can reflect only one direction, since it cannot show both sides at once while you are holding it. If you want to see both directions simultaneously, you would have to rise high above your original position so that left and right unite into one direction and nothing could be called first or last, beginning or end.

    Divine Destiny, in some respects identical with Divine Knowledge, is described in a Prophetic saying as containing all time and events as a single point, where first and last, beginning and end, what has happened and what will happen are all united into one. As we are not excluded from it, our understanding of time and events could be like a mirror to the past.[2]

- We do not create our actions. If we actually did so, we also would have to be their ultimate cause. If that were the case, we could not have free will, for, according to logic, a thing exists if its existence is absolutely necessary and all necessary conditions are prepared for its existence. Thus whatever comes into existence has to have a real, complete cause. But a complete cause would make the existence of something compulsory, meaning that there would be no room for choice.

- Although our free will cannot cause something to happen, Almighty God has made its operation a simple condition for bringing His universal Will into effect. He uses our free will to guide us in our chosen direction, and so we are responsible for our actions. If you place your child on your shoulders and, at her request, take her outside, she might catch a cold. Could she blame you for her cold? Indeed, you might even punish her for her request. In a similar manner, Almighty God, the Most Just of Judges, never forces His servants to do anything, and so has made His Will somewhat dependent on human free will.

We may summarize the discussion so far in seven points:

1. Divine Destiny, also called Divine determination and arrangement, dominates the universe but does not cancel or negate our free will.

2. Since God is beyond time and space and everything is included in His Knowledge, He encompasses the past, present, and future as one undivided and united point. For example: If you are in a room, your view is restricted to the room. If you look from a higher point, you can see the whole city. As you rise higher and higher, your vision continues to broaden. The Earth, when seen from the moon, appears to be a small blue marble. It is the same with time.

3. Since all time and space are included in God's Knowledge as a single point, God recorded everything that will happen until the Day of Judgment. Angels use this record to prepare a smaller record for each individual.

4. We do not do something because God recorded it; God knew beforehand what we would do it and recorded it.

5. There are not two destinies: one for the cause, the other for the effect. Destiny is one and relates simultaneously to the cause and the effect. Our free will, which causes our acts, is included in Destiny.

6. God guides us to good things and actions, and allows and advises us to use our willpower for good. In return, He promises us eternal happiness in Paradise.

7. We have free will, although we contribute almost nothing to our good acts. Our free will, if not used properly, can destroy us. Therefore we should use it to benefit ourselves by praying to God. This will make it possible for us to enjoy the blessings of Paradise, a fruit of the chain of good deeds, and attain eternal happiness. Furthermore, we always should seek God's forgiveness so that we might refrain from evil and be saved from the torments of Hell, a fruit of the accursed chain of evil deeds. Prayer and trusting in God greatly strengthen our inclination toward good, and repentance and seeking God's forgiveness greatly weaken, even destroy, our inclination toward evil and transgression.

DIVINE DESTINY AND DECREE, AND DIVINE GRACE

Divine Decree means carrying out Destiny's decisions or judgments. It simultaneously includes our actions and God's creation of them, for God allows us to do what we will to do by bringing it into existence. The Arabic word translated here as Divine Grace is *'ata'*, which means "God's lavishness in giving, His favor, liberality and benevolence."

God has two main records or registers: the Supreme Preserved Tablet (corresponding to Destiny or Divine Knowledge) and the Manifest Record (corresponding to the reality of time). The Supreme Preserved Tablet never changes, since God also has absolutely unrestricted Will and is therefore not restricted by the Destiny He established for His creatures. However, He may change what He records in the Manifest Book: *God effaces whatever He wills and confirms whatever He wills, with Him is the Mother of the Book* (13:39).

This subtle matter is difficult to understand. Although we cannot fully understand the reality of this effacement and confirmation, we frequently witness it in our lives. For example, one day we leave home with the intention of going to a place where sins are freely committed. However, out of His mercy and favor,

God arranges for us to meet some good friends who persuade us to go to a good place. Likewise, we commit sins too freely and therefore are subject to misfortune. But instead of dealing with us by His Justice, God, out of His grace, treats us with utmost grace and pardons us, thereby saving us from misfortune.

Divine Grace exists so that we will not despair of being forgiven, so that we may turn to Him despite our sins, and so that we should not see ourselves as absolutely bound by the consequences that Divine Destiny and Decree establishes for our deeds. This is made explicit in the following verses:

> Whatever misfortune befalls you, is for what your own hands have earned, and for many (of them) He grants forgiveness. (42:30)

> If God were to punish people for their wrongdoing, He would not leave on the Earth a single living creature; but He reprieves them to an appointed term. (16:61)

> Relate (to them from Me): "O My slaves who have transgressed against their selves! Do not despair of God's mercy! Surely God forgives all sins, for He is the All-Forgiving, the Most Compassionate. (39:53)

Divine grace or liberality manifests itself more clearly in human history. As we are responsible and accountable for our acts, we direct our own history. Such historical philosophies as historicism are quite mistaken, for there is no determination in history or historical events.

Many historical peoples, such as those of the 'Ad, the Thamud, and Pharaoh, deserved to perish because of their dissolute lifestyles, injustice, and atrocities. So God eradicated them. However, Prophet Jonah's people turned to God with utmost sincerity and deep repentance, and reformed themselves morally after they saw signs of impending destruction. As a result, *God spared them the penalty of disgrace in the life of this world, and gave them comfort for a while* (10:98). Emphasizing this point, God's Messenger said: "Fear does not prevent misfortunes, but prayer and charity prevent them."[3]

Therefore, believers should never cease praying and giving charity. When they feel misfortune coming, they should immediately turn to God in prayer, repent, give charity, or perform some service for Islam.

THE DIVINE WISDOM IN CREATING PEOPLE DIFFERENTLY

Why did God create us with different levels of provision and intelligence, lifestyle and physiology? Why does He allow hardship and poverty amidst ease and luxury? Such questions, besides relating to Destiny, also have some bearing on understanding the Divine way of acting.

We Must Try to Know God

Before discussing this issue, we should point out that all such questions arise from not knowing the Divine Being. If we had as much desire to learn everything about God as we do about a movie star or a sports figure, if we had access to the necessary resources from which we could learn something about our Master, if we studied the Book of the Universe according to the criteria established by the Qur'an, and if we followed the principles preached by the Prophet to establish a true life—if we did all of this, we could discern the immaterial dimension of things and events through the prism of our conscience. If we could reach that level, we would not need to ask such questions. But as long as science isolates itself from religion, and healthy meditation is replaced by mechanical life and mass information, we will continue to ask such questions and find it hard to know our Creator.

God Controls Everything and Does as He Wills

Consider our claims of ownership and control over what we regard as our property. What share do we have in producing the food we consume? Each morsel of food requires the existence of the entire universe. Given this, and if we can claim ownership and control over our private property in which we have so little share, why should God, the Creator and unique Owner of the universe and all of its contents, not have complete control of His property?

God Almighty's Names Have Different Manifestations

The Name All-Providing supplies beings with what they need to live, the Name All-Healing enables patients to recover, and the Name All-Answering comes to the aid of the needy. He warns the heedless with His Name All-Distressing, and relieves the distressed with His Name All-Relieving. If we study the manifestations of God's Names, we can see the beauty in the variety they bring to the universe, and understand the wisdom underlying the differences in creation. God makes Himself known by manifesting His Names. For example, flowers smile at us as the result of the manifestation of His Names originating in His Grace, while natural catastrophes remind us of His Wrath as the manifestation of His Names originating in His Majesty.

Everything is God's Blessing

We cannot question God Almighty for what He gives or does not give. Remember that God did not create you as a lifeless element, a plant or an animal, but as a human being. Also, just as there are always people who are wealthier and healthier than you, there are also people who are poorer and sicker than you. So, with respect to wealth and health, consider those who are poorer and sicker than you. With respect to honesty and morality, learning and altruism, truthfulness and generosity, and so on, emulate those who are better than you.

Suppose a rich person gives three destitute people an apartment flat, a large house, and a palace, respectively. Does the one who is given an apartment flat have the right to ask the rich person why he was not given a house or a palace? Should he not, rather, thank his benefactor for the apartment? Similarly, all that we have is from God. Thus, whether we are rich or poor, sound or disabled, healthy or sick, we are obliged to thank God.

We Plant Here and Harvest in the Hereafter

This world is an arena of trial, a place where we seek to acquire the state appropriate for the other life. This is not easy. Like a tailor designing the best possible suit for a client by cutting and stitching the material and then having the client try it on, God Almighty causes us to "turn about" in diverse conditions to "shape" us for the afterlife.

We are like raw minerals that have to be refined. Just as there are many types of minerals, our social life requires that we have different levels of intelligence, physical strength, and sensitivity. Depending upon the final product desired, whether gold or diamonds, coal or copper, different (and more exacting and demanding) processes and methods must be applied to the raw mineral. Similarly, each of us may need a different test, trial, or training to be refined and reach our destined final level of attainment. This means that God subjects each of us to different levels of suffering and affliction to elevate us to a state appropriate for the other world.

This world is also the realm of trouble. When God warned Adam not to eat of the forbidden tree, He reminded him:

> Adam, surely this [Satan] is an enemy to you and your wife. So let him not expel you both from the Garden, so that you are unprosperous. It is assuredly given to you neither to hunger therein nor to go naked, neither to thirst therein, nor to suffer the sun. (20:117-19)

That means that we will experience hunger, thirst, tiredness, and encounter hardship in the world. This must be so, because in this world we sow the seeds that will be harvested in the Hereafter. Those seeking only to gratify their desires most probably are the ones God will address in the other world with the following words:

> You dissipated your good things in your worldly life, and you took your enjoyment in them; therefore today you will be recompensed with the chastisement of humiliation because you waxed proud on the Earth without right, and for your ungodliness. (46:20)

On the other hand, those who endure hunger, thirst, and other hardship here for the sake of God will be admitted to Paradise and addressed thusly by angels: *Peace be upon you. Well you have fared; enter in, to dwell forever* (39:73); and *Eat and drink with wholesome appetite for that you did long ago, in the days gone by* (69:24).

More Blessings Mean More Responsibility

As God gives you more bounties and blessings, your responsibility grows. For example, almsgiving is compulsory for the wealthy, while the disabled, blind, or sick do not have to bear arms in the way of God. To express the utmost degree of piety, the Prophet Jesus says:

> You have heard that it was said: "Do not commit adultery." But I tell you that anyone who looks at a woman lustfully has already committed adultery with her in his heart. If your right eye causes you to sin, gouge it out and throw it away. It is better for you to lose one part of your body than for your whole body to be thrown into Hell. And if your right hand causes you to sin, cut it off and throw it away. It is better for you to lose one part of your body than for your whole body to go into Hell. (Matthew 5:27-30)

So, we do not know if being rich or poor, or healthy or sick, is better for us. And, the Qur'an tells us that: *It may be that you dislike a thing although it is good for you, and love a thing although it is bad for you. God knows but you know not* (2:216).

Furthermore, many rich people cannot enjoy food and drink or the world's beauty as much as poor people do, due to their lack of appetite or bad health. Although poverty is not something to be desired and indeed, as stated by Prophet Muhammad, can even cause unbelief, it is difficult to claim that the rich are always happier than the poor. No one can assert that people in the Middle Ages, when living standards were relatively low, were less happy than today's rich people. Happiness lies in spiritual satisfaction, not in having the material facilities to gratify bodily desires.

Another point to emphasize is that no one should complain about hardship. When compared with times of good health, comfort, and happiness, times of illness or hardship often are not worth mentioning. Also, we usually live unaware of the constant bounties we receive. For example, the sun rises every day and sends us its heat and light for free. We are never deprived of air, without which we would die instantly although we pay nothing for it. All the natural events necessary for producing rain occur without our help. What we should do is thank God for these and all other bounties (none of which we can provide for ourselves), for the greatest part of our life (spent in health and comfort), and not to complain to God about illness, hardship, or the lack of some additional blessing.

Equality in material resources, as well as in intellectual and physical ability, should not be considered a desirable social objective, for it is incompatible with the requirements of social life. These differences, as well as those in individual temperament, disposition, and preference, sustain the variety of human occupations, a fundamental element of human social life. This variation causes people to need one another and to establish mutual good relations.

However, these relations should be based on justice and mutual love, respect, understanding, and care. They should not lead to oppression, usurpation, and cheating, or to class-based social hostility and contempt. According to Said Nursi (d. 1960), a Muslim scholar, thinker, and activist who started a major Islamic revival in Turkey in the first half of the twentieth century, two major reasons for all the revolutions and upheavals of the last few centuries are the attitudes: "I do not care if others die of hunger so long as I am full," and "You work so that I may eat."

Islam tackles the first attitude with zakat, the obligatory alms-tax on wealthy Muslims, principally for redistribution among the poor and needy. Islam tackles the second attitude by prohibiting all interest-based transactions. Further, Islam extols the virtue helping the poor and needy and commends moderate, disciplined living. The lives of the Prophet and his four immediate political successors (known collectively as the Rightly Guided Caliphs) are good examples for the Muslim élites to follow.

The Purpose of Misfortune

Before closing, we should point out that however undesirable and even appalling in appearance, affliction and illness usually bear good results. Just as punishing our children to train them, amputating a gangrenous limb, or deriving medicine from a snake's venom, most afflictions or illnesses usually produce good results.[4]

A sparrow-hawk's swooping contributes to a sparrow's agility and develops its ability to escape. People may be hurt by rain or electricity or fire, but no one actually curses them. Fasting may be difficult, but it provides the body with energy, activity, and resistance. A child's immune system usually gains strength through illness. Exercise is not easy, but it is almost essential for the body's health and strength. Our spirit is refined and acquires the state deserving Paradise through worship and meditation, as well as through illness, suffering, and hardship. God gives a large reward for a small sacrifice. Hardship and suffering promote us to higher spiritual degrees and will be rewarded in the other world with a generosity that we cannot even imagine. For this reason, Prophets suffer the most grievous hardship and difficulty, and they are followed by saints and other believers, each according to their degree of belief.

Hardship, illness, and calamity cause believers' sins to be forgiven and remind them to be alert to sin and the attempted seductions coming from Satan and their carnal selves. They also help us appreciate God's blessings, express our gratitude, and encourage the rich and healthy to help the poor and the sick. Those who never experience hunger cannot fully appreciate the conditions of the hungry. Nor can one who has never been sick be aware of what sick people live through. So, hardship, illness, and calamity may establish closer relations between different groups or classes of people.

Calamity and suffering increase our resistance to hardships of life and train us to persevere and endure. They also separate the strong and sincere supporters of a cause from those who are supporters out of convenience or some other personal (and therefore inappropriate) reason.

QUESTIONS ON DESTINY AND HUMAN FREE WILL

Question: Are we victims of Destiny? Do we have any part in the calamities befalling us?

Answer: As this question has been discussed earlier, I will present a summarized account.

No one is a victim of Destiny. God does not destine our acts; rather, He creates whatever we will to do. Destiny's decrees or verdicts are based on its consideration of our free will.

We are directly responsible for whatever happens to us. If we experience misfortune, it is either because we have misused our free will or because, as with Prophets, God wills to promote us to higher ranks. For example, the sun is absolutely necessary for and indispensable to life. If we stay outside too long and die of sunstroke, can we blame the sun? Of course not, for we could have gone inside or taken sufficient precautions. In the same way, our free will (not Destiny) is responsible for any misfortune that comes our way. Blaming Destiny only causes the misfortune to worsen.

To cite another example: God Almighty created and endowed us with certain faculties or powers, one of which is lust. If we use this power improperly and thus harm ourselves, it can only be our fault. God gave us this power so that we may reproduce the species in the proper manner and be promoted to higher spiritual ranks by resisting our carnal self's illicit suggestions. It is the same with anger. God Almighty gave it to us so that we can defend ourselves and our religious and social values, not to hurt others. Therefore, if an uncontrolled burst of anger causes us to kill someone, it is our fault, not Destiny's.

Destiny relates to both the cause and the effect simultaneously. If we judge only by considering the effect, usually we make mistakes. For example, if we accuse a father of abusing his son while he is only trying to discipline him because he loves his son or so that the son may reform himself and learn how to behave properly, we would be wronging the father. We should consider all related information while judging any event. If we cannot see any good in it, we should tell ourselves that whatever God does is good either in itself or in its consequences, and never accuse Destiny. This is what is meant by: *It may be that you dislike a thing although it is good for you, and love a thing although it is bad for you. God knows but you know not* (2:216).

In such calamities as earthquakes or floods, God usually does not choose between the good and the evil or the innocent and the guilty. Such calamities fall on everyone, for they are part of the tests and trials prepared for us and serve His purpose. However, in return for undergoing such calamities, good and innocent people will receive a great reward in the Hereafter. Also, it should be pointed out that sometimes God uses calamities to punish such people, because they do not try to enjoin what is good and prevent what is evil.

Whatever God does is the best and most proper. So, we should try to see His wisdom behind the good He bestows on us and the suffering to which He subjects us.

Question: Why does so insignificant a thing as free will cause one to deserve eternal Paradise or Hell?

Answer: When we compare God's acts and creation with our own function in existence, we see that the role of human free will is really insignificant. As a result, some have denied it. Followers of the middle path in this matter have concluded that human free will is an inclination, or something like inclination, or more of a preference for our internal inclinations, and then acting upon that inclination. It is actually like flicking a switch to light a house or a city.

Before asking why God Almighty may condemn us to eternal Hellfire if we misuse our free will during our short lifespan, we should think about whether we really can deserve eternal Paradise by using our free will correctly. Should we not consider whether we ever can thank God enough for the bounties He pours upon us? If we worshipped Him during our entire life unceasingly, we could not thank Him enough even for our eyes.

As pointed out earlier, a pomegranate or a cherry has the same cost as the universe, for its growth or production requires the cooperation of air, water, soil, and the sun, none of which we could produce. Furthermore, God Almighty asks us to assign only a small amount of time for worship. We seldom need more than one hour to perform the five prescribed daily prayers. The amount of wealth we are enjoined to give in charity is, in most cases, only one-fortieth of what we have. We have to go on pilgrimage (hajj) only once, and only if we can afford it. The rest of our life and wealth is for worldly things. Despite this, God, the All-Merciful, promises us eternal Paradise, the blessings and beauties of which are beyond imagination. So first of all, we should think about God's infinite mercy, which enfolds us and invites us to Paradise.

Now we will answer the question.

Intention

Our intention is critical. The Messenger says:

> Actions are judged according to intentions. Whatever you intend to do, you get the reward thereof. So, whoever emigrates for God and His Messenger has emigrated for God and His Messenger; whoever emigrates to acquire something worldly or to marry a woman emigrates to what is intended.[5]

Intention is the spirit of our actions and determines how we will be rewarded (or punished). If you do not eat or drink during the day, but made no intention to fast, you are not counted as having fasted. If you fast without intending to obtain God's good pleasure, you receive no reward. If you are killed fighting to exalt or strengthen the Word of God, you die as a martyr and go, by God's will, to Paradise. If you are killed while fighting for any other cause, such as fame or wealth, you are not considered a martyr and most probably will not be admitted to Paradise. So, you are rewarded (or punished) according to your intention.

If you have a firm belief in God and the pillars of faith, and intend to believe in them [as if you were to live eternally], you will be rewarded with eternal happiness in Paradise. If you have removed your inborn tendency to believe, and thus intend not to believe even if you were to live forever, you will cause your own eternal punishment. In the case of people whose unbelief is deeply ingrained and who have lost the capacity to believe, the Qur'an says:

> As for the unbelievers, it is the same whether you warn them or warn them not. They will not believe. God has set a seal on their hearts and on their hearing, and on their eyes is a covering (2:6-7)

Punishment For Unbelief

A given punishment is determined by the nature and result of the crime and the person's intention, not by the duration of the act.

Murder, which takes only a couple of minutes or even seconds to commit, is often punished by many years in jail or the death sentence. Unbelief is infinitely more serious than murder. Unbelief means denying numerous Prophets and saints as the witnesses for the existence of the Creator of the whole universe and thus it means accusing these truthful people of lying and deception. Unbelief also means the following:

- Denying the true testimony of innumerable creatures, from atoms to huge galaxies, to their Creator's existence and Unity, and accusing them of lying or giving false testimony.

- Denying God, the Unique Creator, Sustainer, and Administrator of existence, and degrading His innumerable works of art.

- Accusing more than 100,000 Prophets of the most abased form of lying, deception, and trickery, and doing this despite the fact that according to the testimony of history and the people to whom they were sent, they are the most truthful of all humanity.

- Accusing believers of following the greatest liars of human history. Such a view also insults innumerable believers since the time of Adam and accuses them of deception and deviation.

For these and other similar reasons, it is pure justice to condemn unbelievers to the eternal punishment of Hell.

However insignificant our free will appears, and however slight a sin unbelief may seem to be at first sight, unbelief is a denial and negation and therefore destructive. Remember that we likened free will to flicking a switch to illuminate a room. Flicking a switch off can throw a whole city into darkness. A match can destroy a huge, magnificent palace in a couple of minutes, even though it took hundreds of workers several years to build it. Remember that a single bullet fired by a Serbian ignited World War I and led to massive death and destruction.

Also, suppose there is a garden containing all kinds of flowers and trees in which birds sing and animals live. These plants and animals need water, reaching them through the canals, in order to survive. Someone is responsible for opening those canals so that water can flow through them. If that person, for whatever reason, did not allow water to flow and thus killed everything in the garden, what would be an appropriate punishment? The act of unbelief is equivalent to such an act, but on the scale of the creation as a whole.

Unbelief is an unforgivable ingratitude. How can you deny Him Who brought you into existence from non-existence, gave you so many faculties (e.g., reason, intellect, heart, memory, insight, inner and outer senses), and nourishes you with numerous varieties of food and drink? Such people prepare their own doom, and their punishment must be equal to their action (of denial).

Even if we all worked together, we could not create even one fruit, one leaf, or one blade of grass. Denying the existence of the One Who can do all of this, and Who created this huge universe and gave us dominion over it, is the worst sin that we can commit, and so deserves the most lasting and severest punishment.

Satan tries to lead us astray by inviting us to unbelief and dissipation. Our evil-commanding self was given to us so that we could rise to higher ranks by refining it. Our conscience innately feels the existence of God, the Creator and Sustainer of beings, and feelings that long for eternity can be satisfied only with eternity. Followers of Satan, unbelievers who are ruled by their desires and their evil-commanding selves, close their conscience to innumerable signs of God in themselves and the universe, extinguish their feelings related to eternity, and blind themselves to the Creator's most manifest signs: the Qur'an, Prophet Muhammad, and all other Prophets, peace and blessings be upon them.

Punishment Varies

The punishment for violating a trust is proportional to its significance and its true owner. A child who breaks a window does not receive the same punishment as an aide-de-camp who loses or breaks the king's crown. If a private and a commander spend the money they received (based on their rank) on petty things and so waste it, the commander certainly would receive a much greater punishment than the private. If a scientist responsible for carrying out scientific investigations spent the resources entrusted to him on studying trifling things, certainly he would be punished far more severely than a shepherd who spent the resources assigned to him on meeting his own needs instead of those of his animals.

Animals do not misuse or waste the capital of life assigned to them. They do whatever they must: some carry loads, some give milk and meat, and others produce honey or silk for our use. Only we can spend our resources according to our own desires. Given this fact, as well as the earlier-mentioned bounties that God has given us due to our status as His vicegerents on Earth, our misuse of these resources results in a very severe punishment. If we allow ourselves to be dominated by our evil-commanding self instead of our heart (which must overflow with knowledge and love of the Creator), we are destined to become fuel for the fire of Hell.

Question: The Prophet says that at the sixth week of an embryo's development, God sends an angel to write whether it will be righteous and prosperous or wicked and condemned. What does this mean, and how can we reconcile it with human free will?

Answer: In addition to what has been said above, we will make the following comments.

Destiny is a title of Divine Knowledge. It does not cancel our free will or force us to behave in a preordained way. Since God knows beforehand what we will do and say (as He is not constrained by our concept of time), He orders an angel to write down our life-history. We behave according to the dictates of our free will, not because God wrote down our future life.

Destiny is related both to the cause and the effect. There are not two separate destinies, one for the cause, the other for the effect. God knows beforehand how we will behave in a given circumstance, and His preknowledge does not negate our free will.

Only God knows whether we will go to Paradise or Hell. Although unbelief deserves eternal punishment, we may not say that unbelievers are going to Hell, for one day they might accept belief and go to Paradise. Many atheists have become Muslims. Islam came to guide unbelievers to faith and worship, and consequently to eternal happiness in Paradise.

Question: What does fitra (primordial nature) mean?

Answer: In an authentic *hadith*, the Prophet says that all infants are born with this *fitra*, and then their parents cause them to adopt another faith (or no faith at all).

This *hadith* means that everyone has the innate potential to become a Muslim. Islam is the natural religion of all creatures, as it means "peace, salvation, and obedience." Since everything obeys God absolutely and functions according to His laws, all creatures are *muslim*. Every being's bodily structure, regardless of religion or lack thereof, whether they are human or jinn, are *muslim*, for all bodies operate according to the laws God Almighty determined for them. If a new-born could lead a completely monastic life free of environmental effects, he or she would remain a natural Muslim.

This *hadith* also means that a new-born's mind is like a tape on which anything can be recorded, a lump of dough that can be shaped in any way, a blank paper on which anything can be written. If you could protect your mind from any external source of corruption, you could receive anything related to Islam easily and become a perfect Muslim. But if your mind becomes impure, or you inject into it the tenets, beliefs, and conduct of another religion (or of atheism), you either will adopt another faith or encounter many problems on your way to becoming a good Muslim.

New-borns resemble seeds that can produce good Muslims, for they are all seeds of future Muslims. Adverse conditions cause these seeds to be deformed or spoiled, and these people eventually adopt another faith or none at all. Therefore, to raise good Muslims, we have to do our best to improve our familial and surrounding social conditions. After children reach puberty, sins are a primary cause of deformed seeds. As every sin has the potential to lead people to unbelief, we must protect ourselves against sin. Family, education, and social environment are also of great importance.

Question: What does guidance mean, and can we guide someone else?

Answer: Guidance is a light that God kindles in you because you use your own free will in the way of belief. Only God guides one to the truth, as pointed out repeatedly in the Qur'an: *If God willed, he could have brought them all to the guidance* (6:35); *If it had been your Lord's will, all who are on Earth would have believed, altogether* (10:99); *You do not guide whom you like, but God guides whom He wills* (28:56); and *For verily You cannot make the dead hear, nor can you make the deaf hear the call when they have turned to flee. Nor can you guide the blind out of their deviation. You can make none hear save those who believe in Our Revelation so that they surrender and become Muslims* (30:52-53).

Since God guides, we implore Him in every *rak'a* of our daily prescribed prayers, saying: *Guide us to the Straight Path* (1:6). God's Messenger says: "I have been sent to call people to belief. Only God guides them and places belief in their hearts."

The Qur'an also states that God's Messenger calls and guides people to the Straight Path, such as in: *Surely you call them to the Straight Path* (23:73); and *Thus We have revealed a Spirit to you from Our Command. You did not know what was the Scripture, nor what the Faith was, but We have made it a light whereby We guide whom We will of Our servants. You are indeed guiding to a Straight Path* (42:52).

The verses do not contradict each other. God creates everyone with the potential to accept belief, but both the family and existing educational and social conditions have a certain role in one's guidance or misguidance. To call people to belief, God sent Messengers, some of whom received Revealed Books, so that people could reform themselves. Prophet Muhammad is the last Messenger, and the Revealed Qur'an is the last and only uncorrupted Divine Book.

The Qur'an contains the principles of guidance. The Messenger provides guidance, whether through the Book or his personality, conduct, and good example. He recites the Divine Revelations, shows God's signs to his people (or to humanity at large, in the case of Prophet Muhammad), and points out their misconceptions, superstitions, and sins.

Every thing, event, and phenomenon is a sign pointing to God's Existence and Unity. Therefore, if we believe sincerely and without prejudice, struggle against carnal desire and the temptations of the evil-commanding self and Satan, and use our free will to find the truth, God will guide us to a way leading to Him. He declares in the Qur'an:

> Fear God and seek the means [of approach to and knowledge of] Him, and strive in His way in order that you may succeed and be prosperous [in both worlds]. (5:35)

> As for those who strive in Us [in Our way and for Our sake and to reach Us], We guide them to Our paths; and God is with the good. (29:69)

> Those who fear God [and keep their duty to Him], He will appoint a way out for them. (65:2)

In order to find or deserve guidance, we must sincerely strive for it and search for the ways leading to it. Those whom God blesses with guidance should first show that they have received it by setting a good example, and then call others to it through every lawful (Islamic) means. God repeatedly commands His Messenger to do just that in these, and other, verses:

> Warn your tribe of near kindred [of their end, the consequences of their deeds, and the punishment of Hell]. (26:214)

> Remind and give advice, for you are one to remind. (88:21)

> Proclaim openly and insistently what you are commanded. (15: 94)

> Call to the path of your Lord with wisdom and fair exhortation, and reason with them in the most courteous manner. (16:125)

> Surely in the Messenger of God you have a good example for him who hopes for God and the Last Day, and remembers God oft. (33:21)

God's Messenger conveyed God's Revelations to people, called them to belief in the best and most effective way, and endured great difficulty and persecution for doing so. He refused the most alluring bribes designed to make him stop calling people to belief in One God, and continued his mission without expecting any worldly reward. Seeking only God's pleasure and the prosperity of people in both worlds, when he conquered Makka (with God's help) and made God's Word prevail, he forgave the Makkans who had persecuted him ruthlessly for 21 years, saying: "No reproach, this day, shall be on you. God will forgive you, (for) He is the Most Merciful of the Merciful. Go! You are freed!"[6]

God's Messenger once said to 'Ali: "If someone finds guidance at your hand, this is better for you than having red camels."[7] According to the rule of "the one who causes is like the doer," one who leads someone else to guidance receives whatever the latter earns, without any decrease in his or her own reward. Similarly, God's Messenger says:

> Whoever establishes a good path receives the same reward as those who follow that path thereafter until the Last Day without any decrease in their reward; whoever establishes an evil path is burdened with the same sins as those who follow it thereafter until the Last Day, without any decrease in their burden.[8]

If you lead other people to guidance, never remind them by saying, for example: "You found guidance only because of me." This is a grave sin and ingratitude to God, for only God guides and causes you to lead others to guidance. Similarly, those guided through you should never say, for example: "Without you, I would never have been guided."

If you lead others to guidance, you should think: "Praise be to God, for He has used such a poor and needy one like me to achieve this meritorious deed. God is so powerful, merciful, and munificent to His servants that He creates clusters of grapes on wood. As wood has no right to ascribe to itself the grapes growing on it, I cannot attribute another's guidance to myself." As for those who find guidance, they should think: "God, my Master, saw my need and helplessness and allowed His servant to lead me to guidance. All praise be to Him."

Nevertheless, those who are led to guidance can feel thankful to the one whom God used to guide them. After all, since God created us and our actions, He also creates the means that enable guidance and misguidance. But this does not negate or diminish the part of our own free will in our guidance or misguidance.

ENDNOTE: Qur'anic point of view about human free will

Most Western Orientalists accuse Islam of being fatalistic, although only one small Islamic sect (the *Jabriya*) has ever defended fatalism. On the contrary, almost all Western philosophies of history and, to some extent, Christianity, are fatalistic and based on the supposed irresistibility of historical laws. The outlines of those philosophies of history may be summed up as follows:

- Humanity is steadily progressing toward the final happy end.
- This progress depends on the fatalistic, irresistible laws of history, which are completely independent of humanity. Therefore, we must obey these laws if we do not want to be eliminated.
- We cannot criticize the stages (e.g., primitive, feudal, or capitalistic) through which we must inevitably pass, because we have nothing to do other than to pass through them.

Such views imply the following: Present socioeconomic and even political conditions are inevitable, because they were dictated by nature, which decrees that only the able and the powerful can survive. If these laws favor the West, the communities that choose to survive must concede to the West's dominion.

What distinguishes the Qur'anic concept of history from other philosophies is the following:

- While philosophers of history or sociologists build their conceptions on the interpretation of past events and present situations, the Qur'an deals with the matter from the perspective of unchanging principles.
- The Qur'an stresses individual and communal free choice and moral conduct. Although Divine Will could be regard-

ed as, in some respects, the counterpart of Geist in Hegelian philosophy and of absolute, irresistible laws of history in other philosophies, the Qur'an never denies human free will. God tests humanity here so that it should sow the "field" of the world to harvest in the next, eternal life. For this reason, all that happens here are occasions that God causes to follow one another so that good and evil people may be distinguished. Testing requires that the one being tested have free will to choose. Thus, according to the Qur'an, we are the ones who make history, not a compelling Divine Will. God simply uses our choice to bring His universal will into effect. If this point is understood, the Western philosophies of history and their conception of some "inevitable end" are seen to be groundless. (Tr.)

CHAPTER 4

The Resurrection and the Afterlife

THE RESURRECTION AND THE AFTERLIFE

THE BENEFITS OF BELIEF IN THE RESURRECTION

After belief in God, belief in the Resurrection has the primary place in securing a peaceful social order. Why should those who do not believe that they will be called to account strive to live an honest, upright life? But those of us who are convinced of this final reckoning in the other world certainly try to live a disciplined and upright life. The Qur'an declares:

> In whatever affair you may be, and whichever part of the Qur'an you recite, and whatever deed you do, We are witness over you when you are deeply engrossed therein. Not an atom's weight in the Earth and in the heaven escapes your Lord, nor is there anything smaller or greater, but it is in a Manifest Book. (10:61)

Certain angels are entrusted with recording everything that we do. God also has full knowledge and awareness of all our deeds, intentions, thoughts, and imaginings. Those who understand this (and act accordingly) will find true peace and happiness in both worlds. A family and community composed of such individuals would feel that they were living in Paradise.

Belief in the Resurrection prevents young people from wasting their lives in transitory and trivial things, and gives hope to the elderly as they move closer to the grave. It also helps children endure the death of loved ones. Children who believe that they will be reunited with their deceased loved ones in a far better world find true consolation in the Resurrection. Everyone, regardless of age, gender, and any other artificial human-devised difference, needs belief in the Resurrection as much as they need air, water, and bread.

As this belief leads people to a life of peace, intellectuals who seek public peace and security should emphasize it. Those who are convinced of what the Qur'an declares—*Whoever does an atom's weight of good shall see it, and whoever does an atom's weight of evil shall see it* (99:7-8)—live a responsible life, and a community composed of such people finds true peace and happiness. When this belief is inculcated in the hearts of young people, they will no longer be a harmful social element, but rather will seek to serve their nation and humanity.

Children are very sensitive and delicate. Extremely susceptible to misfortune, they also are easily affected by what happens to them and their families. When they lose a family member or become orphans, their world is darkened and they fall into deep distress and despair. When one of my sisters died during my childhood, I was devastated. I frequently went to her grave and prayed from the bottom of my heart: "O God! Please bring her back to life again and let me see her beautiful face once more, or let me die so as to be reunited with her." So, what else other than belief in the Resurrection and reunion with deceased loved ones can compensate for the loss of parents, brothers and sisters, and friends? Children will find true consolation only when they are convinced that their beloved ones have flown to Paradise, and that they will be reunited with them.

How can you compensate the elderly for their past years, their childhood and youth that have been left behind? How can you console them for the loss of their loved ones who preceded them in death? How can you remove the fear of death and the grave from their hearts? How can you make them forget death, which they feel so deeply? Will more and newer worldly pleasures console them? Only convincing them that the grave, which seems to them like an openmouthed dragon just waiting to devour them, is really a door to another and much better world, or simply a lovely waiting room opening onto that world, can compensate and console them for such losses.

In its inimitable style, the Qur'an voices such feelings through Prophet Zechariah:

This is a mention of your Lord's mercy unto His servant
Zechariah; when he invoked Him with a secret, sincere call,
saying: "My Lord, my very bones have become rotten and my
head is shining with gray hair. My Lord! I have never been dis-
appointed in my prayer to You." (19:2-5)

Fearing that his kinsmen would not be sufficiently loyal to
his mission after his death, Prophet Zechariah appealed to his
Master for a male heir to his mission. This is the cry of all old
people. Belief in God and the Resurrection gives them the good
news: "Do not be afraid of death, for death is not eternal extinction. It is only a change of worlds, a discharge from your life's
distressing duties, a passport to an eternal world where all kinds
of beauty and blessings wait for you. The Merciful One Who
sent you to the world, and has kept you alive therein for so long,
will not leave you in the grave's darkness and dark corridors
opening onto the other world. He will take you to His Presence,
give you an eternal and ever-happy life, and bless you with all
the bounties of Paradise." Only such good news as this can console the elderly and enable them to welcome death with a smile.

Our free will, which we use to direct our life, makes us unique
among all creatures. Free will is the manifestation of Divine Mercy
and, if used properly, will cause us to be rewarded with the fruits
of Mercy. Belief in the Resurrection is a most important and compelling factor urging us to use our free will properly and not to
wrong or harm others.

Sahl ibn Sa'd narrates that God's Messenger was told of a
young man who stayed at home for days. The Messenger went
to visit him. When the young man saw him appear unexpectedly, he threw himself into the Messenger's arms and died instantly. The Messenger told those around him: "Lay out your friend's
corpse. Fear of Hell frightened him deeply. I swear by Him in
Whose hand my life is that God will surely protect him from
Hell."[1] The Qur'an declares: *Those who fear to stand before their
Lord and curb the desires of the carnal self, Paradise will be their
dwelling place* (79:40-41).

In a *hadith qudsi*, God says: "I will not unite two securities,
nor two fears."[2] In other words, those who fear His punishment

here will be protected from His punishment there, while those who do not fear His punishment here will not be saved from it there.

'Umar said, upon seeing a young man bravely protesting and resisting an injustice: "Any people deprived of the young are doomed to extinction." Young people have a transforming energy. If you let them waste it in triviality and indulgence, you undermine your own nation's future. Belief in the Resurrection stops young people from committing atrocities and wasting their energies on passing pleasures, and directs them to lead a disciplined, useful, and virtuous life.

Belief in the Resurrection also consoles the sick. A believer with an incurable illness thinks: "I am dying; no one can prolong my life. Everyone must die. Fortunately, I am going to a place (Paradise) where I will recover my health and youth, and enjoy them forever." Secure in this knowledge, all beloved servants of God, Prophets, and saints welcome death with a smile. The Last Prophet said during the final minutes of his life: "O God, I desire the eternal company in the eternal world." He had informed his Companions the day before: "God let one of His servants choose between enjoying the beauty of this world as long as he wishes and what is with Him. The servant chose what is with Him."[3] That servant was the Messenger himself. The Companions understood whom he meant and burst into tears.

Similarly, when 'Umar ruled over a vast area stretching from the western frontiers of Egypt to the highlands of Central Asia, he prostrated himself before God and sighed: "I can no longer fulfill my responsibility. Let me die and be taken to Your Presence." Such a strong desire for the other world, the world of eternal beauty, and being blessed with the vision of the Eternally Beautiful One caused the Prophet, 'Umar, and many others to prefer death to this world.

The world is a mixture of good and evil, right and wrong, beauty and ugliness, and oppressors and oppressed. Many instances of wrong (appear to) go unnoticed, and numerous wronged people cannot recover their rights. Only belief in being resurrected in another world of absolute justice consoles the wronged and oppressed, and dissuades them from seeking vengeance. Similarly, those stricken with affliction and misfortune find consolation in the Resurrection, because they believe that whatever befalls them purifies them, and that anything lost in a catastrophe will be restored in the Hereafter as a blessing, just as if they had given these items as alms.

Belief in the Resurrection changes a house into a garden of Paradise. In a house where the young pursue their pleasures, children have nothing to do with religious sentiment and practices, parents are engrossed in procuring all fantasies of life, and grandparents live in an old-folks or nursing home and console themselves with pets, for there are no grandchildren around whom they can love and who can show them the respect they desire—in such a house, life is a burden difficult to bear. Belief in the Resurrection reminds people of their familial responsibilities, and as they implement these duties, an atmosphere of mutual love, affection, and respect begins to pervade the house.

This belief leads spouses to deepen their love and respect for each other. Love based on physical beauty is temporary and of little value, for it usually disappears shortly after marriage. But if the spouses believe that their marriage will continue eternally in the other world, where they will be forever young and beautiful, their love for each other remains even though they gradually age and lose their physical beauty.

Such a belief-based family life makes its members feel that they are already living in Paradise. Similarly, if a country orders itself according to this same belief, its inhabitants would enjoy a life far better than what Plato imagined in his *Republic* or al-Farabi (Alpharabios) in his *Al-Madinat al-Fadila* (The Virtuous City). It would be like Madina in the time of the Prophet or the Muslim lands under 'Umar's rule.

To have a better understanding of how the Prophet built that society, we provide several examples of his sayings concerning the Resurrection and the afterlife:

> O people! You will be resurrected barefoot, naked, and uncircumcised. Listen to me with full attention: "The one who will

be first clothed is Abraham, upon him be peace." Heed what I will say: "That day some from my Umma will be seized on the left side and brought to me. 'I will say: O Lord! These are my Companions.' I will be told: 'You do not know what disagreeable things they did after you.' Then I will say as the righteous servant [meaning Jesus] said: 'I was a witness over them while I continued to stay among them. When You took me You became the watcher over them. You are Witness over all things. If You punish them, they are Your slaves; if You forgive them, surely You are the All-Mighty, the All-Wise.'"[4]

Since God created them, the children of Adam have not experienced an event more terrible than death. However, death is easier than what will follow it. They will suffer such terror that sweat will cover their bodies until it becomes like a bridle around their chins, until it grows into something like a sea on which, if desired, vessels could be sailed.[5]

People will be resurrected in three groups: those who combined fear of God with expectation [fearing His punishment but never despairing of His mercy and forgiveness], those who [because they frequently "faltered"] will try to go to Paradise "mounted on a mule" in twos, threes, fours ... or tens. The rest will be resurrected into Fire; [since they constantly pursued sins worthy of Hellfire], if they want to sleep in the forenoon, Hell will go to sleep with them; when they reach night, Hell will reach night with them; when they reach morning, Hell will reach morning with them, and when they reach evening, Hell will reach evening with them.[6]

God's Messenger made sure that his Companions understood exactly what Hell was, and roused in them a great desire for Paradise by conveying its good tidings to them. As a result, they lived in great consciousness of Divine reward and punishment. They were so sensitive to religious obligations and the rights of people that, for example, two of them once appealed to the Messenger to solve a disagreement. After hearing them, the Messenger said:

I am a human being like you, so I will judge according to what you say. It is possible that one of you speaks more convincing-

ly and I may judge in his favor. However, God will judge rightly in the Hereafter according to the truth of the matter. The
wrongdoer will meet his due punishment, while the innocent
will meet his reward.[7]

This was enough for each Companion to concede his claimed
right. The Messenger advised them: "Divide the disputed goods
in half, and then draw lots. Each one should consent to his share
wholeheartedly and without regret."

Sa'd ibn Rabi' was severely wounded at the Battle of Uhud.
In his last breath, he whispered to Muhammad ibn Maslama, who
brought him greetings from the Messenger: "Take my greetings
to God's Messenger. By God, I sense the fragrance of Paradise
behind Mount Uhud."

QUR'ANIC ARGUMENTS

Although scientific findings like the second law of thermody-
namics show that existence is gradually disappearing, and even
a collision of two planets could destroy the universe. If existence
began with a big bang, why should it not end with another big
bang or collision? Existence is an extremely delicately calculated
organism, a system with parts subtly dependent upon each other. A human body is made up of about trillions of cells. Just as
a single deformed, cancerous cell can kill the entire body, any
serious deformation anywhere in the universe also could "kill"
it. Our death sometimes comes unexpectedly and without any
visible, diagnosed reason. Do we know whether or not the universe might "die" all of a sudden, unexpectedly, from a "disease"
or a "heart attack"? Maybe our old world has terminal cancer
because we abuse it.

God's Universal Acts Point to the Resurrection

The Qur'an argues for the Resurrection. To impress upon our
hearts the wonder of what the Almighty will accomplish in the
Hereafter, and to prepare our minds to accept and understand it,
the Qur'an presents the wonder of what He accomplishes here.
It gives examples of God's comprehensive acts in the macro-cos-

mos and, at times, presents His overall disposal of the macro-, normo-, and micro-cosmoses (the universe, humanity, and atoms, respectively).

For example, the following Qur'anic verse stresses God's Power and, by mentioning specific instances of It, calls us to have conviction in our meeting with Him in the Hereafter:

> God is He Who raised the heavens without any pillars that you can see, then He established Himself upon the Throne (of authority; having shaped the universe and made it dependent upon certain laws, He exercises His absolute authority over it), and subjected the sun and the moon (to His command); each runs (its course) for an appointed term. He regulates all affair, expounding the signs, that you may believe with certainty in the meeting with your Lord. (13:2)

The First Origination of the Universe and Humanity Indicate Their Second Origination

The Qur'an presents the phenomenon of the universe's creation, which it defines as the first origination (56:62), while describing the raising of the dead as the second origination (53:47), to prove the Resurrection. It also directs our attention to our own origin, arguing:

> You see how you progressed—from a drop of sperm to a drop of blood, to a blood clot suspended on the wall of the womb, from a suspended blood clot to a formless lump of flesh, and from a formless lump of flesh to human form—how, then, can you deny your second creation? It is just the same as the first, or even easier [for God to accomplish]. (22:5; 23:13-16)

The Qur'an makes analogies between the Resurrection and His deeds in this world, and sometimes alludes to His deeds in the future and in the Hereafter, in such a way that we can become convinced of that which we cannot fully understand. It also shows similar events here and compares them to the Resurrection. One example is as follows:

> Has not man seen that We have created him from a sperm-drop? Then lo, he is a manifest adversary. And he has coined for Us a

similitude, and has forgotten the fact of his creation, saying:
"Who will revive these bones when they have rotted away?"
Say: "He will revive them Who produced them at the first, for
He is Knower of all creation."[8] Who has made for you fire from
the green tree, and behold! You kindle from it. Is not He Who
created the heavens and the Earth able to create the like of them.
Aye, that He is! For He is the All-Wise Creator. (36:77-81)

The Qur'an likens the universe to a book unfolded. At the
end of time, its destruction will be as easy for God as rolling up
a scroll. As He unfolded it at the beginning, He will roll it up
and, manifesting His absolute Power without any material cause,
will re-create it in a much better and different form:

> On that day We shall roll up the heavens like a scroll rolled up
> for books. As We originated the first creation, so We shall bring
> it forth again. It is a promise (binding) upon Us. Truly We shall
> fulfill it (as We promised it). (21:104)

> Have they not seen that God, Who created the heavens and the
> earth and was not wearied by their creation, is able to give life
> to the dead? Surely He has power over everything. (46:33)

The Qur'an likens the Resurrection to reviving soil in spring
following its death in winter, and mentions how God disposes of
atoms and molecules while creating us in stages. Dried-out
pieces of wood blossom and yield leaves and fruits similar, but
not identical, to those that existed in previous years. Innumerable
seeds that had fallen into soil now begin to germinate and grow
into different plants without confusion. God's raising the dead
on the Day of Judgment will be like this:

> Among His signs is that you see the soil dry and barren; and
> when We send down rain on it, it stirs to life and swells. Surely
> God Who gives the dead soil life will raise the dead also to life.
> Indeed, He has power over all things. (41:39)

> O humankind! If you are in doubt concerning the Resurrection,
> (consider that) We created you of dust, then of semen, then of
> a fertilized ovum suspended on the wall of the womb, then of
> a lump of flesh shaped and unshaped, so that We demonstrate

to you Our power. And We keep in the wombs what We please to an appointed term, and afterwards We bring you forth as infants, then We cause you to grow up, that you reach your prime. Among you some die (young) and some are sent back to the feeblest phase of age so that they know nothing after they had knowledge. You sometimes see the soil dry and barren. But when We pour down rain on it, it trembles, and swells, and grows of every pleasant pair. That is so because God is the Truth, and He it is Who gives life to the dead, and He is powerful over all things. (22:5-6)

Look at the prints of God's Mercy: how He gives life to the soil after its death. Lo! He verily is the Reviver of the dead (in the same way), and He is able to do all things. (30:50)

God has brought you forth from the soil like a plant. And to the soil He will restore you. Then He will bring you back fresh. (71:17-18)

Especially in *suras* 81, 82, and 84, the All-Mighty alludes to the Resurrection and its attendant vast revolutions and Lordly deeds. Due to what we have seen here, such as seasonal changes, we can formulate an analogy that will help us understand and then, with awe in our hearts, accept what the intellect might otherwise refuse.

As giving even the general meaning of these three *suras* would take a great deal of time, let's take one verse: *When the pages are spread out* (81:10). This implies that during the Resurrection, everyone's deeds will be revealed on a written page.

At first, this strikes us as strange and incomprehensible. But as the *sura* indicates, just as the renewal of spring parallels another resurrection, "spreading out the pages" has a very clear parallel. Every fruit-bearing tree and flowering plant has its own properties, functions, and deeds. Its worship consists of glorifying God and thereby manifesting His Names. Its deeds and life record are inscribed in each seed that will emerge next spring. With the tongue of shape and form, these new trees or flowers offer an eloquent exposition of the original tree's or flower's life and deeds, and through their branches, twigs, leaves, blossoms, and fruits spread out the page of its deeds. He Who says: *When the pages are spread out* is the same Being Who achieves these feats in a very wise, prudent, efficient, and subtle way, as dictated by His Names All-Wise, All-Preserving, All-Sustaining and Training, and All-Subtle.

In many verses, the Qur'an warns us that we were created to achieve specific goals, not to do whatever we want. As we are responsible beings, whatever we do is recorded. Our creation from a drop of fluid through several stages, the utmost care shown to our creation and the importance attached to us, demonstrate that we have great responsibilities. After death, we will be called to account for our lives. In addition, our creation through stages is a manifest evidence for God's Power, Who raises the dead to life.

> Does man think he will be left to himself uncontrolled (without purpose)? Was he not a drop of fluid which gushed forth? Then he became a clinging clot; then He shaped and fashioned, and made of him a pair, the male and female. Is He then not able to raise the dead to life? (75:36-40)

A close analysis of the universe's functioning shows that two opposed elements are prevalent and firmly rooted everywhere. These elements result in good and evil, benefit and harm, perfection and defect, light and darkness, guidance and misguidance, belief and unbelief, obedience and rebellion, and fear and love. The resulting continual conflict causes enough alteration and transformation to produce the elements of a new world. These opposite elements eventually will lead to eternity and materialize as Paradise and Hell. The eternal world will be made up of this transitory world's essential elements, which then will be given permanence.

Paradise and Hell are the two opposite fruits growing on the tree of creation's two branches, the two results of the chain of creation, the two cisterns being filled by the two streams of things and events, and the two poles to which beings flow in waves. They are the places where Divine Grace and Divine Wrath manifest themselves, and will be full of inhabitants when Divine Power shakes up the universe.

In this world, oppressors depart without paying, and the oppressed are still humiliated. Such wrongs will be brought before the Supreme Tribunal, for God would be unjust and imperfect if He allowed them to be ignored. Indeed, God sometimes punishes the guilty in this world. The suffering endured by previous disobedient and rebellious peoples teaches us that everyone is subject to whatever correction God Almighty's Splendor and Majesty chooses to apply. So, as declared in the verse: *Keep apart on this day, O you criminals* (36:59), God's absolute Justice requires that He separate the good from the wicked in the Hereafter and treat each group accordingly.

GENERAL ARGUMENTS

Universal Wisdom Requires the Resurrection

God is absolutely free to do what He wills, and no one can call Him to account. Being All-Wise, He acts with absolute purposiveness and wisdom, and never does something that is in vain, futile, or pointless.

When we analyze ourselves, as well as our nature, physical and spiritual identity, structure and body, we realize that we were created for certain important purposes. Nothing in our body is superfluous. The same is true of the universe, which is also viewed as a macro-human being by many Muslim scholars, for each part of it manifests great purposes and innumerable instances of wisdom.

We are unique, for we contain some aspect of all that exists in the universe. Our mental and spiritual faculties represent angelic and other spiritual worlds, such as the world of symbols or immaterial forms. But due to our inborn capacity to learn and to our free will, we can excel even the angels. Our physical or biological being represents plants and animals. Although contained in time and space, our spiritual faculties and such other powers as imagination allow us to transcend them. Despite our unique and priceless value when compared with other members of creation, some of us die at birth and some others quite young.

In addition, we long for eternity and desire eternal life—some of our senses or feelings cannot be satisfied with something less. If we could choose between eternal life with severe hardship during this life and eternal nonexistence after a short luxurious life, probably we would choose the former, maybe even preferring eternal existence in Hell to eternal nonexistence. The All-Merciful and All-Wise did not condemn us to eternal nonexistence or implant within us the desire for eternity to make us suffer while trying to fulfill an impossible, yet heart-felt, desire. So Divine Wisdom requires the existence of an eternal world.

This World Cannot Judge Our Actual Worth

Although we have a small physical body, our mental and spiritual faculties allow us to embrace the universe. Our acts are not restricted only to this world, and therefore cannot be bound by time and space. Our nature is so universal that even the first man's acts affects the last man's life and character and all of existence. Restricting us to a physical entity, a very short lifespan, and a limited part of space, as materialists do, shows a complete misunderstanding and lack of appreciation of what each of us really is.

This world's scales cannot weigh the intellectual and spiritual value of the Prophets and their achievements, or the destruction caused by such monsters as Pharaoh, Nero, Hitler, and Stalin. Nor can they weigh the true value of sincere belief and moral qualities. What is the proper reward for a martyr who has sacrificed everything for the sake of God, or for such universal human values as justice and truthfulness; or for a believing scientist whose dedicated research results in an invention that benefits all people until the Last Day?

Only the other world's delicate scales, which account for an atom's weight of good and evil, can weigh such deeds accurately: *We set up a just balance for the Day of Resurrection. Thus, no soul will be treated unjustly. Even though it be the weight of one mustard seed, We shall bring it forth to be weighed; and Our reckoning will suffice* (21:47). Even if nothing required the Resurrection, the necessity of weighing our deeds would require an infinitely just and sensitive balance to be established.

All of God's Acts have a purpose, and sometimes several purposes. Based on this fact, His universal Wisdom requires the

Resurrection. If It did not, we would have to deal with the following issues, among others. The Majestic Being manifests the Sovereignty of His being Master via the universe's inclusive and perfect order and purposiveness, justice and balance. How could He not reward believers who seek His protection as Master and Sovereign, believe in His Wisdom and Justice, and obey them through worship? Would He allow those who deny His Wisdom and Justice, who rebel against or ignore Him, to remain unpunished? As this impermanent world contains hardly any of His Wisdom and Justice with respect to humanity, most unbelievers depart unpunished and most believers unrewarded. Thus, God's Justice is necessarily deferred to a Supreme Tribunal, where each individual will be rewarded or punished in full.

It is clear that the One administering this world does so in accordance with infinite wisdom. Just look at how everything's use and benefit is manifested. Every bodily limb, bone, and vein, as well as every brain cell and cellular particle, serves many wise purposes. These facts show that everything is arranged according to infinite wisdom. Look at the absolute orderliness in the fashioning of everything, another proof.

In short, we were created for universal purposes. This is even stated in the Qur'an: Did you reckon that *We only created you in vain, and that to Us you would not be returned? So, exalted is God (from exerting Himself in what is vain), the Sovereign, the Truth. There is no god but He; Lord of the Noble Throne* (23:115-16). We were not created for mere play or sport, and eternal nonexistence in the grave is not our ultimate destiny. Rather, we were created for an eternal life prepared for us by all of our actions, and for an eternal world full of eternal beauty and blessing (Paradise) or evil and wickedness (Hell).

Divine Mercy and Munificence Require the Resurrection

We notice that the more needy and helpless a creature is, the better it is nourished. For example, during the first stages of human life, we are nourished in the best way and without effort on our part both before and immediately after birth. As we pass through childhood, youth, and adulthood, becoming ever more aware of our personal strength and willpower, we try to meet our own needs as well as those of our family members, often with great difficulty.

Similarly, foxes and other animals that rely on their power and cunning are barely nourished despite much effort and toil, while fruit-worms live on the best food and quite easily, and plants take their food without effort. Such examples clearly show that One absolutely Merciful and Munificent rules, sustains, and maintains all creatures.

God's Mercy and Munificence are Eternal

An Eternal One manifests Himself eternally and requires the existence of eternal beings. His eternal Mercy and Munificence demand eternal manifestation and thus eternal beings on whom to confer eternal bounties. But our world is only temporary, and millions of its living creatures die each day. What can such a fact indicate, other than this world's final and complete death?

This world cannot receive the comprehensive manifestation of the Divine Names and Attributes. Nor can living beings, who experience great hardship and difficulty in maintaining themselves. For example, we cannot satisfy all our desires and appetites. Our youth, beauty, and strength, upon which we set our hearts, leave without a word and cause us great sorrow. Also, we have to exert ourselves even to obtain a cluster of grapes. If we were denied eternal nourishment after having tasted it, would this not be an insult and a mockery, a source of great pain? For a blessing to be real, it must be constant. Without an eternal life in which we can satisfy our desires eternally, all of God Almighty's bounties bestowed upon us would change into pain and sorrow. Therefore, after destroying this world, God will transform it into an eternal one that can receive the comprehensive manifestations of His Mercy and Munificence without obstruction, one in which we can satisfy all our desires eternally.

Divine Pity and Caring Require the Resurrection

These heal wounds and wounded hearts and feelings, cause a patient to recover, end the pain of separation, and change pain and sorrow into joy and pleasure. They help human beings and animals throughout their lives, especially before and right after birth. Their mothers' wombs are well-protected homes in which they are nourished directly without any effort on their part. After birth, Divine Pity and Caring provide them with breast-milk, the best possible food, and their parents' feelings of pity and caring. All of these are a single manifestation of Divine Pity and Caring.

Although Divine Pity and Caring encompass the universe, here we encounter wounds, hurt feelings, incurable illness, hunger, thirst, and poverty. Why? As above, the answer is that this world cannot receive the comprehensive manifestation of Divine Pity and Caring. Our inability to do so, as well as our injustice to others and abuse of our innate abilities, intervenes between beings and the manifestations of Divine Pity and Caring. Above all, every living thing dies. This arouses great sorrow in the heart, a sorrow that can only be compensated for by belief in another, eternal world.

Once when God's Messenger was sitting in the mosque, some prisoners of war were brought to him. A woman looking for something with great anxiety caught his attention. Whichever boy the woman saw, she took him to her bosom and then left him. When she finally found her son, she embraced him, pressed him to her bosom, and caressed him with great affection. This caused the Messenger to burst into tears and, pointing to the woman, he asked his Companions:

> "Do you see that woman? Would she throw that child in her arms into Hell?" The Companions answered that she would not, and the Messenger, upon him be peace and blessings, added: "God is much more compassionate than that woman. He would never throw His servants into Hell [unless the servants absolutely deserve it]."[9]

Divine Pity and Caring will be manifested fully in the other world, for that world allows no intervention, sorrow, and pain.

Divine Justice and Honor Require the Resurrection

God's Names and Attributes are absolute and eternal. Therefore, He is absolutely and eternally Merciful, Relenting, and Forgiving, as well as absolutely and eternally Mighty, Just, and Dignified. Although His *Mercy embraces all things* (7:156) and, as stated in a *hadith*, "exceeds His Wrath," some people's sins are so serious (e.g., unbelief and associating partners with God) that they deserve eternal punishment. Besides, the verse: *whoever kills a human being unjustly, it is as if he (or she) has killed humanity* (5:32) cannot be ignored. This is especially true today, where might is right, thousands of innocent people are killed daily, and many others are wronged and deprived of their basic human rights. Even worse, many of the most serious sins and injustices go unpunished.

Death does not discriminate between oppressed and oppressor, innocent and guilty, sinless and sinful. This only can mean that while minor sins may or may not be punished here, major sins (e.g., unbelief, associating partners with God, murder, and oppression) are referred to the Hereafter's Supreme Tribunal, where God will dispense absolute Justice.

One day, those who thanked God will be welcomed with: *Eat and drink to your hearts content because of what you did in days gone by* (69:24) and *Peace be upon you! You have done well. Enter here to dwell forever* (39:73). In this place, God has prepared for us things we cannot even begin to imagine. Meanwhile, those who engaged in bloodshed, sin, and other prohibited activities will be thrown into Hell with the shout: *Enter (through) the gates of Hell to dwell therein forever: what an evil abode for the arrogant!* (39:72).

Divine Grace and Generosity require the Resurrection. A saint once asked Harun al-Rashid, an 'Abbasid caliph, the following:

> "If you desperately needed a glass of water, would you abandon your kingdom in return for it?" The caliph answers that he would. "If you could not discharge it from your body, would you again give up kingdom in order to be able to discharge it?" The caliph answers that he would. The saint concludes: "Then all of your wealth and kingdom consist of a glass of water."

We are provided with whatever we need for almost nothing. The more necessary for life an item is, the more abundant and cheaper it is in nature. Our most pressing need is air, which we receive free of charge. Then comes water, which is almost free. God sends both of these from His infinite Mercy, and we make absolutely no contribution. Then come heat and light, which we receive from the sun for nothing. When we look at the rest of His bounties, we see that they are extremely cheap. And yet we still demand that He perform a miracle so that we might believe in Him! Our effort to procure these blessings is minuscule when compared to how they were produced. However, if these bounties or blessings were only temporary and imperfect, our fear of death would change them into poison.

Thanks to God's being eternal, He will provide for us eternal and ever-better forms of bounties, through His Names and Attributes, free of charge. As these will be eternal, they will not become a source of pain engendered by our fear of death. For us as believers, death is a changing of worlds, a discharge from worldly duty, an invitation to the eternal abode He has prepared for us, and a passport to that abode.

Divine Beauty Requires the Resurrection

Listen to a bird's singing on a spring morning, the murmur of a brook flowing through green fields or deep valleys. Look at the beauty of spectacular green plains and trees in blossom. Watch the sun rise or set, or the full moon on a cloudless, clear night. All of these, and many more that God presents to our senses, are but a single gleam of His absolute and eternal Beauty manifested through many veils. By observing such manifestations, through which He makes Himself known, we are enraptured.

Temporary blessings leave unbearable pain in our heart when they disappear. If spring came only once, we would sigh over it until we died. So, a true blessing must necessarily be eternal. In this world, the Eternally Beautiful One shows us only shadows of His Beauty in order to arouse our desire to see Its eternal and perfect manifestation. Moreover, He will allow us to see Him in Paradise in a manner free of any qualitative and quantitative measure or dimension: *On that day there will be shining faces, gazing upon their Master* (75:22-23).

The Relation Between Things and Humanity
Indicates the Resurrection

There is a basic relation between humanity and this world. We are born into an amiable environment and equipped with the required senses. We have feelings like compassion and pity, as well as caring and love, for there are many things here to which we can apply them. We feel hunger and thirst, cold and heat. Fortunately, these feelings can be satisfied with that which was prepared before or with only a slight exertion on our part.

Consider an apple. Its color and beauty appeal to our eyes and our sense of beauty. Its taste addresses our sense of taste, and its vitamins nourish our bodies. Despite our need of its nutriments, we might refuse to eat it if it were ugly and tasteless, and thereby deprive ourselves of its nourishment. This, as well as many other natural facts, shows that One with infinite Knowledge and Power created us and prepared a suitable environment for us. He knows all of our needs, capacities, and qualities, just as He knows nature down to its smallest building blocks.

Another example is reproduction, which depends on mutual love and attraction between a man and a woman. If our Creator had not placed such things in us, if He had not allowed us to enjoy the process of reproduction, and if He had not implanted a great love and caring for our resulting children, we would never have reproduced. The first and final members of our species would have been Adam and Eve.

Death ends all pleasure and makes everything as if it had never been. Given this, if there were no Resurrection our life would be a meaningless existence of suffering and pain. However, this world is a shadowy miniature of the other, eternal one. The bounties God bestows here are only examples of their eternal and much better forms in the eternal world, and are displayed here to encourage us to act in order to deserve them:

> Give glad tidings to those who believe and do good deeds. For them there will be Gardens beneath which rivers flow. Every time they are served with the fruits therein, they will say: "This

is what was given to us aforetime." They shall be given in perfect semblance. And there will be pure spouses for them, and they will abide there forever. (2:25)

All joy and beauty, reward and happiness in this world point to their perfect and eternal forms in Paradise; all pain and punishment, ugliness and unhappiness point to their likes in Hell. God will use the debris from this world, after He destroys it, to build the other world. Thus, the interrelations among things here and between this world and the other point to the Resurrection.

Recording and Preservation Point to the Resurrection

Nothing disappears completely from this world. While our every word and act is recorded and preserved, why should we not be able to understand that God records all of humanity's words and deeds in a way unknown to us? Advances in science and technology constantly provide new evidence for His Existence and Unity and affirm, with the Divine origin of the Qur'an, the truth of Islamic beliefs. The Qur'an declared centuries ago that: *We shall show them Our signs in the outer world and within themselves until it will be manifest to them that (the Qur'an) is the truth. Does not your Lord suffice, since He is witness over all things?* (41:53).

If people sincerely search for the truth and are not blinded by prejudice, ignorance, and worldly ambition and desire, every new scientific advance displays the truth of the Qur'an. We see that God enfolds everything in small things like seeds. For example, each human being is enfolded in a sperm or in his or her 46 chromosomes. If we had 44 or 48 chromosomes, we would be something completely different. Similarly, when we die and disappear into the soil, our most essential part does not disappear, as discussed earlier, for God will use it rebuild us on the Day of Resurrection. God preserves everything, and so nothing can disappear forever. For example, a plant that dies in autumn or winter continues to live in innumerable memories as well as in its seeds that will bring it back in an almost identical form next spring.

Just as God preserves things in their seeds, He preserves sounds and voices, as well as appearances and sights to display them in another world. Maybe one day these sounds and sights will be discovered.

One time I heard of an experiment carried out by a scientist trying to find a killer. The suspects were brought singly under the tree where the crime was committed. The tree showed nothing unusual until the guilty person was brought close to it, at which time it began to react negatively. Somehow, the tree had recorded the killer's voice, manner, posture, or whatever he had displayed during the crime. God preserves a human being in a sperm, a plant in a seed, a hen in an egg, and shows us that He records everything by enabling us to record and preserve sounds and images. Given this, would He leave us, the noblest and perfect pattern of existence, to our own devices or allow our record to disappear? Of course not; rather, He will resurrect us in a different, eternal world.

Divine Power Proves the Resurrection

Consider an atom. How it is formed and maintains its relationships with other atoms are astounding miracles. Creating a solar system or an atom, both of which have orbiting bodies, and then regulating their movements and establishing their relationships are equally easy for God. Similarly, a cell is like an autonomous government. It has its own departments, each of which is interrelated with others and ruled by a center, as well as a "ministry of finance" that manages its income and expenditure. It is as if each cell were as smart as the smartest person on the planet. In addition, there are very close and substantial relations between these cells, all of which are ruled by a center: the brain.

These are only a few examples of the Creator's Power. Everything is equally easy for Him. Creating and administering the universe is as easy as creating and administering an atom. If all people worked together, we could not create even one atom. So, if the absolutely Powerful One says He will destroy the universe and rebuild it in a different form, He will do so. As God does not lie and is without defect, His promises can be believed. As stated in the Qur'an: *The Day of Final Decision and Judgment is*

*a fixed time, a day when the Trumpet is blown, and you come in mul-
titudes, and the heaven is opened and becomes as gates* (78:17-19).

Death and Revival Indicate the Resurrection

An overall death and revival is repeated every year.[10] In winter,
a white "shroud" covers the soil, whose yearly life cycle ends in
autumn. Nature has already turned pale and shows fewer traces
of life. The shell has fallen in and, ultimately, trees become like
lifeless, hard bones; grass has rotted away and flowers have
withered; migrating birds have left; and insects and reptiles have
disappeared.

Winter, which is only temporary, is followed by a general
revival. Warm weather causes trees to bud and, wearing their finery, present themselves to the Eternal Witness. The soil swells,
and grass and flowers start to bloom everywhere. Seeds that fell
into ground during the previous autumn have germinated and,
having annihilated themselves, are transformed into new forms
of life. Migrating birds return, and the planet hosts countless insects
and reptiles. In short, nature appears before us with all its splendor and finery.

Consider the phenomenon of photosynthesis. A tree's leaves
are lungs that, in the presence of sunlight, separate carbon dioxide into carbon and oxygen by giving off oxygen and retaining
carbon, which it combines with the hydrogen of the water
brought up through its roots. Out of such "magical" chemistry,
God makes sugar, cellulose, various other chemicals, and fruits
and flowers [all having a different smell, taste, color, and shape].
This same carbon dioxide and water help innumerable kinds of
fruit, each of which has a unique taste, to grow. However simple
a process this seems, the collective wisdom of humanity cannot
produce a single fruit.

This process of respiration causes a tree to spend a great deal
of energy, but also brings it much greater benefits. During the
night, this process is reversed: the tree takes in oxygen and gives
off carbon dioxide.

Consider what deliberate results these unconscious actions
produce. Then ask yourself if something so completely ignorant

and unconscious of its own existence, and totally devoid of any power of choice, could do such comprehensive things that obviously require an all-comprehensive knowledge, power, and choice. So, the Power that gives a tree such significant purposes and makes it bear many deliberate results certainly will not abandon the fruit to its own devices. Humanity is the fruit of the tree of creation. Would God abandon us and condemn us to eternal annihilation? It would be illogical for God to create us for many deliberate purposes and then let us remain eternally mixed in the soil. He preserves a fruit in memories and through its seeds, just as He returns the like of it next summer after promoting it to a higher level of life in an animal or human body. Given that, He will promote us to a higher level of life in another world following the total destruction of this one.

God created the world and humanity when nothing of either thing existed. He brought our body's building blocks together from soil, air, and water, and made them into a conscious, intelligent being. Is there any doubt that the person who made a machine can tear it apart and reassemble it, or that an army commander can gather his dispersed soldiers through a trumpet-call?

Similarly, while reconstructing the world, God Almighty will gather our atoms and grant them a higher, eternal form of life: *Say: "Travel in the land and see how He originated creation, then God brings forth the later growth. Assuredly, God is able to do all things"* (29:20); and *Look at the imprints of God's mercy (in creation): how He gives life to the earth after its death. He surely is the reviver of the dead (in the same way), and He is able to do all things* (30:50).

Many Other Phenomena Point to the Resurrection

Great care and many purposes are attached to even the most insignificant seeming things. For example, cellulose is the structural tissue forming the chief part of all plants and trees. Its elasticity allows plants to bend, and thus protects them from breaking. It is also important in making paper.

Cellulose is hard to digest; only enzymes secreted by cud-chewing animals can dissolve it. However, cellulose aids excretion, for it accelerates the bowel workings and prevents constipation. Thus cud-chewing animals are like factories that change substances with cellulose into useful matter. Their manure makes an excellent fertilizer, for innumerable bacteria in the soil consume it. This process increases the soil's productivity and rids it of foul-smelling things.

If such bacteria did not exist, living beings could not survive. For example, if all the flies born in spring did not disappear into the soil, they would form a thick cover over the entire planet. Through the manifestation of His Name All-Purifying, God Almighty uses bacteria to clean the soil. Have you ever considered why forests are so clean although many animals die in them every day? They are so clean because carnivorous animals and bacteria consume animal corpses. Would God, Who employs the most insignificant-seeming creatures for many great purposes, allow us to rot in the ground and thereby reduce our existence to utter futility?

Again, a healed wound shows the body's vigor. A fruit reminds us of the tree that bore it, footprints point to the one who has passed by, and water leakage indicates a water source. Similarly, our innate feeling of and desire for eternity are signs of an eternal One and the eternal world. Moreover, this world and its contents cannot satisfy us. We overflow with subtle, refined feelings and aspire to lofty ideals that could not have originated in matter and the material world. These are reflections of the infinite, immaterial dimensions of existence.

Philosophers, especially Muslim ones, call the universe a macrohuman and humanity a *normo-cosmos* or a micro-cosmos. Like us, the universe is a whole entity consisting of innumerable interrelated parts. Maybe an angel has been assigned to represent it by serving as its spirit. Who knows? Like us, the universe also can be injured and have, as Einstein puts it, new bodies formed in its remote corners. It also has an appointed time of death, just as we do.

We have so little knowledge about existence. As we increase in such knowledge, we also increase, paradoxically, in our ignorance of it. Existence is in a process of continuous flux, and we are little more than ignorant bystanders. Prophet Muhammad, God's Last Messenger used to pray: "O God, show me the reality of things."

Everything in the universe has a purpose. The universe's ecological system is so complex, and its parts are so interrelated, that the lack or removal of one part would cause the entire universe to be destroyed. If a tree's bacteria were killed, we could not obtain fruit.

Every species and thing has an important and unique place in the universe's structure. Such a magnificent universe cannot be purposeless. It functions according to a moving timeline: seconds point to minutes, minutes to hours, and hours to the end of today and the coming of tomorrow; days point to weeks, weeks to months, months to years, and years to the end of our lifespan. Existence has its own days in every sphere and dimension, and its appointed lifespan one day will cause it to end.

Also, time goes in cycles. For example, a scientist has established that corn is abundantly produced every 7 years, and that fish are abundant every 14 years.[11] The Qur'an points to this in *Sura Yusuf*. The "life" of existence has certain terms or cycles: the life of this world and of the grave, for example. The afterlife, the last cycle, has many cycles or terms of its own. The Qur'an refers to them as days, for a day is the shortest time-cycle unit. It corresponds to the entire life of existence. Daytime reminds us of this world's divisions of dawn, morning, noon, afternoon, and evening, which have their counterparts in our lives: birth and infancy, childhood, youth, old age, and death, respectively. Night, on the other hand, resembles the intermediate life of the grave and the next morning: the Resurrection.

Almost all previous people believed in the Resurrection[12]

Even the self-proclaimed divine Pharaohs of ancient Egypt believed in the Resurrection, and so wanted to be buried with their most precious things and slaves. We read in the inscriptions found in their tombs: "After death, the sinful will take on ugly forms and remain under the ground forever until eternity, while pure souls will join angels and live among exalted ones."

On the sheets buried together with the dead, we also read petitions like the following:

> Greetings to You, O Divine Being Exalted! I have come to Your presence in order to observe Your infinitely beautiful Face. Please favor me with this observation. I wronged no one, nor betrayed anyone. I caused no one to weep, nor killed anyone. I oppressed no one, either. I am here in Your presence to present my situation to You. I only desire to observe Your Face.

If we search through the tombs, epitaphs, documents, and art of bygone peoples, we hear humanity's sighs for eternity echoing throughout time. Despite the alterations and distortions that have crept in over time, we find clear evidence of a belief in eternity in ancient India, China, and Greece, as well as in most Western philosophies.

For example Shahristani, a Muslim historian and theologian, writes that Zarathustra said: "Humanity has a duty in the world. Those who do their duties satisfactorily will gain purity and join the dwellers of the higher abodes. However, those who fail to do their duties will be condemned to stay under the ground until eternity."

India has always been home to many religions although it is highly probable that they are all distorted versions of one true religion. Despite this, however, almost all contain a belief in the Resurrection and eternity. In many of them, belief in eternity has led to belief in reincarnation. One exception is Buddhism. Buddha did not believe in eternal cycles of reincarnation, but rather that souls would ultimately return to the Absolute Being and find eternal peace and contentment. Souls that enter other bodies are evil ones, and do so in order to be purified. When they are purified, they also return to the Absolute Being and find peace and happiness. (See Chapter IV Endnote)

Homeros, an ancient Greek poet, writes about a soul's shelter. He believed that souls, which manifest themselves here in bodies, have shelters in another place. Pythagoras, a Greek mathematician, believed in the Resurrection and argued that purified souls would join the exalted dwellers of higher worlds, while evil ones would remain imprisoned on the Earth, which would be enveloped in fire. Plato attributes to Socrates many arguments for the Resurrection and eternal life, some of which are as follows:

> Man should be virtuous. To become virtuous requires resistance against carnal desires. This means a deprivation on the part of man. This deprivation will be compensated with an eternal, happy life.

> Opposites follow each other in the world. Light and darkness, spring and winter, day and night follow each other. Death follows life, so another life will follow death. However, this second life will be eternal.

> Everyone sometimes feels as if he experienced something before which is just happening to him now. This means that we live this life in another world, the world of the spirits, before we come here. So, this life is the result of a previous life and a "rehearsal" of another life to come.

Although it is highly questionable whether this last argument is correct, and although it suggests reincarnation, it is an undeniable fact that Socrates and his student Plato believed in an afterlife.

Aristotle diluted the idealism of his teacher, Plato, with some elements of materialistic philosophy. However, he also believed in the spirit's existence and immortality, as he said: "Apart from man's material body, something immaterial exists in him, which is immortal."

Xenophanes and Heraclitus, both ancient Greek philosophers, believed in an afterlife. The former held that, apart from our body, we have a soul that continues to live after we die. Among the principles of good morality he argued was that it is impossible for the One Who has created the universe so beautifully and adorned it because of His love for man, that He will not bring him back to life again after he has made him die. Heraclitus argued that during the Last Day, stars will fall onto the earth and envelop it as a circle of fire. Evil souls will remain in this fire as a punishment, while pure ones will escape it and rise to higher abodes.

Except for materialists like Epicurus and Democritus, all ancient philosophers in the East and West believed in the afterlife. Most Western rationalists who prepared the ground for the Renaissance believed in the Resurrection and the afterlife. Among them, Descartes argued convincingly for the soul's immortality and analyzed issues pertaining to the afterlife.

Leibniz and Spinoza also believed in another life. The former resembled Plato in that, corresponding to Plato's ideas, he spoke of *monads* as the immaterial parts of beings that must develop infinitely. As this cannot occur in this time-limited world, there must be an eternal world in which they can realize their infinite development. Spinoza, a pantheist, believed in an eternal, collective life of beings. Pascal and Bergson also believed in an afterlife.

In the Muslim world, almost all philosophers believed in eternal life. Even the irreligious Abu al-A'la al-Ma'arri tried to describe, in his *Risalat al-Ghufran*, the Day of the Resurrection according to Qur'anic verses. Dante appears to have adapted this scholar's writings for his descriptions of Paradise, Hell, and Purgatory.

To sum up: Except for a few materialists, the long history of Eastern and Western philosophy witnesses to belief in the Resurrection and an afterlife.

THE RESURRECTION IN REVEALED SCRIPTURES

The Qur'an, the last heavenly Scriptures, has four main themes: God's Existence and Unity, the Resurrection and afterlife, Prophethood, and worship and justice. It emphasizes the Resurrection far more than all previous Scriptures.

Despite the distortion it has suffered, the Torah still has verses concerning the Resurrection. The Gospel came to restore this corruption and to affirm what had remained intact. However, it also was distorted. Not long after Jesus' departure from this world, about 300 Gospels appeared and were circulated. Their internal contradictions and those with other Gospels led to many distortions that only grew over time. However, there are still some Gospel passages about the Resurrection and the Hereafter, such as the following:

Blessed are the poor in spirit, for theirs is the kingdom of heaven... Blessed are the merciful, for they will be shown mercy. Blessed are the pure in heart, for they will see God...Blessed are those who are persecuted because of righteousness, for theirs is the kingdom of heaven... Rejoice and be glad, because great is your reward in heaven. (Matthew 5:3, 7-8, 10, 12)

Woe to the world because of the things that cause people to sin! Such things must come, but woe to the man through whom they come! If your hand or your foot causes you to sin, cut it off and throw it away. It is better for you to enter life maimed or crippled than to have two hands and two feet and be thrown into eternal fire. And if your eye causes you to sin, gouge it out and throw it away. It is better for you to enter life with one eye than to have two eyes and be thrown into the fire of Hell. (Matthew 18:7-9)

The dead will be raised physically and spiritually. According to the context, the Qur'an mentions either spiritual or bodily resurrection. For example: *O soul at peace! Return unto your Lord well-pleasing and well-pleased! Enter among My (righteous) servants. Enter My Paradise!* (89:27-30).

These verses mention the soul's return to its Lord. Many other verses describe the Resurrection and the other world in such material or physical terms that we must accept that it also will be physical. The Qur'an discusses the truth of Paradise and Hell, either in detail or in brief, in 120 places. While describing these realms and explaining who deserves which one, it stresses the combination of our soul and our body.

For example, the faces of the people of Paradise will shine with happiness, and they will find prepared for them whatever they desire. They will be together with their spouses and family members who deserve Paradise. God will rebuild the women of Paradise without defect and as virgins, and they will excel Paradise girls in beauty. The people of Paradise will live in magnificent palaces set in gardens full of splendid trees, beneath which will flow rivers of honey, pure water, milk, and other beverages. On the other hand, the people of Hell will suffer great remorse and burn in fire. When their skins are scorched or burned completely, they will be exchanged for new ones. In addition, those bodily parts with which they sinned will witness against them.

Hell, because of its terror, warns people to reject unbelief and sin, and Paradise urges those with sublime feelings to strive for perfection. And so the Qur'an mentions both Paradise and Hell as a favor or grace:

> This is Hell which the guilty deny. They go circling round between it and fierce, boiling water. Which is it, of the favors of your Lord, that you deny? But for him who fears the standing before his Lord there are two gardens. Which is it, of the favors of your Lord, that you deny? (55:43-47)

ENDNOTE: Further explanation on Buddhism

Buddhism is regarded as a religion without a God or an eschatology. This must be largely due to its concentration on the individual's spiritual perfection and purification and a harmonious social life. The Buddha stressed the supremacy of ethics, and his outlook was definitely practical and empirical. In fact, he did not tolerate any doctrines that appeared to divert the mind from the central problem of suffering, the cause of suffering and its removal, and the urgency of the moral task. Therefore it cannot be said that Buddhism directly and absolutely rejects belief in a Supreme Being.

The conclusion of Wendy Erickson, a Canadian writer who became an agnostic while an atheist after her studies on God and Revelation, drew on the "objective" nature of God is significant on this point:

> In his book, *Medusa's Hair*, Gananath Obeyesekeri has shown us that even today Buddhist ascetics in India mystically experience the divine as a painful (and simultaneously ecstatic) possession by another being that completely takes over their bodies.
>
> Experience has led people in all religious traditions to make very different faith statements about the "objective" nature of God or Ultimate Reality. Buddhists experience the Ultimate as Oneness, Creativity, or Consciousness. Jews, Christians and Muslims have sensed the Ultimate as transcendent Love, Power,

and, yes, Creativity too. Monistic Hindus perceive the Ultimate as a hidden Self, or Atman, which is one with the Godhead, Brahman. When Love is the predominant sense, transcendence is often sought after through worship and compassion toward others. Believers seek to get beyond themselves by recognizing that the world does not revolve around them; there is an Ultimate Reality that exists beyond their selves, is much bigger than them and, in some sense, more real. Prayer can be seen as one way for a believer to cultivate a sense of being in God's presence. This Reality (God) also exists within each individual. [http://atheism.about.com]

What Buddha said about his faith and mission demonstrates that, rather than rejecting a faith or a transcendent reality, his real aim was to found a society on moral values and the cessation of pain in individuals:

Bear always in mind what it is that I have not elucidated, and what it is that I have elucidated. And what have I not elucidated? I have not elucidated that the world is eternal; I have not elucidated that the world is not eternal; ... I have not elucidated that the soul and the body are identical; I have not elucidated that the monk who has attained (the *arahat*) exists after death; I have not elucidated that the arahat does not exist after death; ... I have not elucidated that the arahat neither exists nor does not exist after death. And why have I not elucidated this? Because this profits not, nor has to do with the fundamentals of religion; therefore I have not elucidated this. And what have I elucidated? Misery have I elucidated; the origin of misery have I elucidated; the cessation of misery have I elucidated; and the path leading to the cessation of misery have I elucidated. And why have I elucidated this? Because this does profit, has to do with the fundamentals of religion, and tends to absence of passion, to knowledge, supreme wisdom, and Nirvana. [Henry Clarke Warren, *Buddhism in Translation* (Harvard University Press: 1922), 122; *Majjhima Nikaya* 63, in John B. Noss, *Man's Religions* (New York: Macmillan, 1956), 166. (Tr.)]

CHAPTER 5

Prophethood and Muhammad's Prophethood

PROPHETHOOD AND MUHAMMAD'S PROPHETHOOD

God creates every community of beings with a purpose and a guide or a leader. It is inconceivable that God Almighty, Who gave bees a queen, ants a leader, and birds and fish each a guide, would leave us without Prophets to guide us to spiritual, intellectual, and material perfection.

Although we can find God by reflecting upon natural phenomena, we need a Prophet to learn why we were created, where we came from, where we are going, and how to worship our Creator properly. God sent Prophets to teach their people the meaning of creation and the truth of things, to unveil the mysteries behind historical and natural events, and to inform us of our relationship, and that of Divine Scriptures, with the universe.

Without Prophets, we could not have made any scientific progress. While those who adopt evolutionary approaches to explain historical events tend to attribute everything to chance and deterministic evolution, Prophets guided humanity in intellectual—and thus scientific—illumination. Thus, farmers traditionally accept Prophet Adam as their first master, tailors accept Prophet Enoch, shipmakers and sailors accept Prophet Noah, and clock makers accept Prophet Joseph. Also, the Prophets' miracles marked the final points in scientific and technological advances, and have urged people to accomplish them.

The Prophets guided people, through personal conduct and the heavenly religions and Scriptures they conveyed, to develop their inborn capacities and directed them toward the purpose of their creation. Had it not been for them, humanity (the fruit of the tree of creation) would have been left to decay. As humanity needs social justice as much as it needs private inner peace,

Prophets taught the laws of life and established the rules for a perfect social life based on justice.

Whenever people fell into darkness after a Prophet, God sent another one to enlighten them again. This continued until the coming of the Last Prophet. The reason for sending Prophets Moses and Jesus required that Prophet Muhammad should be sent. As his message was for everyone, regardless of time or place, Prophethood ended with him.

Due to certain sociological and historical facts, which require a lengthy explanation, Prophet Muhammad was sent as "a mercy for all worlds." For this reason, Muslims believe in all of the Prophets and make no distinction among them:

> The Messenger believes in what has been sent onto him by his Lord, and so do the believers. They all believe in God and his angels, His Scriptures and His Messengers: "We make no distinction between any of His Messengers"—and they say: "We hear and obey. Grant us Your forgiveness, our Lord; to You is the journeying." (2:285)

That is why Islam, revealed by God and conveyed to humanity by Prophet Muhammad is universal and eternal.

Describing Prophethood and narrating the stories of all Prophets is beyond the scope of this book. By focusing on the Prophethood of the Seal of the Prophets who told us about the other Prophets and Divine Scriptures and made our Lord known to us, we will make the other Prophets known and prove their Prophethood.

Belief in God, the source of happiness, and following the Last Prophet and Messenger of God are the keys to prosperity in both worlds. If we want to be saved from despair and all negative aspects of life and attain intellectual, spiritual, and material perfection, we must believe wholeheartedly that Muhammad is the Messenger of God and follow his guidance.

PROPHET MUHAMMAD IN THE BIBLE

Almost all previous Prophets predicted Prophet Muhammad. Despite the distortions suffered by the Torah, the Psalms, and the Gospels, we find indications of his coming. For example, the Torah promises this:

> The Lord said to me [Moses]: "What they say is good. I will raise up for them a Prophet like you among their brothers; I will put My words in his mouth, and he will tell them everything I command him. If anyone does not listen to My words that the Prophet speaks in My Name, I will Myself call him to account." (Deuteronomy 18:17-19)

The phrase *a Prophet like you among their brothers* clearly refers to a Prophet from the line of Ishmael, the brother of Isaac, who is the forefather of Moses' people (the Children of Israel). The only Prophet who came from this line after Moses and resembled him in many ways (e.g., bringing a new law and waging war on his enemies), is Prophet Muhammad. Also, Deuteronomy 34:10 clearly states that no Prophet like Moses ever appeared among the Israelites: *"[With respect to his virtues and awesome deeds,] a Prophet like Moses, whom the Lord knows face to face, no longer appeared among Israel."*[1] The Qur'an points to the same fact: *We have sent to you a Messenger as a witness over you, even as We sent to Pharaoh a Messenger* (73:15).

The sentence I *will put My words in his mouth, and he will tell them everything I command him*, in the above Biblical verse, means that the promised Prophet will be unlettered and speak whatever is revealed to him. God states this in the Qur'an: *He does not speak out of [his own] desire. It is but a Revelation revealed* (53:3-4).

The following verse: *The Lord came from Sinai and dawned over them from Seir; He shone forth from Mount Paran* (Deuteronomy 33:2), refers to the Prophethood of Moses, Jesus, and Muhammad, respectively. Moses spoke to God and received the Torah at Sinai; Prophet Jesus received Divine Revelation at Seir, a place in Palestine; and God manifested Himself to humanity for the last time through His Revelation to Prophet Muhammad at Paran, a mountain range near Makka. The Torah mentions (Genesis 21:21) Paran as the desert area where Abraham left Hagar and Ishmael. The Zamzam well is located there. As stated in the Qur'an (14:35-37), Abraham left them in the valley of Makka, at that time an uninhabited place within Paran's mountain ranges.

The verse in Deuteronomy, according to the Arabic version published in London (1944) and the Ottoman Turkish version (Istanbul: 1885), continues: *He came with myriads of holy ones; in his right hand appeared to them the fire of the Shari'a.* It is almost the same in King James' version: And he came with ten thousands of saints: from his right hand went a fiery Law for them. This verse refers to the promised Prophet, Muhammad, who would have numerous Companions of the highest degree of sainthood. The fire of the Shari'a alludes to the fact that he would be allowed, even ordered, to fight his enemies.

In the Gospel of Matthew, we come across an interesting verse in which Jesus said:

> Have you never read in the Scriptures: "The stone the builders rejected has become the capstone; the Lord has done this, and it is marvelous in our eyes? Therefore I tell you that the kingdom of God will be taken away from you and given to a people who will produce its fruit. He who falls on this stone will be broken to pieces, but he on whom it falls will be crushed." (Matthew 21:42-44)

This capstone cannot be Prophet Jesus, for the verses refer to crushing victories won by the "capstone's" followers. No people were ever crushed because they resisted Christianity. Christianity spread in the Roman Empire only after it underwent some changes and was reconciled with Roman religion(s). Western dominion of the world came via scientific thought's triumph over the Medieval Church, and took the form of ruthless colonialism.

Islam, on the other hand, ruled almost half of the Old World for centuries. Its original purity was never diluted, its enemies were defeated many times, and it successfully defended itself against Crusaders. Currently, Islam is once again rising as a pure, authentic religion, way of life, and hope for human salvation. Moreover, Prophet Jesus himself alludes to this by stating that the kingdom of God will be taken away from his followers and given to a people who will produce its fruit, as seen above.

Moreover, in a telling detail recorded in *Sahih al-Bukhari* and *Muslim*, Prophet Muhammad describes himself as the "capstone," thereby completing the building of Prophethood.

Another reference to the Prophet is in the Gospel of John as the "Paraklit, the Spirit of Truth," referred to by Jesus in the following verse:

> But I tell you the truth: It is for your good that I am going away. Unless I go away, the Paraklit will not come to you; but if I go, I will send him to you. When he comes, he will convict the world of guilt in regard to sin and righteousness and judgment. (John 16:7-8)

In these verses, Prophet Muhammad is referred to as *Paraklit*. It derives from the Greek word Períklytos (the "Much-Praised"). Its Aramaic counterpart is Mawhamana, meaning Ahmad. Ahmad and Muhammad are derived from the same root word "ha-mi-da" meaning to praise, and mean the praised one. However, Ahmad also means one who praises. It is highly interesting that Bediüzzaman Said Nursi records that Prophet Muhammad was mentioned in the Torah also with the name Munhamanna, meaning Muhammad, the praised one. The Qur'an also states that Jesus predicted Prophet Muhammad with the name Ahmad, a synonym of Muhammad (61:6).

Further, Jesus mentioned and predicted the Paraklit with various other names, but always with the same function, as seen in the following verses:

> When the Paraklit comes—the Spirit of Truth—who comes from the Father, he will testify about me. (John 15:26)

> I have much more to say to you, more than you can now bear. But when he, the Spirit of Truth, comes, he will guide you into all truth. He will not speak on his own; he will speak only what he hears, and he will tell you what is yet to come. He will bring glory to me by taking what is mine and making it known to you. (John 16:12-14)

These are only a few of the Bible's allusions to Prophet Muhammad. The late Hussayn Jisri found 114 such allusions and quoted them in his *Risalat al-Hamidiya*.

HIS LIFE

Prophet Muhammad's life proves his Messengership and fore-tells his Prophethood. Consider the following facts:

- The extraordinary events on the night of his birth,[2] the different character he displayed even as a child, and the meaningful signs people of insight observed on him all meant that he would undertake a great mission.

- Prior to his Prophethood, he opposed injustice and joined organizations like the *Hilf al-Fudul*, which defended the helpless and restored usurped rights.

- Although of honorable descent, he did not live in luxury; rather, he grew up as an orphan under the protection of his grandfather and then his uncle. Whatever money he may have earned by trading before and after his marriage went to support orphans, widows, and the poor. Thus, he was never wealthy and had no powerful backers.

- Despite his community's moral corruption, he lived an extraordinarily chaste, disciplined, and morally upright life. During his childhood, he intended only twice to attend wedding ceremonies, but was overpowered by sleep on both occasions. (Thus, he did not see improper things and practices that Islam would later outlaw.) When he was 25 years old, he married Khadija, a respected 40-year old widow. He only married again after her death 25 years later. Those who knew him said he was as shy as a young girl when he was proposed marriage.

- Muhammad's childhood and youth were a prelude to his Prophethood. Even his enemies called him "the Trustworthy," for no one could deny that he was completely truthful and trustworthy. People said: "If you travel, you can entrust your family and belongings to Muhammad without hesitation." Once while the Quraysh were repairing the Ka'ba, a question of individual and clan honor arose over who would reinsert the sacred Black Stone. To prevent violence, they all agreed to let Muhammad decide. He asked them to bring a piece of cloth, which he then spread on the ground. Placing the Black Stone on it, he told each chief to raise their corner. When the Black Stone was raised to the required height, he set it in its place.

- Muhammad was unlettered. During his whole life, no one taught him and no written culture influenced him. Toward his fortieth year, he began retreating to Hira cave. One day he emerged with a new, wholly authentic message to heal humanity's wounds, and challenged all literary geniuses to produce something like it.

- His enemies never accused him of lying or cheating. To prevent Islam's spread, they labeled him a poet, a sorcerer, a magician, or a lunatic. Sometimes they attempted to justify their rejection by such false pretexts as: "If only this Qur'an had been sent down to one of the great men of the two cities (Makka and Ta'if)."

- How could a 40-year-old man, universally acclaimed by his society as completely honest and trustworthy, one who had no moral and intellectual imperfection, suddenly and unexpectedly begin to lie and deceive his people without ever being caught? Even enemies who had known him for years never accused him of this. They never caught him in a lie, could not meet his challenge to produce a similar document, and could not discredit him. After years of warfare driven by base motives, even his bitterest enemies (e.g., Safwan ibn Umayya, Abu Sufyan ibn Harb, 'Amr ibn al-'As, and Ikrima ibn Abi Jahl) finally accepted the truth of his message.

When he was entrusted with the duty of Prophethood, his life did not change at all. There are also several other points to consider:

- If Prophet Muhammad nursed selfish aims and intentions, why did he wait until he was 40 to claim Prophethood?

- Until he was 40, no one had ever heard Muhammad give an eloquent speech, talk on religious and metaphysical issues, formulate laws, or handle a sword. How could he have changed so suddenly from a reserved, quiet, and completely apolitical man into the greatest reformer history has ever known? He explains intricate metaphysical and theological problems, why nations decline and fall, and ethical canons; gives laws related to social culture, economic organization, group conduct, and international relations; and becomes so brave that he never retreats in battle. He reformed his people's modes of thought, worldviews, beliefs, habits, and morals.

- Prophet Muhammad blended many roles and his own personal excellences into one personality. He is a man of wisdom and foresight, a living embodiment of his own teachings; a great statesman and military genius; a legislator and teacher of morals; a spiritual luminary and religious guide. He sees life comprehensively, and all that he touches is improved and adorned. His teachings regulate everything from international relations to eating, drinking, sleeping, and personal hygiene. He used these teachings to establish a civilization and a culture that produced such a fine, sensitive, and perfect equilibrium in all aspects of life that no trace of a flaw, deficiency, or incompleteness has ever been found in it. What alleged shortcomings and imperfections deny him his rightful status as Prophet and Messenger of God?

- Prophet Muhammad lived as the poorest of his community. All of his resources were used to spread Islam. Despite his greatness, he presented himself as the humblest and most ordinary person. He sought no material reward or profit, left no property for his heirs, and ordered his followers not to set something aside for himself or his descendants. In fact, he forbade his family and progeny from receiving zakat (alms).

- Prophet Muhammad was extremely merciful. In Makka, persistent persecution eventually forced him to emigrate to Madina. However, when he finally conquered Makka without bloodshed after 5 years of warfare, he forgave all of his enemies, including the Hypocrites and unbelievers. He knew who the Hypocrites were, but concealed their identities so they could enjoy the rights of full citizenship to which their outward confession of faith and practice entitled them.

- Prophet Muhammad was particularly fond of children. Whenever he saw a child crying, he would sit beside him or her and share his or her feelings. He felt a mother's pain for her child more than the mother herself. Once he said: "I stand in prayer and wish to prolong it. However, I hear a baby cry and shorten the prayer for the sake of its mother, who is praying in the congregation." He took children in his arms and hugged them, sometimes carrying them on his shoulders. As for animals, he once said that a prostitute was guided to truth by God and ultimately went to Paradise for giving water to a dog dying of thirst, while another woman was condemned to Hell for letting a cat starve to death.

- Prophet Muhammad was extremely mild and never took anything personally. When people slandered his wife 'A'isha, he did not punish them after she was cleared. Bedouins often came to his presence and behaved impolitely; he did not even frown at them.

- He was the most generous of people, and liked to distribute whatever he had. After Prophethood had been bestowed upon him, he and his wealthy wife Khadija spent all they had in the way of God. When Khadija died, they were so poor that he had to borrow money to buy a shroud in which to bury the first person to embrace Islam and his first supporter.

- According to the Prophet, this world is like a tree whose shade is enjoyed by people on a long journey. No one lives forever, so people must prepare for the journey's second part: Paradise or Hell. His mission was to guide people to truth by all permissible means, which he did. Once 'Umar saw him lying on a rough mat and wept, saying:

> O Messenger of God! While kings sleep in soft feather beds, you lie on a rough mat. You are the Messenger of God and therefore deserve an easy life more than any other person. The Messenger answered him: Do you not agree that [the luxuries of] the world be theirs but those of the Hereafter ours?

Islam does not approve of a monastic life. It came to secure justice and humanity's well-being, and warns people against over-indulgence. For this reason, many Muslims chose an ascetic life. Although Muslims generally became rich after the death of the Messenger, caliphs Abu Bakr, 'Umar, and 'Ali preferred austerity partly because of their own inclination and partly to follow the Prophet's example strictly. Many other Muslims made this same choice.

- Prophet Muhammad was the most modest person. As he attained higher ranks, he increased in humility and servant-hood to God. He preferred being a Prophet–slave to being a Prophet–king. While building the mosque in Madina, he carried two sun-dried bricks while everybody else carried one. While digging the trench around Madina to defend it during the Battle of the Trench, the Companions bound a stone around their bellies because of hunger; the Messenger bound two. When a man began to tremble because of his awe-inspiring appearance, the Messenger calmed him, saying: "Don't be afraid, brother. I am a man, like you, whose mother used to eat dry bread." A mentally unbalanced woman once pulled him by the hand and said: "Come with me and do my housework." God's Messenger did as she asked. 'A'isha said the Messenger patched his clothes, repaired his shoes, and helped his wives with the housework.

'Ali describes the Prophet as follows:

> God's Messenger was the most generous of people in giving out and the mildest and foremost of them in patience and per-severance. He was the most truthful of people in speech, the most amiable and congenial in companionship and the noblest of them in family. Whoever sees him first is stricken by awe of him but whoever knows him closely is attracted to him deeply, and whoever attempts to describe him says: "I have, either before him or after him, never seen the like of him, upon him be peace and blessings."

Other than conveying God's Message by performing the mission of Divine Messengership, who led such an austere life as Muhammad? What can he be other than a Prophet? What substantial argument can one put forward against his Prophethood?

HIS CHARACTER AND HIGH MORALITY

- If a man's universally admired accomplishments, wealth, and fame do not change him, and he remains as humble as he was at the beginning of his career, this shows an impressive strength of character, morality, and virtue. Despite his unparalleled achievements, which force even non-Muslims and atheists to consider him the greatest person of all times, Prophet Muhammad was poorer and more humble when he entered Makka victoriously than he was at the beginning of his mission.

- One's face reveals one's inner world and character. Those who saw Prophet Muhammad could not help but admire his appearance and, if unprejudiced, acknowledge his truthfulness. For example, 'Abd Allah ibn Salam, the most renowned Jewish scholar of the time, believed in him at first sight, saying: "One with such a face cannot lie."

- If a firefly declares itself to be the sun, its lie lasts only until sunrise. Turkish people say that a liar's candle only burns till bedtime, meaning that a lie is short-lived. So, a deceitful person pretending to be a Prophet would soon be unmasked, and no one would accept his or her claim.

- Even an unimportant person in a small group cannot lie shamelessly and openly without somehow being discovered. Prophet Muhammad challenged everybody to come until the Last Day. He gave many important speeches to a large community concerning a great cause, all with great ease and freedom, without hesitation or anxiety, with pure sincerity and great solemnity, and in an intense and elevated manner that provoked his enemies.

- An unlettered person cannot speak on something requiring expert knowledge, especially to specialists in that area. However, Prophet Muhammad spoke on every issue from theology and metaphysics to medicine and history, physics and biology, and has never been contradicted. He challenged his people's strengths (literature, eloquence, and oratory), yet nothing they composed could compare with the Qur'an.

- People do not risk their life, wealth, and reputation, and bear hardship and persecution for a lie, unless they want even more wealth and higher worldly position. Before claiming Prophethood, Prophet Muhammad was well off and respected. After Prophethood, he confronted great hardship and persecution, and spent all he had for his cause. His enemies slandered, mocked, and beat him. Finally forcing him out of his homeland, they took up arms against him. He bore all of this without complaint and asked God Almighty to forgive them, for all he wanted was to see everybody believing in and worshipping the One God exclusively, thereby prospering in both worlds and being saved from the torments of Hell.
- History is full of people who, saying one thing and doing another, never attained a large and devoted following. Their ideas did not change people permanently, nor did their systems outlive them for any length of time. However, Prophet Muhammad sincerely and honestly practiced what he taught, and was the most obedient worshipper of the Creator and follower of the religious law. This shows his full conviction in his cause and that he is a Messenger of God sent to guide humanity to the True Path.
- People's characters are usually well-established by the time they are 30, and do not change significantly after that. To change one's character after 40 is practically impossible. If, God forbid, there had been any imperfection and blemish in Prophet Muhammad's character, it certainly would have appeared before his Prophethood. Is it logical that a person recognized by his community as its most honest and upright member would suddenly, at age 40, assume the role of a great liar and fraud to his own people?
- Liars can neither acquire nor maintain a large group of dedicated followers eager to sacrifice themselves. Even though being Prophets who never lied, Moses and Jesus did not have such devoted followers. The Jews betrayed their Prophet— Moses—when he left them for 40 days to receive the Torah on Mount Sinai, by worshipping a golden calf made by Samiri.

Even after so many years of intellectual and spiritual training in the desert, only two God-fearing men obeyed when Moses ordered them to fight the Amalekites. As for Jesus, one of his most devoted twelve followers [Judas Iscariot] betrayed him.

The Companions were so devoted that they willingly sacrificed everything for the Prophet Muhammad. Although brought up among a primitive, ignorant people without any positive idea of social life and administration or a Scripture, and immersed in spiritual and intellectual darkness, Prophet Muhammad soon transformed them into the masters, guides, and just rulers of the region's most civilized, socially, and politically advanced peoples and states. Their subsequent rule has been widely admired ever since—even by those who continue to oppose Islam and Muslims.

Also, innumerable universally acclaimed profound scholars, famous scientists, and pure, spiritual masters have been produced by the generations following the Companions. How could they establish a civilization, the most magnificent and advanced of all times, by following a liar? God forbid such a thought!

- Prophet Muhammad was the perfect exemplar of high moral conduct and virtue. He appeared among a desert people possessing only the most rudimentary level of civilization and devoted to immorality. Who brought him up as the most virtuous and moral person? His father died before he was born; his mother died when he was 6 years old. He was then raised by his grandfather and uncle, but how could they give these perfections to him when they did not embody them to such a degree? His teacher was God, as he himself said: "My Lord educated me and taught me good manners, and how well He educated me and how beautifully He taught me good manners."

- History has seen many virtuous people. However, no one has ever combined all virtues and good qualities as perfectly as Prophet Muhammad. Many generous people cannot show enough courage when and where necessary, and many courageous people cannot be so lenient and generous. But Prophet Muhammad combined in his person all virtues and laudable qualities at the highest level.

Virtue and good morality require balance. Excessive generosity becomes extravagance, excessive thrift becomes miserliness, courage is confused with rashness, and dialectics or demagogy with intelligence. Virtue requires knowing how to act in certain conditions. For instance, the self-respect of the weak for the strong, when assumed by the latter, becomes self-conceit; the humility shown by the strong to the weak, when assumed by the latter, becomes self-abasement. A person's voluntary forbearance and sacrifice (of one's rights) is good and a virtue; when done on behalf of others, however, it is treason. People may bear their own conditions patiently, but they cannot do so for the nation. Pride and indignation on behalf of the nation are commendable, whereas they are not on behalf of oneself. Prophet Muhammad was perfectly balanced in his virtues and good moral qualities; perfectly courageous when necessary; perfectly mild, forgiving, and humble among people; perfectly dignified but gracious; and more generous than all others, but also thrifty and opposed to extravagance. In short, he was the most perfect balance of all virtues and good qualities.

- According to Muslim theologians, there are six essentials of Prophethood: truthfulness, trustworthiness, communication of God's commands, intelligence, infallibility, and freedom from any mental and physical defect. History records that Prophet Muhammad had these six essential attributes in the most perfect fashion.

- People often have to make quick decisions that might cause them problems in the future. Prophet Muhammad's great achievements, made during the relatively short time span of 23 years, are without parallel in human history. He never faltered, and his decisions always proved to be correct. Moreover, his actions and words were both for his own people and for all future generations regardless of time and place. As none of his statements have ever been contradicted, no one can criticize his actions, words, and decisions. Can one who is not a Prophet taught by God, the All-Knowing, have such intelligence, foresight, sagacity, insight, sound reasoning, and prudence?

HIS ACHIEVEMENTS

• People usually consider their own occupations as more important, necessary, beneficial to social life, and more challenging than others. However, although every occupation has some degree of difficulty and social use, educating people is far more difficult and more necessary for a healthy social life.

Raising really educated people requires true educators who have clear goals. But if such people are to succeed, they must embody what they teach and advise to their students; intimately know their students' character and potential, as well as their desires and ambitions, shortcomings and strengths, and level of learning and understanding; and know how to treat them in all circumstances, approach their problems, and get them to replace their bad qualities with good ones.

People may not live according to their asserted "strong" beliefs, have only superficial good moral qualities, or have weak spots (e.g., open to bribery, insensitivity, hoarding). How should we view educators who transform their students by completely replacing their bad qualities with good ones, and then proceed to establish a community to serve as a model for future generations; who transform the base rock, copper, iron, and coal in their hands into silver, gold, precious stones, and diamonds? Would such an educator not be considered extraordinary? What Prophet Muhammad achieved in his 23 years as the educator of his people is far more than what such educators do.

• Not using force is another important dimension of a good education. Penal sanctions, coercion, and military and police forces can only succeed in "guiding" people for a short while. If a transformation is to be permanent, people must undertake it willingly, meaning that they must be convinced of its truth. No one has ever known people so comprehensively as Prophet Muhammad, or has managed to transform such a pitiless, crude, war-mongering, ignorant, and unyielding people into a community that provides a perfect and complete life and moral example for all future generations.

- No one can guide people in every field of life. It is very difficult for anyone, however able and clever, to be an able statesman, commander, brilliant scientist, and successful educator simultaneously. However, Prophet Muhammad was the most perfect spiritual and intellectual master, the most able statesman and commander, the most efficient educator, and the greatest scholar history has ever seen.

- Prophet Muhammad was the foremost practitioner of all forms of Islamic worship, and the most God-conscious Muslim. He perfectly observed all details of worship, even when in danger. He never imitated anyone, and excellently combined the beginning and end of spiritual perfection. He is unparalleled in prayer and knowledge of God. In his supplications and prayers, he describes his Lord with such a degree of Divine knowledge that no Muslim has ever attained a similar degree of knowledge and description of God.

- His faith was so extraordinarily strong, certain, miraculous, elevated, and enlightened that no contemporary prevalent (and opposed) idea, belief, philosophy, or teaching ever caused him to doubt or hesitate. Moreover, all saintly people of all times, primarily his Companions, benefited from his faith, which they admit to be of the highest degree. This fact proves that his faith is matchless.

- Just as the Prophets' consensus is a very strong proof of God's Existence and Oneness, it also is a firm testimony of the truthfulness and Messengership of Muhammad. History confirms that all sacred attributes, miracles, and functions indicating the truthfulness and Messengership of Prophets, are found in Muhammad to the highest degree. Prophets predicted his coming by giving good tidings of him in the Torah, the Gospels, the Psalms, and other Scriptures (known as "Pages" in the

Qur'an). Through their missions and miracles, they affirmed and "sealed" the mission of Muhammad, the foremost and most perfect Prophet.

Thousands of saints attained truth and perfection, performed miracles, gained insight into the reality of things, and made spiritual discoveries by following the Prophet's example. All of them assert God's Oneness and the Prophet's truthfulness and Messengership. Their testimony confirms his truthfulness, for they affirm the truth he proclaimed through the light of faith and certainty coming from knowledge, sight, or experience.

Thousands of exacting scholars of purity, meticulous scholars of truthfulness, and believing sages have reached the highest station of learning through the sacred truths brought by this unlettered man. The number of those who attribute their success to the truth brought by him prove and affirm the Oneness of God, the foundation of his mission, and the truthfulness of the Prophet, the greatest teacher and supreme master.

His family and Companions, whose insight, wisdom, and spiritual accomplishment make them the most renowned, respected, celebrated, pious, and intelligent people after the Prophets, declared that he was the most truthful, elevated, and honest person. This was their conclusion after having examined and scrutinized all of his thoughts and states, whether hidden or open, with the utmost attention to detail.

- He displayed such steadfastness, firmness, and courage while preaching and calling people to the truth that no hostility from the contemporary powers and great religions, or of his own people, tribe, and uncle, ever caused him to hesitate or feel anxiety or fear. He successfully challenged the world, and made Islam triumphant over all other religions and systems.
- Let us go to Arabia in the Era of Happiness. That unlettered man, who had never set foot in a school for military or civil affairs, or for the law or science, presented a religion and law that, when followed, ensure happiness in both worlds. People of all times listen to his words. He easily solves all social, political, and economic problems, and establishes such perfect rules

that they leave permanent imprints everywhere. A great part of his life is spent on the battlefield, where he functions as the most able commander of all times. His behavior shows him as the best husband, the most eminent and yet most compassionate father, and the most amiable and loyal friend. He does all this in so short a time as 23 years.

- A leader must know his people thoroughly to educate them and lead them to realize a great cause. Alexis Carrel, a great twentieth-century French scientist and philosopher, still describes human beings as unknown, as the most complex and intricate of creatures.[3] However, Prophet Muhammad had such a comprehensive knowledge of his people that he could educate them in such a way that they transformed themselves willingly to realize his cause. Knowing how to act in every situation, his decisions never had to be changed or his appointments to office rescinded. He succeeded in bringing the most refined, well-mannered, and civilized society out of an extremely backward, uncivilized, and rough people.

- Not only did he eradicate his people's savage customs and immoral qualities to which they were addicted, he also equipped and adorned these same desperate, wild, and unyielding peoples with all praiseworthy virtues and made them the teachers and masters of the world, including civilized nations. His domination was not outward; rather, he was the beloved of hearts, the teacher of minds, the trainer of souls, and the ruler of spirits.

Despite all the advanced techniques and methods, modern communities cannot remove permanently so small a vice as smoking. However, Prophet Muhammad quickly removed many ingrained bad habits with little effort, and replaced them with good habits in such a way that they became inherent in his people's very being. If people do not believe this, let them go there with hundreds of philosophers, sociologists, psychologists, pedagogues, and educators and see if they can achieve in 100 years even a small portion of what the Prophet achieved in a year.

- The Prophet met all of his detractors with a smile. When the Qurayshi leaders told Abu Talib to make his nephew abandon his mission, the Prophet answered:

  > O uncle! Should they place the sun in my right hand and the moon in my left, so as to make me renounce this mission, I shall not do so. I will never give it up; either it will please God to make it triumph or I shall perish in the attempt.

  On another occasion, a deputation of the Qurayshi elite offered him all the worldly glory they could imagine if he would abandon his mission:

  > If you want wealth, we will amass for you as much as you wish; if you aspire to win honor and power, we are prepared to swear allegiance to you as our overlord and king; if you have a fancy for beauty, you shall have the hand of the most beautiful maiden of your own choice.

  The terms would be extremely tempting for anyone, but they had no significance in the eyes of the Prophet. He responded:

  > I want neither wealth nor power. God has commissioned me as a warner to humanity. I deliver His Message to you. Should you accept it, you shall have felicity in this life and eternal bliss in the life Hereafter. Should you reject the Word of God, surely God will decide between you and me.

  The faith, perseverance, and resolution with which he carried his mission to ultimate success prove the supreme truth of his cause. Had there been the slightest doubt or uncertainty in his heart, he could not have withstood the opposition that continued for 21 long years.

- Great leaders have changed the course of history through their states, empires, or revolutions. However, almost none of them engendered so strong a unity of belief, thought, and ideal among their followers as Prophet Muhammad. After 40 years of a completely apolitical life, he suddenly appeared on the world stage as such a great political reformer and statesman that, without any media or mass communications, he united the scattered inhabitants of Arabian deserts. From belligerent, ignorant, unruly, and uncultured tribes, he raised a nation under one banner, law, religion, culture, civilization, and form of government.

- A leader must know people very well in order to win them over to his or her cause. Most leaders promise power, wealth, position, or a bright future; Prophet Muhammad conquered minds and hearts and promised his followers God's pleasure and Paradise. His followers sacrificed themselves willingly and preferred poverty and God's pleasure and Paradise. He set the example in his own family, always preparing them and his Companions for eternal peace and permanent bliss, and displaying it in his own life.

  His daughter Fatima, his most beloved family member, once came to him wearing a necklace. The Prophet asked: "Do you want people here and in the heavens to say that my daughter wears a chain from Hell?" These words were enough for her, for they were coming from the mouth of one whose throne was established in people's hearts and who had conquered their minds. She continues:

  > I immediately sold the necklace, bought a slave and emancipated him, and then went to the Messenger of God. When I told him what I had done, he rejoiced. He opened his hands and thanked God, saying: "All thanks to God, Who protected (my daughter) Fatima from Hell."

- Suppose you are a school teacher or director who wants to raise your students and employees to your own ideal. You also are prepared to undergo any hardship to realize this goal. Now, what would you do if they spit in your face when you pass by, place a tripe over your head while you pray, slap you in the face, throw stones at you and scatter thorny plants where you walk, ambush you with daggers, mock you in front of others, slander your wife, kill your relatives and mutilate their bodies, attack you many times and even injure you, and expel you from your native land? Could you bear such cruelty and continue on your way without hesitation? More than that, could you forgive and even pray for them, saying: "O God forgive them and guide them to truth, for they do not know." If you were taken to a Paradise-like place and could choose between living there or returning to resume your mission, would you choose to go back? The Prophet underwent all of this and still chose to return to his people and transform them into the best community known to history. Would you?

- The Prophet sent envoys to the Adal and al-Qarah tribes to teach them Islam. However, members of the Hudhayl tribe attacked them on the way, killed some and gave the survivors to the Quraysh. Zayd ibn Dasina was among the envoys. Before the Qurayshi polytheists executed him, Abu Sufyan, who had not yet embraced Islam, asked him:

> "I adjure you by God, Zayd, don't you wish that Muhammad was with us now in your place so that we might cut off his head, and that you were with your family?" "By God," said Zayd, "let alone wishing that Muhammad were here in my place so that I were with my family, I do not wish that even a thorn should hurt his feet in Madina."

Abu Sufyan remarked: "I swear by God that I have never seen a man who was so loved by his Companions as Muhammad." This remains true even now, for history has never produced a person who was (and is) more loved by his or her followers than Prophet Muhammad.

- Prophet Muhammad answered innumerable questions from the polytheists, Jews, and Christians of his time on such widely divergent issues as religion, history, metaphysics, astronomy, medicine, and so on. He answered without faltering, and his answers have never been proven wrong.
- Prophet Muhammad brought a law, a religion, a way of life, a code of worship, a way of prayer, a message, and a faith that was (and remains) unique. The law this unlettered man brought is matchless in that it has administered, both justly and precisely, one-fifth of humanity for fourteen centuries. The daily practices of Islam, which originated in the Qur'an and his own sayings, precepts, and example, have served for centuries

as the peerless guide and authority for billions of people. They have trained and refined their minds and souls, illumined and purified their hearts, and perfected their spirits.

After the Companions, who led humanity in all scientific, political, social, administrative, economic and other fields of life, many other worthy people appeared. I list only a few of countless such people: such saints and purified, meticulous scholars as Abu Hanifa, Shafi'i, Bayazid al-Bistami, 'Abd al-Qadir al-Jilani, Imam Ghazali, Imam Rabbani, and Bediuzzaman Said Nursi; such scientists as al-Biruni, al-Zahrawi, Ibn Sina (Avicenna), and Ibn Haytham; and hundreds of thousands of literary geniuses, commanders, statesmen, and other stars of humanity. All of them followed in the Prophet's footsteps.

In addition, such Western intellectuals and statesmen as Lamartine, William Muir, Edward Gibbon, John Davenport, L. A. Sedillot, Goethe, P. Bayle, Stanley Lane-Poole, A. J. Arberry, Thomas Carlyle, Rosenthal, Elisee Reclus, Andrew Miller, Bismarck, Leopold Weis, Marmaduke Pickthall, Martin Lings, and Roger Garaudy have admitted that he is the greatest person ever to have lived. Some of them even embraced Islam. This is another proof of his Prophethood.

HIS KNOWLEDGE OF THE PAST

- History is an important branch of knowledge. Unlike most sciences, it mostly depends on historical documents or artifacts. Although we can acquire some knowledge of the past, it is often very difficult to know the underlying facts, intentions, and motives, for accurate knowledge depends on reliable documents. But reliable documents are rare, for personal inclinations, interests, prejudices, and other motives distort what actually happened. For example, since We have only the translations of the Old and New Testaments, in which so many changes have been made, if the Qur'an had not been revealed, we would not have true knowledge of the

Israelite Prophets, especially Prophet Jesus, and the original beliefs of Christianity and Judaism.

- Prophet Muhammad related many facts about past peoples and events. Much of this information is in the Qur'an, which informs us of past civilizations (e.g., 'Ad, Thamud, Iram, Sodom and Gomorra, and ancient Egypt) and peoples (e.g., those of Noah, Abraham, and Shu'ayb). It also provides a general historical outline of the Jewish people from the beginning to the time of Jesus, particularly in the times of Prophets Moses, David, and Solomon. Much of this information was revealed while the Prophet was in Makka and had no contact with either Christians or Jews. When he emigrated to Madina, Jewish and Christian scholars questioned him on many topics and could not refute his answers.

- Some of this historical information is found in *Sahih al-Bukhari*, *Sahih al-Muslim*, *Sunan al-Tirmidhi*, and other books of Traditions. The Qur'an and the books have retained their original, uncorrupted texts, and none of their information has ever been contradicted; rather, much of it has been affirmed, and we can expect further affirmations in the future. This is an absolute, undeniable proof of Muhammad's Prophethood.

- Prophet Muhammad analyzed the causes and results of these bygone civilizations and peoples. His historical accounts presented laws of history and broad psychological, social, and economic principles concerning human individual and collective life. In addition, these masterpieces of literary style and eloquence have never been equaled.

HIS PREDICTIONS

Normally, no one can know exactly what will take place at some future date. Scientists are not even sure about natural events that occur according to so-called deterministic laws, and state that they cannot guarantee that the world will be in the same state even a few seconds later as it is now. Sociologists and historians speak of historical laws supposedly based on historical events or the flow of history. History, however, has contradicted almost all of them, including such historians and supporters of various concepts of a continual historical progress as Karl Marx, Max Weber, Johann Fichte, Georg Hegel, and Johann Herder.

Only God Almighty knows the future. However, He may favor whomever He pleases with some of this knowledge. Those who are convinced about the news they give concerning the future can only be Messengers of God.

Prophet Muhammad predicted many things, all of which either have been confirmed by history or remain to be confirmed. These are also found in the Qur'an and in books of Tradition. Among them are the following:

- The Byzantine and Persian empires were the superpowers of that time. While the Makkans were persecuting the small Muslim community, the Persians utterly defeated the Byzantines and seized Aleppo, Antioch, and the chief Syrian provinces (including Damascus). Jerusalem fell in 614-15; Christians were massacred and their churches burnt. The Persian flood of conquest spread over Egypt, reaching as far as Tripoli in North Africa. Another Persian army ravaged Asia Minor right up to the gates of Constantinople.

  As a result, the Makkan pagans rejoiced greatly and redoubled their opposition to the Prophet whose Message was a renewal of the Message of Jesus preached in Palestine. The following Qur'anic verses, revealed just at that time, gave certain tidings of a very near victory of the Romans over the Persians:

  > Alif Lam Mim. The Romans have been defeated in a land close by, but they, after their defeat, will be victorious, within nine years. God's is the command in the former case and in the latter, and on that day believers will rejoice, with the help of God. He helps to victory whom He wills. He is the All-Mighty, the All-Compassionate. (30:1-5)

  No one at that time could have predicted such a reversal of events. But the Prophet, conveyed these Divine Revelations to his followers. Abu Bakr immediately bet the Makkan polytheists that the Romans would be victorious in 9 years. Heraclius, the Roman Emperor, attacked the Persians by sea in 622 (the year of the Hijra) and, after decisive battles and three successive campaigns, routed them after a few years. His victories happened at the same time as the believers defeated the Makkan polytheists at Badr. And so the predictions in those two verses were proven true.

- Six years after the Prophet emigrated to Madina, he left for Makka to perform the minor pilgrimage. The Makkans met him at Hudaybiya. After reaching a suitable compromise, the Muslims returned to Madina. Some believers were not pleased with this treaty. But the Qur'anic verses revealed after the treaty proclaimed it a manifest victory and gave them a decisive glad tiding:

> In truth, God fulfilled the vision of His Messenger: You will surely enter the Sacred Mosque, if God wills, in full security; you will have your heads shaved, your hair shortened, and you will have nothing to fear. He knew what you knew not, and He granted, besides this, a near victory. He it is Who has sent His Messenger with guidance and the religion of truth, that He may cause it to prevail over all religion. God is enough for a witness. (48:27-28)

One year later the Muslims performed the minor pilgrimage, and the year after they conquered Makka. Also, Islam prevailed over all other religions for centuries and, if God wills, will have global superiority in the near future.

- Pharaoh enslaved the Children of Israel. God sent Prophet Moses there to call Pharaoh to belief in One God and allow the Israelites to leave Egypt with Moses. Pharaoh's refusal opened a long struggle. One night when Moses succeeded in marching toward the frontier with his people, Pharaoh learned of his attempt and set out after him. When Moses reached the Red Sea, he touched it with his staff and a path opened. Pharaoh followed him, but was engulfed with his legions.

While narrating this event, the Qur'an makes a very interesting prediction: *Today We shall preserve your body that you may be a sign to those after you: although most men give no heed to Our signs* (10:92). Pharaoh's corpse was later found floating on the

Sinai's western shore. Residents can still show you this land, now known as Jabal Fir'awn (Hill of Pharaoh). A few miles away is a hot spring called Hammam Fir'awn (the Bath of Pharaoh).

• A considerable part of the Qur'an concerns the Last Day. It describes how the world will be destroyed and rebuilt, and how the dead will be raised, assembled in the Place of Mustering, judged and sent to Paradise or Hell. The Qur'an also gives vivid descriptions of life in those two realms.

Among his predictions in the books of Tradition are the following:

• 'Umar reports in a narration recorded in Sahih al-Muslim:

> 'Before the Battle of Badr started, God's Messenger, upon him be peace and blessings, walked around the battlefield and pointed to some locations, saying: "Abu Jahl will be killed here, 'Utba here, Shayba here, Walid here, and so on." By God, we found, after the battle, the dead bodies of all those men in the exact places that God's Messenger had pointed out.[4]

• Bukhari and Abu Dawud quote Habbab ibn Arat, who said:

> Once, during the days of trouble and torture in Makka, I went to God's Messenger, who was sitting in the shade of the Ka'ba. I was still a slave of the Makkans. They tortured me severely. Unable to endure those tortures any longer, I asked God's Messenger to pray to God for help and salvation. But he turned toward me and said: "By God, previous communities had to endure more pitiless tortures. Some were made to lie in ditches and cut in two with saws, but this did not make them forsake their faith. They were skinned alive, but they never became weak against the enemy. God will perfect this religion, but you display undue haste. A day will come when a woman will travel by herself from San'a to Hadramawt fearing nothing but wild beasts. However, you show impatience."

Habbab concluded: "By God, what God's Messenger predicted that day, have all come true. I have personally witnessed it all."[5]

- Bukhari, Muslim, and Ahmad ibn Hanbal record:

  > While building the Prophet's Mosque in Madina, the
  > Messenger told 'Ammar: "What a pity O 'Ammar, a rebel-
  > lious group will kill you." 'Ammar was killed in the Battle
  > of Siffin by the supporters of Mu'awiya, who rebelled against
  > Caliph 'Ali.[6]

- Before his death, the Messenger called his daughter Fatima
  to his bedside and informed her that she would be the first
  family member to join him after his death.[7] She died 6 months
  later.

- He predicted the Mongol invasion, saying: "The Hour will not
  come before you fight against a people with red faces, small,
  slanting eyes, and flat noses. They wear hairy leather boots."[8]

- As related by Hakim, Tirmidhi, Ibn Hanbal, and Ibn Maja,
  by repeatedly declaring: "After my death, you should follow
  the way of Abu Bakr and 'Umar,"[9] the Prophet meant that
  Abu Bakr and 'Umar would succeed him as caliphs. He also
  predicted that Abu Bakr's reign would be short, whereas 'Umar
  would remain longer and make many conquests.

- According to authentic narrations, the Prophet, told his community that they would conquer Damascus, Jerusalem, Iraq,
  Persia, Istanbul (Constantinople), and Cyprus, and that Islam
  would reach as far as the easternmost and western-most parts
  of the world.[10]

- The Prophet declared: "This affair began with Prophethood
  and as a mercy; then it will be mercy and Caliphate; afterwards
  it will change into a cruel monarchy, and finally into an iniq-
  uity and tyranny." He also foretold: "Surely, the Caliphate
  after me will last 30 years; afterwards it will be a monarchy."[11]
  Whatever the noble Prophet predicted came true.

- According to an authentic narration, the Prophet declared:
  "'Uthman will be killed while reading the Qur'an. God will
  dress him in a shirt, but they will want to remove it from
  him."[12] In other words, 'Uthman would become Caliph,
  but his deposition would be sought and he would be mar-

tyred while reading the Qur'an. This happened exactly as predicted.

- As narrated in an authentic Tradition, the noble Prophet of God said to Sa'd ibn Abi Waqqas when the latter was gravely ill: "It is hoped that you will be spared so that some people may benefit through you and some others be harmed through you."[13] By this, he suggested that Sa'd would be a great commander and make many conquests, and that while many would benefit from him by converting to Islam, many others would be harmed through him after their states collapsed. As predicted, Sa'd assumed command of the armies during the Caliphate of 'Umar and, by destroying the Persian Sassanid Empire, brought many people within the fold of Islam.

- Once the Prophet woke up in the house of Umm Haram, the aunt of Anas ibn Malik (his servant for 10 years in Madina), and said with a smile: "I dreamed that my community would fight in the sea sitting on thrones like kings." Umm Haram asked: "Pray that I may be with them." He said firmly: "You shall be."[14] All this came true 40 years later, when Umm Haram accompanied her husband 'Ubada ibn Samit on the conquest of Cyprus. She died there, and her tomb remains a visited place.

- According to an authentic narration, the Prophet declared: "A liar who claims Prophethood, as well as a blood-thirsty tyrant, will appear from the Thaqif tribe."[15] By this, he gave tidings of the notorious Mukhtar, who claimed Prophethood, and the criminal Hajjaj, who killed tens of thousands of people.

- Again, according to an authentic narration, the Prophet declared: "Surely, Constantinople (Istanbul) will be conquered (by my community); how blessed the commander who will conquer it, and how blessed his army."[16] He thus foretold the conquest of Istanbul by the Muslims, indicated the high spiritual rank of Sultan Mehmed the Conqueror, and the virtuousness of his army. What he foretold took place centuries later.

- God's Messenger made about 300 predictions, the great majority of which have already come true. Some of his predictions are, interestingly enough, about advances in science and technology. For example, as recorded in *Sahih al-Muslim* and *Sunan al-Tirmidhi*, he foretold that a pomegranate would suffice for as many as 20 people, with its rind providing shade for those who ate it, and that the wheat grown in a small house balcony would be enough to feed a family for a year. By these predictions, he must have indicated that humanity would realize great advances in genetic engineering.

Consequently, in his predictions, the Prophet never said "I think," "I guess," "It may be," or "It will probably happen," all of which express doubt. Instead, he spoke as if he were watching the past and future on a television screen. This means that either he had a very keen and far sight capable of penetrating the past and future at the same time, which is impossible for any mortal, or that he was a Prophet taught by the Knower of All Things, the One for Whom all time and space is but a single point.

HIS MIRACLES

A miracle is an extraordinary event that God Almighty brings about at the hands of a Prophet to prove his Prophethood, strengthen the believers' faith, and break the unbelievers' obstinacy.

The universe operates according to God's fixed laws. In the absence of His laws and the uniform character of natural events, everything would be in continual flux. In such an environment, we would be unable to discover the Divine laws of nature or make any scientific progress. Although recent discoveries in atomic physics have shown that whatever exists is a wave in continuous motion, on the surface everything occurs according to classical or Newtonian principles. This has forced scientists to admit that they cannot state that anything will exist in the same state as it did even one second ago.

Normally, life has its own laws according to which we behave. We need food and water to satisfy our hunger and thirst, and go to a doctor when we are sick. We use animals for labor, but cannot talk to them. Trees are fixed in their places, and neither they nor stones and mountains greet us. We conform to the laws of gravitation and repulsion, and do not attempt to rise into the sky without first making the relevant calculations.

All of these and other laws make human life possible. However, since God has determined them, He is not bound by them. Therefore, He may sometimes annul a law or change the ordinary flow of events to allow a Prophet to perform what we call a miracle or to show that He can do whatever He wills at whatever time He desires. The original word in Islamic literature translated as miracle is *mu'jiza* (something that no one else can do). If God allows a saint to perform such an event, it is called *karama* (an extraordinary favor). These favors constitute another proof of Muhammad's Prophethood and the truth of Islam.

God created innumerable *karama* at the hands of Muslim saints. One kind is foretelling the future. For example, Muhyi al-Din ibn al-'Arabi died almost 50 years before the establishment of the Ottoman State, and yet wrote in his Shajarat al-Nu'maniya about the Ottomans, predicted their conquest of Damascus and Egypt, that Sultan Murad IV would march on Baghdad and conquer it after a siege of 41 days, and that Sultan 'Abd al-'Aziz would be killed by cutting his wrists. He also wrote that: "When 'S' enters 'SH,' the burial-place of Muhyi al-Din will be discovered." Using symbols in his predictions, "S" means "Selim" and "SH" means "Sham" (Damascus). Like his other predictions, this one came true when Sultan Selim I conquered Damascus, discovered Ibn al-'Arabi's burial-place, and ordered a tomb built upon it.

Mushtaq Dada of Bitlis, an eastern province of Turkey, predicted 71 years in advance that after many wars and convulsions Ankara would replace Istanbul as the capital city. Interestingly enough, Mushtaq Dada gives the name of the man who would do this: by combining the initial letters of his lines of verse, you get the name Kemal.

God Almighty allowed His Prophets to perform miracles. However, since all previous Prophets were sent to their own people, and their Prophethood was thereby restricted, their miracles were related to the widespread arts and crafts of their time. For example, since at the time of Moses, sorcery enjoyed great prestige in Egypt, God Almighty caused his staff to change into a snake and swallow those of the sorcerers. At the time of Jesus, the healing arts enjoyed great prestige, and so most of his miracles involved healing. As for Prophet Muhammad, since his Prophethood is universal and he is the last Prophet, his miracles are very diverse and connected with nearly all parts of creation.

When a glorified ruler's aide-de-camp enters a city with various gifts from the ruler, a representative of each group of people or from each professional group, society, or association welcomes him cheerfully. Similarly, when the Eternal Sovereign's supreme Messenger honored the universe as an envoy to the Earth's inhabitants, bringing from the Creator the light of truth and spiritual gifts related to the truths of the universe, every entity—from mineral elements and plants to animals and human beings, and from the moon and sun to stars—welcomed him in its own way and language, and became a means for one kind of miracle.

Every word, act, and state of the noble Prophet testifies to his Prophethood and his faithfulness. But not all of them need to be miraculous. The Almighty sent him as human being so that he could guide and lead men and women, in all their individual and collective affairs, to happiness in both worlds, and so they could view the wonders of His art and the works of His Power. Each of these are in fact miracles, but they appear to us as ordinary and familiar events.

If the Prophet had been extraordinary in all his acts, he could not have guided and instructed us. God allowed him to perform some extraordinary phenomena to prove his Prophethood to unbelievers, and so he occasionally worked miracles. But these were done in a way that did not compel belief, as this would negate the purpose of our testing and exercise of free will. If miracles forced people to believe, thereby depriving them of their choice to believe or not, our whole existence and purpose would be meaningless.

The majority of the Prophet's approximately 1,000 miracles were related first by Companions, then by numerous reliable narrators and authorities, and subsequently recorded in authentic books of Tradition. As for the rest, although related by only one or two Companions, they also must be indisputable, as they later were judged true by all reliable authorities and narrated by more than one chain of transmission. In addition, most occurred in the presence of many people (e.g., a military campaign, wedding ceremony, or feast), and one or more of those present related it and the others confirmed it by keeping silent. Therefore, the miracles recorded in authentic books of Tradition are indisputable and cannot be denied or rejected.

Examples of the Prophet's Miracles

The Qur'an declares:

> Glorified be He Who carried His servant by night from the Sacred Mosque (Masjid al-Haram) to Masjid al-Aqsa, the neighborhood of which We have blessed, that We might show him of Our signs. Surely He is the All-Hearing, the All-Seeing. (17:1)

> Then he drew nigh and came down, till he was two bows' length or even nearer, and He revealed unto His servant what He revealed. The heart (of His servant) lied not (in seeing) what he saw. (53:8-11)

The Ascension is one of the greatest miracles of the Prophet Muhammad. Having been favored with spiritual perfection and full refinement through belief and worship, God took him to His holy Presence. Escaping the imprisonment of natural laws and material causes and transcending bodily existence, the Prophet crossed distances swiftly and rose above all dimensions of the material world until he reached the holy Presence of God.

Atomic physics has changed many concepts in physics. It also has established that this world is only one dimension or appearance of existence among many, each of which has its own particularities. Einstein posited that time is only one dimension of existence. Science has not yet drawn any final conclusions about existence, for new findings and developments continually change our view of it. Therefore, how can one question the Ascension? People have difficulty in understanding how one can penetrate all time at the same moment as a single point. To better understand this subtle matter, consider the following analogy:

Imagine that you are holding a mirror. Everything reflected on the right represents the past, while everything reflected on the left represents the future. The mirror can reflect one direction only while you are holding it. If you want to see both sides, you must rise so high above your original position that left and right are united into one and nothing remains to be called first or last, beginning or end.

In the Ascension, the Prophet must have moved with the speed of the spirit, as he traveled through all time and space and all dimensions of existence in a very short period. During that heavenly journey, he met with previous Prophets, saw angels, and beheld the beauties of Paradise and the terrors of Hell. He observed the essential realities of all Qur'anic issues, as well as the meanings and wisdom of all acts of worship. He also reached the realms where even the greatest angel, Gabriel, cannot reach, and was honored with a vision of God's "Countenance," free from any qualitative and quantitative dimension and restriction. Then, to bring humanity out of the darkness of material existence and into the illumined realm of belief and worship, so that all men and women can experience their own "spiritual" ascension, he returned to the world.

Another miracle, that of splitting the moon was performed before people who persisted in denying Muhammad's Prophethood. As related by 'Abd Allah ibn Mas'ud, one night while they were in Mina', the Prophet split the moon into two with a gesture of his index finger. One half appeared behind the mountain, and the other in front of it. Then the Prophet turned to us and said: "Be witnesses!"[17] The Qur'an relates this miracle: *The Hour has approached, and the moon split. But whenever they see a sign, they turn away and say: "This is evident magic."* (54:1-2).

We will now relate several other miracles, all of which are thoroughly documented in Islamic literature.

- Anas ibn Malik relates that Abu Talha, seeing that God's Messenger was hungry, invited him to a meal. The Messenger

came with a crowd of people. Abu Talha had only one loaf of
rye bread at home. His wife Umm Sulaym spread some but-
ter on it. The Messenger prayed for abundance, and at least
70 to 80 people ate as much as they wanted before leaving.[18]

• 'Abd al-Rahman ibn Abi Bakr relates that 130 Companions
were with God's Messenger during an expedition. The
Messenger asked them whether they had something to eat.
Someone had one or two sacks of flour. Dough was prepared,
and a sheep was bought from a polytheist passing by with
his flock. After roasting the sheep's liver, the Messenger gave
a piece to each one present, and put aside the shares of those
who were not present. They cooked the meat in two bowls,
and everyone ate of it. After they finished eating, there was
just as much meat as there had been before they had started
eating.[19]

Many similar miracles were transmitted through various
(sometimes as many as 16) channels. Most of them took place
in the presence of large assemblies and were narrated by many
persons of truth and good reputation.

The One Who created the universe and made it dependent
on certain laws obviously can change those laws for His special,
beloved servant and envoy. Especially in our day, when scientists
have abandoned mechanistic ideas in favor of relativity, it is neither rational nor scientific to deny miracles on the basis of
absolute determinism or causality.

Furthermore, miracles are never completely free of material
causes, however slight and insignificant they may be. Given that
God Almighty causes the smallest things to produce very great
entities, how can we deny miracles? Human beings, weak enough
to be defeated by germs, nevertheless are intelligent enough to
make computers that can hold knowledge that would fill many
libraries. Is this a lesser miracle than enabling His servant to give
some food or drink a blessed increase? Indeed, is not every occurrence in the universe, every act of God, really a miracle, the like of
which we are unable to make?

There are many examples of the Prophet's miracles concerning water. They were related by numerous Companions and

transmitted through various reliable channels. We mention two of them here.

- Once when they were in Zarwa, the Companions could not find enough water for *wudu'* (ritual ablution). God's Messenger asked them to bring a bowl of water. He dipped his hands into it, and water began to run from his fingers like a fountain. Anas ibn Malik says that on that day they were 300 people, and thus relates this incident on behalf of 300 people. If he were lying, is it logical to assume that not even one person would contradict him?[20]

- During the campaign of Hudaybiya, the Companions complained to God's Messenger about the lack of water. He took an arrow out of his arrow-bag and told them to put it in the well called Semed. When they did so, water began to gush forth. During the campaign, all Companions drank from it and performed *wudu'* with it.[21]

Authentic books of Tradition, including primarily *Sahih al-Bukhari* and *Sahih al-Muslim*, report many miracles of healing sick and wounded people, among them the following:

- During the Battle of Khaybar, God's Messenger asked where 'Ali was. Informed that 'Ali's eyes were hurting him," he sent for him and, after he arrived, applied his healing saliva to 'Ali's eyes. At the same moment the pain ceased, and 'Ali's eyes became better than before.[22]

- 'Uthman ibn Hunayf relates:

> A blind man came to God's Messenger and requested him to pray to God to recover his sight. The Messenger said: "If you desire, I'll not pray—being blind may be better for your after-life—or I'll pray." The man chose to be relieved of blindness and the Messenger told him: "Go and do an ablution. Then pray two rak'as and say: 'O God, surely my appeal is to You and I turn toward You through the Prophet Muhammad, the Prophet of mercy. O Muhammad, surely I turn toward God through you, that He uncover my sight. O God, make him my intercessor.'"

The man did as he was told, and his sight was restored.[23]

The animal kingdom recognized God's Messenger, upon him be peace and blessings, and became the means for him to work miracles. Although there are many examples, we will mention here only a few that are well-known and agreed on by exacting authorities.

- During the Hijra, when God's Messenger took shelter from the unbelievers in Thawr cave, two pigeons guarded the entrance (like two sentries) and a spider (like a doorkeeper) covered its entrance with a thick web. While Ubayy ibn Khalaf, a Qurayshi chief, was examining the cave, his friends suggested that they should enter. He answered: "There is a web here, which seems to have been spun before the birth of Muhammad." The others added: "Would those pigeons, standing there, still be there if someone were in the cave?"[24]

- Jabir relates:

   > I was with God's Messenger during a military campaign. When my camel became exhausted and left behind, God's Messenger prodded it slightly. This made the camel so fast that I had to pull on the reins to make it go slower so that I could listen to the Messenger, but I was unable to [slow it down].[25]

- Anas ibn Malik reports:

   > After the conquest of Khaybar, a Jewish woman offered God's Messenger a roasted sheep. God's Messenger, upon him be peace and blessings, ate a piece but, according to the narration of Abu Dawud, stopped eating and said: "This sheep says it has been poisoned." He turned to the woman and asked her why she offered him poisoned meat. When the woman replied that she wanted to kill him, the Messenger responded: "God will not let you attack and annoy me."[26]

- 'A'isha reports:

   > We had a pigeon in our house. When God's Messenger, upon him be peace and blessings, was at home, it would stay quiet. As soon as he left, it would continually pace to and fro.[27]

- Anas ibn Malik relates:

> God's Messenger, upon him be peace and blessings, was the most generous and courageous person. One night the people of Madina heard some voices and set out in fear to investigate. On their way, they saw a man coming toward them, who appeared to be God's Messenger, upon him be peace and blessings. He said to them: "There is nothing to be distressed about." He had mounted Abu Talha's horse and investigated the matter before anybody else. He turned to Abu Talha and said: "I found your horse fast and comfortable," whereas it had been very slow before that event. After that night, no other horse could race against it.[28]

According to many accounts in the books of Traditions, he used inanimate objects while performing his miracles.

* Jabir ibn Samura reports: God's Messenger, upon him be peace and blessings, once said: "Prior to my Prophethood, a rock in Makka used to greet me. I still recognize it."[29] 'Abd Allah ibn Mas'ud reports: We could hear food glorifying God while we were eating with God's Messenger, upon him be peace and blessings.[30]

* Traditionists unanimously report from Anas, Abu Hurayra, 'Uthman, and Sa'id ibn Zayd, who said:

> God's Messenger, upon him be peace and blessings, climbed up Mount Uhud, with Abu Bakr, 'Umar, and 'Uthman. The mountain, either in awe or because of its joy, trembled. He said: "Be still, O Uhud, for on you is a Prophet, a truthful one, and two martyrs."[31]

Thus did the Messenger predict the martyrdom of 'Umar and 'Uthman.

* It is established through authentic narrations from 'Ali, Jabir, and 'A'isha that rocks and mountains would greet God's Messenger, saying: "Peace be upon you, O Messenger of God." 'Ali says: "Whenever we walked in the suburbs of Makka in the early times of his Prophethood, trees and rocks would say: 'Peace be upon you, O Messenger of God.'"[32] The Prophet's protection was itself a miracle.

* As related through various channels:

During the military campaigns of Ghatfan and Anmar, a courageous chief named Ghowras unexpectedly appeared at the side of God's Messenger, who was lying under a tree. Unsheathing his sword, he asked God's Messenger: "Who will save you from me now?" "God will," the Messenger replied. Then he prayed: "O God, protect me from him as You will." At that moment, Ghowras was knocked down, and his sword slipped from his hand. God's Messenger, upon him be peace and blessings, took the sword and asked him: "Now, who will save you from me?" Ghowras began to tremble and entreated God's Messenger to spare his life. "You are a noble, forgiving one; only forgiveness is expected of you," he pleaded. God's Messenger forgave him, and when Ghowras returned to his tribe, he said to them: "I have just come from the best of humanity."[33]

- Abu Hurayra relates:

  Abu Jahl once asked those near him: "Does Muhammad still rub his face against earth [i.e. make prostration]?" "Yes, he does," they answered. Abu Jahl added: "By Lat and 'Uzza, if I see him doing that again, I will tread on his neck or bury his face with soil."

A short while later God's Messenger came and began to pray. While he was prostrating, Abu Jahl approached him but suddenly turned back in fear and amazement, trying to protect himself with his hands. When asked why he had done so, he answered: "Truly, between him and me is a trench filled with fire, and something horrible and some wings."

God's Messenger commented on the event: "If he had approached me, the angels would have torn him to pieces."[34] God promised to guard him against people:

  O Messenger! Make known whatever is revealed unto you from your Lord, for if you do it not, you will not have conveyed His Message. God will protect you from people. Surely, God guides not the unbelievers. (5:67)

The acceptance of his prayers is also a miracle, as can be seen in the following accounts:

- The authorities of Tradition, including Imam al-Bukhari and Imam Muslim, all report that the Messenger's prayer for rain always was accepted immediately. Sometimes it would begin before he lowered his hands while on the pulpit. Rain clouds would appear when his army ran out of water. Even in his childhood, his grandfather 'Abd al-Muttalib would go out with him to pray for rain, and rain would come out of God's love for him. 'Abd al-Muttalib immortalized this in a poem. After the Prophet's death, 'Umar once invoked the name of 'Abbas while praying for rain, saying: "O God, this is the uncle of Your beloved Prophet. Give us rain for his sake." Thereafter it rained.[35]

- Anas ibn Malik reported that one Friday when God's Messenger was giving a sermon, a man came into the mosque and said: "O Messenger of God, there is drought. Please ask God to send rain." The Messenger prayed, and it rained until the next Friday. On that day, while God's Messenger was on the pulpit again giving a sermon, a man stood up and said: "O Messenger of God, please pray to God to turn the rain from us." The Messenger prayed: "O God, send the rain onto the places around us, not onto us." Anas, who reported the event, says: "By God, I saw the clouds scatter and rain fall onto other places, and it stopped raining on the people of Madina."[36]

- 'Abd Allah ibn 'Umar relates: When there were about 40 Companions, God's Messenger, upon him be peace and blessings, prayed: "O God, strengthen Islam with which of those two, namely, 'Umar ibn al-Khattab and 'Amr ibn al-Hisham, is more pleasing to You." The next morning, 'Umar came to the Messenger and accepted Islam.[37]

- 'Abd Allah ibn 'Abbas reports: Once when God's Messenger went to relieve himself, I carried water to him for *wudu'*. When he came out, he asked who had put the water there. "I did," I answered. Whereupon he prayed: "O God, make him profoundly knowledgeable in religion and teach him the meaning of the Qur'an."[38] Based on this prayer, he would be called "Profound Scholar of the Umma" and "Interpreter of the Qur'an." When he was still young, 'Umar put him on his consultative assembly of high-ranking scholars and elders of the Companions.

- Anas ibn Malik relates: My mother took me to God's Messenger and said: "O Messenger of God, this is my son Anas. Let him serve you. Please pray for him."[39] The Messenger prayed: "O God, give him abundant wealth and offspring." Anas remarked in his old age, swearing by God: "You see the abundance of my wealth, and my children and grandchildren number about one hundred."

- Abu Hurayra once complained to God's Messenger about forgetfulness. The Messenger told him to spread a piece of cloth on the ground. Then he seemed to fill his hands with invisible things and empty them on the cloth. After repeating this three or four times, he told Abu Hurayra to pick it up. Abu Hurayra, as he himself later swore by God, never forgot anything again. This is also among the well-known events related to the Companions.[40]

- In addition, the Prophet met with and spoke to angels and jinn. 'Umar reports:

> We were sitting with God's Messenger, upon him be peace and blessings, when a man appeared beside us. He had dark black hair and was wearing a white robe. There were no signs of traveling upon him. He sat before the Messenger and, touching his knees to the Messenger's, asked him about faith, Islam, perfection of virtue (ihsan), and the Last Day. After the interview, the man left and disappeared. God's Messenger, upon him be peace and blessings, turned to me and asked who that man was. "God and His Messenger know better," I answered. The Messenger concluded: "He was Gabriel. He came to teach you your religion."[41]

- Sa'd ibn Abi Waqqas relates:

> At the Battle of Uhud, I saw two men (the archangels Gabriel and Michael) dressed in white on either side of God's Messenger, fighting for his sake. I had never seen them before, nor have I seen them since.[42]

- Rifa'a ibn Rafi' reports:

  > Gabriel asked God's Messenger his opinion of the Companions
  > who participated in the Battle of Badr. The Messenger
  > answered like this: "We consider them among the most virtu-
  > ous of Muslims." Gabriel responded: "So do we. We consider
  > the angels who were present there among the most virtuous of
  > angels."[43]

- In his *Musnad*, Ahmad ibn Hanbal reports from 'Abd Allah
  ibn Mas'ud that God's Messenger invited jinn to accept
  Islam and taught them about the Qur'an.[44]

  The Prophet, also performed miracles related to the appearance of invisible objects and realms.

- 'A'isha reports:

  > One day the sun was eclipsed. God's Messenger, upon him be
  > peace and blessings, performed the prayer of eclipse and then
  > explained: "The sun and the moon are two of God's signs.
  > When you witness an eclipse, pray until it ends. By God, in this
  > place where I have performed the prayer I saw everything
  > promised to me. When you saw me move forward during the
  > prayer, I did that to take a cluster of grapes that appeared to me
  > from Paradise. Again, by God, when you saw me move back-
  > ward, I did so because I saw Hell roaring with its parts piling
  > one upon another."[45]

- 'Abd Allah ibn 'Abbas relates: God's Messenger, upon him
  be peace and blessings, passed by two graves and said:

  > Heed what I will tell you: Those lying in those graves are suf-
  > fering torments because of two grave sins. One of them used
  > to backbite and slander others everywhere; the other was not
  > careful [about guarding himself] against urine stains.[46]

  Even such inanimate objects as trees and sticks testified to
  his Prophethood.

- Jabir ibn 'Abd Allah reports:

  > We were walking with God's Messenger, upon him be peace
  > and blessings. We went down into a wide valley, and the

Messenger searched for a place to relieve himself. When he could not find one, he went to the two trees he had seen by the valley. He pulled one of them by a branch next to the other tree. The tree was like an obedient camel being pulled by its reins. He addressed them: "Join together over me, by God's permission." The trees did so and formed a screen.[47]

- 'Abd Allah ibn 'Umar reports:

God's Messenger, upon him be peace and blessings, used to lean against a pole called the "date-palm trunk" when delivering a sermon. When a pulpit was built and the Prophet started giving his sermons from it, the pole moaned because of its separation. The Messenger climbed down and stroked it, after which it stopped moaning.[48]

- Abu Sa'id al-Khudri relates:

God's Messenger gave Qatada ibn Nu'man a stick on a dark night, saying: "This stick will light up your surroundings as far as 7 meters. When you get home, you will see a black shadow. Without allowing it to tell you anything, strike it with this stick."[49]

Qatada did as he was instructed.

MIRACLES CANNOT BE DENIED

- The noble Prophet declared that he was a Prophet and, to prove his Prophethood, presented the glorious Qur'an and nearly 1,000 miracles. Their occurrence cannot be denied, for even the most obstinate unbelievers only charged him with sorcery. Unable to deny the miracles, they took them to be sorcery to justify their unbelief and continued to misguide their followers.

His miracles have been confirmed and reported unanimously by the Hadith authorities. A miracle is the Creator's confirmation of his Prophethood, as it says, in effect: "You have spoken the truth." If a person claims in the ruler's presence that the ruler appointed him or her to such and such a position, the word "Yes" uttered by the ruler proves this claim. Further, if the ruler changes his usual practice and attitude at that person's request, it only further confirms such a claim. In the same way, the noble Messenger claimed that he was the envoy of the Creator of the universe, Who, in turn, changed His unbroken order when necessary so that His envoy could perform a miracle to prove his claim.

- Denying miracles amounts to denying God's existence, Muhammad's Prophethood, as well as the Qur'an's Divine authorship. Such a denial is absurd and meaningless, for while one piece of evidence proves a claim, its denial requires an overall investigation throughout time and space. For example, if you claim that there are black swans, all you have to do is produce one. But if you claim that this is impossible, you must show all swans from the beginning to the end of time. So, the nonexistence of something is almost impossible to prove. Those who deny miracles, which billions of believers, as well as hundreds of thousands of saints, scholars and scientists, have confirmed since the Prophet's claim of Prophethood, are like those who say that since one door of a magnificent palace with 1,000 doors is closed, the palace cannot be entered.

- Almost all Prophets worked miracles. For centuries, millions of Jews and billions of Christians have confirmed the miracles of Moses and Jesus, respectively. When compared to other Prophets, what shortcoming do they find in Prophet Muhammad that causes them to deny his miracles?

- The creation of Adam, Eve, and Jesus are miracles, for they were not born according to God's law. Although currently entangled in materialistic notions, science one day will have to attribute the origin of life to a Divine miracle. Besides, it is highly questionable whether it is scientific to label as myth the beliefs, concepts, or events that science cannot explain.

Science is based on theories and develops through trial-and-error investigations of those theories. Many now-established facts were once considered false, and many once-established facts are now known to be fallacies. Moreover, we unquestionably accept the existence of many things that we cannot prove scientifically. Denying miracles is unscientific, insofar as such a judgment or conclusion must be based on concrete proof. No one can deny, whether based on science or not, the miracles of Prophet Muhammad.

- Some regard miracles as being against reason and logic. However, our reason and intellect cannot grasp everything in existence. Also, no two people have the exact same intellectual capacity. So, in order to decide something reasonable or not, whose intellect will judge? The Qur'an declares: *Whomsoever We will, we raise in degrees. Over every man of knowledge is one who knows better* (12:76).

The magnificent order, harmony, and purposiveness in existence decisively point to One with absolute knowledge, will, and power. That One, God the Creator, does what He wishes, for He is not bound by the laws He established for the universe. Therefore, He can change them or even act and create without any laws if He so wishes. Given this, we should try to discover those laws, as God gave us an intellect to do just that, not to judge His acts. Human intellect is limited, and we all know that what is limited cannot judge that which is not limited.

- Time varies or changes according to the dimensions of existence and place. For example, time measurements differ from planet to planet. The finer or more refined matter is, the quicker its time and movement, as indicated that our spirit travels much faster than our physical body. Also, our imagination can travel through all spheres within a few seconds.

Just as each person is unique in regard to power, there is a great difference between each species' capacity. We are far more powerful than ants or bees, but they can do things that we cannot. Also, invisible things or beings like angels and jinn, and even storms and gales, may be far more powerful than human beings. So all physical and intellectual powers and capacities are included in a single, absolute Power. If that Power can do whatever It wishes, why should we not believe in miracles?

- We witness and even experience certain events that we regard as miraculous, for the law of causality cannot explain everything. Furthermore, modern physics asserts that whatever exists is a wave in continuous motion, meaning that we cannot say that what exists now will exist in the same manner even one second from now. Therefore, the law of causality is only a veil covering the Divine operations so that people do not directly attribute certain disagreeable things and events to God. And so it is the affirmation, not denial, of miracles that is really reasonable and scientific.

HIS MARRIAGES

Some critics of Islam, either because they are unaware of the facts or are biased, revile the Prophet as a self-indulgent libertine. They accuse him of character failings that are hardly compatible with a person of average virtue, let alone with the Prophet, God's last Messenger, and the best model for humanity to emulate. A simple account of these marriages, which are openly discussed in many biographies and well-authenticated accounts of his sayings and actions, shows that they were part of a most strictly disciplined life, and another burden that he bore as God's Last Messenger.

The Prophet entered into these marriages due to his role as the Muslims' leader and guide toward Islamic norms and values. In the following pages, we will explain some of the reasons behind his marriages and demonstrate that the charges are baseless and false.

The Prophet married his first wife, Khadija, when he was 25 and had not yet been called to his future mission. Given the surrounding cultural environment, not to mention the climate, his youth, and other considerations, it is remarkable that he enjoyed a reputation for perfect chastity, integrity, and trustworthiness. As soon as he was called to Prophethood, he acquired enemies who slandered him. However, none dared to invent something unbelievable. It is important to realize that his life was founded upon chastity and self-discipline from the outset, and remained so.

Muhammad married Khadija, a woman 15 years his senior, when he was in his prime. This marriage was very lofty and exceptional in the eyes of the Prophet and God. For 23 years, the couple lived a life of uninterrupted contentment in perfect fidelity. In the eighth year of Prophethood, however, Khadija died and the Prophet had to raise his children by himself. Even his enemies had to admit that during all these years they could find no flaw in his moral character.

The Prophet took no other wife while Khadija was alive, although polygamy was socially acceptable and widely practiced. He remarried only after he was 55, an age by which very little real interest and desire for marriage remains. The allegation that these marriages were due to licentiousness or self-indulgence is thus groundless and without merit.

People often ask how a Prophet can be polygamous. There are three points to be made here. But first, let's recognize that those who continually raise such questions are non-Muslims who do not have accurate knowledge of either Islam and religion in general, and so, either deliberately or mistakenly, confuse right with wrong to deceive others and spread doubt.

Those who do not believe in or practice any religion have no right to reproach those who do. Their lifestyles, especially their multiple extramarital liaisons, are examples of unrestrained self-indulgence unhindered by such considerations as the happiness and well-being of young people in general, and of their own children in particular. Those who advertise themselves as free and liberated condone such practices as incest, homosexuality, and polyandry. One can only wonder how such relationships affect the children of such unions. Such critics have only one motive: to drag Muslims into the moral confusion and viciousness in which they themselves are trapped.

Jews and Christians who attack Prophet Muhammad for his marriages can be motivated only by fear, jealousy, and hatred of Islam. They forget that the great patriarchs of the Hebrew race, named as Prophets in the Bible and the Qur'an and revered by followers of all three faiths as exemplars of moral excellence, all practiced polygamy—and on a far greater scale than Prophet Muhammad.[50]

Here we remember the words of Isaac Taylor, who spoke at the Church Congress of England, on how Islam changes the people who accept it:

> The virtues which Islam inculcates are temperance, cleanliness, chastity, justice, fortitude, courage, benevolence, hospitality, veracity and resignation.... Islam preaches a practical brotherhood, the social equality of all Muslims. Slavery is not part of the creed of Islam. Polygamy is a more difficult question. Moses did not prohibit it. It was practiced by David and it is not directly forbidden in the New Testament. Muhammad limited the unbounded license of polygamy. It is the exception rather than the rule...

Polygamy did not originate with the Muslims. In the Prophet's case, from the viewpoint of its function within the mission of Prophethood, polygamy (or, more strictly, polygyny) had far more significance than people generally realize.

In a sense, polygamy was a necessity for the Prophet, for through it he established the statutes and norms of Muslim family law. Religion cannot be excluded from private spousal relations or from matters known only by one's spouse. Therefore, there must be women who can give clear instruction and advice, rather than hints and innuendoes, so that everything is understood. These chaste and virtuous women conveyed and explained the norms and rules governing Muslim private life.

* Since these women were of all ages, the Islamic requirements and norms could be portrayed in relation to their different life stages and experiences. These provisions were learned and applied within the Prophet's household first, and then passed on to other Muslims by his wives.

* Each wife was from a different clan or tribe. This allowed the Prophet to establish bonds of kinship and affinity throughout the community. As a result, a profound attachment to him spread among many diverse people, thereby creating and securing equality, brotherhood, and sisterhood in a most practical way and on the basis of religion.

- Each wife, both during the Prophet's life and after his death, was of great benefit and service to Islam. Each one conveyed and interpreted his message to her clan: all of the outer and inner experiences, qualities, manners, and faith of the man whose life, in all its public and intimate details, embodied the Qur'an. In this way, all clan members learned about the Qur'an, *hadith*, *tafsir* (interpretation and commentary on the Qur'an), and *fiqh* (understanding of the Islamic law), and so became fully aware of Islam's essence and spirit.

- Polygamy also allowed Prophet Muhammad to establish ties of kinship throughout Arabia. As a result, he was free to move and be accepted as a member in each family, for their members regarded him as one of their own. Given such a relationship, they were not shy to ask him directly about the affairs of this life and the Hereafter. The tribes also benefited collectively from this proximity, considered themselves fortunate, and took pride in that relationship. Some of these tribes were the Umayyads (through Umm Habiba), the Hashimites (through Zaynab bint Jahsh), and the Banu Makhzum (through Umm Salama).

What we have said so far is general and could, in some respects, be true of all Prophets. Now we will discuss the lives of *Ummahat al-Mu'minin* (the mothers of the believers) not in the order of the marriages but in a different perspective.

Khadija was the Prophet's first wife. When they married, she was 40 and he was 25. She bore all of his children, except his son Ibrahim, who did not live very long. As well as being a wife, Khadija was also her husband's friend who shared his inclinations and ideals to a remarkable degree. Their 23-year marriage was wonderfully blessed and passed in profound harmony. Through every insult and persecution, Khadija stood by him and helped him. He loved her very deeply, and did not marry another woman during her lifetime.

This marriage is the ideal marriage of intimacy, friendship, mutual respect, support, and consolation. Though faithful and loyal to all his wives, he never forgot Khadija and often mentioned her virtues and merits. After her death, the Prophet took care of his children for 4 or 5 years, performing the duties of mother and father. To allege that such a man was a sensualist or lustful is not even worthy of consideration. If even 1 percent of it were true, could he have lived such a life during and after his wife's death?

'A'isha was his second wife, though not in the order of marriage. Her father was Abu Bakr, the Prophet's closest friend, devoted follower, and one of the earliest converts. He had long hoped to cement the deep attachment between himself and the Prophet through marriage. By marrying 'A'isha, the Prophet accorded the highest honor and courtesy to a man who shared all the good and bad times with him throughout his mission.

'A'isha, a remarkably intelligent and wise woman, had the nature and temperament to carry forward the work of Prophetic mission. Her marriage prepared her to be a spiritual guide and teacher to all women. She became a major student and disciple of her husband and through him. Like so many Muslims of that blessed time, she matured and perfected her skills and talents and thus joined him in the abode of bliss both as wife and student.

Her life and service to Islam after her marriage prove that she was an exceptional person fully worthy of such an exalted position. She is one of the greatest Hadith authorities, an excellent commentator on the Qur'an, and a most distinguished and knowledgeable expert in Islamic law. She truly represented the inner and outer qualities and experiences of Prophet Muhammad through her unique understanding.

Umm Salama was from the Banu Makhzum clan. Along with her husband, she had embraced Islam at the very beginning and emigrated to Abyssinia to avoid further persecution. After their return, they migrated with their four children to Madina. Her husband, a veteran of many battles, was wounded severely at the battle of Uhud and later died. Both Abu Bakr and 'Umar proposed marriage, aware of her need and suffering as a destitute widow with children. She refused because, according to her judgment, no one could be better than her late husband.

Some time later, the Prophet offered to marry her. This was quite right and natural, for this great woman, who had never shied from sacrifice and suffering for her faith, was now alone after having lived for many years in the noblest clan of Arabia. She could not be neglected and left as a beggar. Considering her piety, sincerity, and all that she had suffered, she certainly deserved to be helped. By taking her into his household, the Prophet was doing what he had done since his youth—befriending those without friends, supporting those without support, protecting those without protection.

Umm Salama, who was an intelligent and fast learner, also had the necessary qualifications to become a spiritual guide and teacher. When the gracious and compassionate Prophet took her under his protection, a new student to whom all women would be grateful was accepted into the school of knowledge and guidance. Let us recall that, at this time, he was approaching 60. For him to marry a widow with many children, and to accept the related expenses and responsibilities, can be understood only as a reflection of his vast reserves of humanity and compassion.

Umm Habiba was the daughter of Abu Sufyan, a long-time bitter enemy of the Prophet and the most determined supporter of unbelief. Yet his daughter was one of the earliest converts. She emigrated to Abyssinia, where her husband died and left her alone as an exile in desperate circumstances.

The Companions were few in number and could barely support themselves, let alone others. Umm Habiba had few options: she could become a Christian and seek their aid (unthinkable); she could go to her father's house, a headquarters of the war against Islam (unthinkable); or live as a beggar, although she belonged to one of the richest and noblest Arab families, and so bring shame upon her family name.

God recompensed Umm Habiba for all that she lost or sacrificed in the way of Islam. She suffered a lonely exile in an insecure environment among people of a different race and religion, and remained devastated by her husband's death. The Prophet, learning of her plight, sent an offer of marriage through the king (Negus). This noble and generous action was a practical proof of: *We have not sent you save as a mercy for all creatures* (21:107).

Through this marriage, Abu Sufyan's powerful family was linked with the Prophet and his household. This development led them to adopt a different attitude to Islam. This marriage also was influential far beyond Abu Sufyan's family: his clan, the Umayyads, ruled the Muslim community for almost a hundred years and produced some of Islam's most renowned warriors, administrators, and governors in the early period. This marriage started the change, for the depth of generosity and magnanimity of the Prophet's soul simply overwhelmed them.

Zaynab bint Jahsh was of noble birth and descent and a close relative of the Prophet. She was very pious, fasted a great deal, kept long vigils, and gave generously to the poor. When the Prophet asked that Zaynab be married to Zayd (his adopted African son), her family and Zaynab herself were at first unwilling, for they had hoped to marry their daughter to the Prophet. Naturally, when they realized that he wanted Zaynab to marry Zayd, they consented out of deference to their love for the Prophet and his authority. The two were married.

Zayd had been captured as a child during a tribal war and sold as a slave. His master, Khadija, presented him to Muhammad when they were married. He immediately freed Zayd and shortly afterwards adopted him as his son. Through this marriage, the Prophet wanted to establish and fortify equality, to make this ideal a reality by ending the ancient Arab prejudice against a slave or even a freed-man marrying a free-born woman. The Prophet therefore was starting this hard task with his own relatives.

The marriage was an unhappy one. The noble-born Zaynab was a good Muslim of a most pious and exceptional quality. The ex-slave Zayd was among the first to embrace Islam, and also was a good Muslim. Both loved and obeyed the Prophet, but they were mutually incompatible. Zayd sought permission to end this marriage several times, but always was told to be patient and remain married to Zaynab.

Once when the Prophet was talking with someone, Gabriel revealed to him that he should marry Zaynab.[51] This new marriage was announced as a bond already contracted: We have married her to you (33:37). This command was one of the severest trials for the Prophet up to that time. Yet he had to marry Zaynab, and thereby violate a tribal taboo, because God had commanded it. 'A'isha later said: "Had the Messenger of God been inclined to suppress anything of what was revealed to him, he would have suppressed this verse."[52]

Zaynab proved herself a most worthy wife. She was always aware of her responsibilities as well as the courtesies expected of her, and fulfilled them to universal admiration.

Before Islam, an adopted son was regarded as a natural son, and his wife was therefore regarded as a natural son's wife. According to the Qur'an, those who have been *wives of your sons proceeding from your loins* (4:23) fall within the prohibited marriages. But this prohibition does not include adopted sons, with whom there is no real consanguinity. This deep-rooted pagan taboo was ended by God's command that the Prophet marry Zaynab.

Juwayriya bint Harith, daughter of Harith, chief of the defeated Banu Mustaliq clan, was captured and held alongside the common people of her clan. When taken to the Prophet, she was in considerable distress due to the fact that her kinsmen had lost everything and because of her profound hatred and enmity toward Muslims. The Prophet understood her wounded pride, dignity, and suffering, as well as how to heal all of them. He agreed to pay her ransom and set her free, and then offered to marry her. How gladly Juwayriya accepted this offer can easily be imagined.

About 100 non-ransomed families were freed when the Ansar (the Helpers) and the Muhajirun (the Emigrants) learned that the Bani Mustaliq were related to the Prophet. A tribe so honored could not be allowed to remain in slavery.[53] In this way, the hearts of Juwayriya and all her people were won.

Safiyya was the daughter of Huyayy, a chief of the Jewish Khaybar tribe. This tribe earlier had persuaded the Banu Qurayza tribe to break their treaty with the Prophet. Since she was small, she had seen her family and relatives oppose the Prophet. Her father, brother, and husband had fallen at the hands of Muslims, and eventually she was captured by them.

The attitudes and actions of her family and relatives might have nurtured in her a deep hatred of Muslims and a desire for revenge. But 3 days before the Prophet arrived at Khaybar and she was captured, she dreamed of a brilliant moon coming from Madina, moving toward Khaybar, and falling into her lap. She later said: "When I was captured, I began to hope my dream would come true." When she was brought before him, the Prophet set her free and offered her the choice between remaining a Jewess and going home or accepting Islam and becoming his wife. "I chose God and His Messenger," she said. They were married shortly after that.

Raised to the Prophet's household, she became a "Mother of the Believers." The Companions honored and respected her accordingly, and so she witnessed at first hand the Muslims' refinement and true courtesy. Her attitude changed completely, and she appreciated the great honor of her new status. This marriage caused many Jews to change their attitudes as they came to see and know the Prophet closely.

Sawda bint Zam'a was Sakran's widow. Both were among the first to embrace Islam. After being forced to emigrate to Abyssinia to escape persecution, Sakran died and left his wife destitute. To help her, Prophet Muhammad, although quite hard-pressed to meet his own daily needs, married her. This marriage took place some time after Khadija's death.

Hafsa was 'Umar ibn al-Khattab's daughter. She had lost her husband, who had emigrated to Abyssinia and then to Madina, where he died from wounds received during a battle. She remained a widow for a while. 'Umar also desired, like Abu Bakr, the honor and blessing of being close to the Prophet in this world and in the Hereafter. Thus, the Prophet wed Hafsa to protect and help the daughter of his faithful disciple.

These are some of the reasons for the Prophet's multiple marriages. Instead of sensuality, he married to provide helpless or widowed women with dignified subsistence; console and honor enraged or estranged tribespeople; establish a degree of relationship and harmony between former enemies; gain certain uniquely gifted individuals for the cause of Islam, in particular some exceptionally talented women; establish new relationship norms among widely differing communities within the unifying bonds of faith in God; and honor with family bonds those men who would become his first two political successors.

These marriages were completely devoid of self-indulgence, personal desire, lust, and all other charges leveled by his detractors. With the exception of 'A'isha, all of these women had been widowed, and all of his marriages (after Khadija's death) were contracted when he was already old. If he had married any woman for pure pleasure, he would have chosen virgins. Far from being acts of self-indulgence, they were acts of self-discipline and self-sacrifice.

The number of the wives he was allowed was a special dispensation within the law of Islam and unique to his person. When the Revelation restricting polygamy came, he had contracted his marriages already. Thereafter, the Prophet also could not marry again.

CHAPTER 6

The Holy Qur'an

THE HOLY QUR'AN

If We had sent down this Qur'an on a mountain, surely you would have seen it humbled, rent asunder by fear of God. Such comparisons do We coin for people that perhaps they may reflect. (59:21)

The Qur'an is the Divine Word or Speech sent down to humanity, the best pattern of creation that is uniquely qualified to receive it. Despite the Qur'an's weight and gravity, many people cannot feel and appreciate its significance, for they have closed their senses and faculties to it. Those who alienate themselves and their inner life from the Qur'an receive nothing from it.

For one who is a good "diver"
The Qur'an is an ocean replete with jewels;
While one indifferent to it
Has nothing to receive from it.

The Qur'an, revealed by God to meet all our needs, diffuses blessing and is peerless in its sublimity and holiness. Those who obey it live a blessed life and acquire (spiritual) superiority over others. The Qur'an changes their world into a kind of Paradise, in which its blessings bloom like flowers. To benefit from its blessing, we must obey its commands, reflect continually on its verses, and use it to answer our questions and solve our problems. The Qur'an is the very essence of life; the more you dedicate your life to it, the more blessed and fruitful your life becomes. The opposite is just as true.

God's Messenger declares: The best among you is one who learns the Qur'an (with all the truths it contains) and then teaches it to others.[1]

If we are to be included among the best, we should go through the Qur'anic truths and teach them to others. The Qur'an is a Divine letter to us. Its contents contain all the principles according to which we must design our lives.

Our Creator has honored us with His Word. The more respectful and obedient we are to this Word, the more honored and respected we are.

God's Messenger, upon him be peace and blessings, also declares: "One who proclaims (the truths) of the Qur'an openly and recites it to announce it to all people is like one who gives alms openly. Another who recites it secretly is like one who gives alms secretly."[2]

Some people give alms openly to encourage others to do so. By reciting the Qur'an publicly, one exhorts others by example. Those who recite in secret should look for themselves in it, and consider it addressed to them personally. Like 'Umar ibn 'Abd al-'Aziz, Muhammad ibn Ka'b al-Qurazi, and others, we should consider that all Qur'anic commands and prohibitions, promises and warnings are directed at us. If we do this, we will understand the Qur'an better and regulate our life according to it.

If we recite the Qur'an sincerely and in full consciousness of its being God's Revealed Word, we will feel revived. If possible, we should recite the Qur'an or hear its recitation as if God's Messenger were reciting it; or better yet, as if Gabriel were reciting it to God's Messenger; or even better still, as if we were hearing it from God Almighty Himself.

ARGUMENTS FOR THE DIVINE AUTHORSHIP OF THE QUR'AN

- When we study the Qur'an's words, styles, and meanings even superficially, we notice immediately that it is unique. So, in rank and worth it is either below—even Satan cannot claim this, nor does he conceive of it—or above all other books. Since it is above, it must be the Word of God.

- The Qur'an declares: *You (O Muhammad) were not a reader of any Scripture before it, nor did you write (such a Scripture) with your right hand, for then those who follow falsehood might (have a right) to doubt it* (29:48). Moreover, it is undeniable that Prophet Muhammad was unlettered and that the Qur'an has presented an open-ended and eternal challenge to humanity: *If you are in doubt concerning that which We have sent down onto Our servant (Muhammad), produce a chapter of the like thereof, and call your witnesses, supporters, who are apart from God, if you are truthful* (2:23). No one has ever met this challenge successfully.

- The Revelation spanned 23 years. How is it that such a book, which deals with Divine truth, metaphysics, religious beliefs and worship, prayer, law and morality, the afterlife, psychology, sociology, epistemology, history, scientific facts, and the principles of a happy life, never contradicts itself? In fact, it openly declares that it contains no contradictions and is therefore a Divine Book: *Will they not then ponder on the Qur'an? If it had been from other than God they would have found therein much contradiction and incongruity* (4:82).

- The Qur'an is a literary masterpiece that cannot be duplicated. Its styles and eloquence, even its actual sentences, words, and letters form a miraculous harmony. With respect to rhythm, music, and even geometric proportions, mathematical measures, and repetition, each is in its exact place and perfectly interwoven and interrelated with others.

- Eloquence, poetry, and oratory enjoyed great prestige in pre-Islamic Arabia. Poetry competitions were held regularly, and winning poems were written in gold and hung on the Ka'ba's walls. The unlettered Prophet had never been heard to say even a couple lines of poetry. However, the Qur'an he brought eventually forced all known experts to surrender.

Even the unbelievers were captivated by it. Nevertheless, to stop Islam from spreading, they said it was magical and should not be listened to. But when poets such as Hansa and Lebid converted and then abandoned poetry out of respect for and awe of the Qur'an's styles and eloquence, the unbelievers had to confess: "If we call it a piece of poetry, it is not. If we designate it a piece of rhymed prose, it is not. If we describe it as the word of a soothsayer, it is not." At times, they could not help listening to the Prophet's recitation secretly at night, but they could not overcome their arrogance long enough to believe in its Divine origin.

• Despite the high level of poetry, Arabic's vocabulary was too primitive to express metaphysical ideas or scientific, religious, and philosophical concepts adequately. Islam, using the words and expressions of a simple desert people, made Arabic so rich and complex that it became the language of the most magnificent civilization, one that made many entirely original contributions to scientific, religious, metaphysical, literary, economic, juridical, social, and political areas. How could an unlettered person launch a philological revolution that has no parallel in human history?

• Despite its apparent simplicity, the Qur'an has many levels of meaning. It illuminates the way for poets, musicians, and orators, as well as for sociologists, psychologists, scientists, economists, and jurists. Founders of true spiritual orders and schools of law and conduct found in it all the principles needed to guide their adherents. The Qur'an shows everyone how to solve their problems and fulfill their spiritual quests. Can any other book accomplish this?

• However beautiful and interesting a book is, we read it at most two or three times and then put it aside forever. Billions of Muslims, on the other hand, have recited portions of the Qur'an during their five daily prayers for the last fourteen centuries. Many have recited it completely once a year, and sometimes even once or twice a month. The more we recite it, the more we benefit from it and the more desire we feel to recite it. People never get tired of its wording, meaning, and content, and it never loses any of its originality and freshness. As time passes, it breathes new truths and meanings into minds and souls, thereby increasing their activity and liveliness.

• The Qur'an describes all our physical and spiritual aspects, and contains principles to solve all social, economic, juridical, political, and administrative problems regardless of time or place. Furthermore, it satisfies the mind and spirit simultaneously, and guarantees happiness in both worlds.

No one, no matter how intelligent, can establish rules to solve all potential problems. Even the best system must be revised at least every 50 years. More importantly, no system can promise eternal happiness, for their principles are restricted to this transient human life, which is infinitely short when compared to the afterlife.

In contrast, no Qur'anic principle has become obsolete or needs revision. For example, it states that wealth should not circulate only among the rich (59:7); that government offices should be entrusted to competent, qualified persons, and that absolute justice should rule in public administration and all disputes (4:58); that people can only have what they strive for (53:39); and that whoever kills a person unjustly is the same as one who would kill all humanity (5:32). These and many other principles (e.g., prohibiting usury, gambling, alcohol, and extramarital sexual relations; enjoining prayer, fasting, almsgiving, and good conduct) are strengthened through love and awareness of God, the promise of an eternal happy life, and the fear of punishment in Hell.

The Qur'an also unveils the mystery of humanity, creation, and the universe. The Qur'an, humanity, and the universe are the three "books" that make the Creator known to us, and are three expressions of the same truth. Therefore, the One Who created humanity and the universe also revealed the Qur'an.

- You cannot find people who do exactly what they ask others to do, or whose deeds reflect them exactly. However, the Qur'an is identical with Prophet Muhammad, and is the embodiment of him in words, just as he is the embodiment of the Qur'an in belief and conduct. They are two expressions of the same truth. When asked about her husband's conduct, 'A'isha replied: "Don't you read the Qur'an? His conduct was the Qur'an." This clearly shows that the Qur'an and Muhammad are the works of God Almighty.

- Authors are usually so influenced by their surroundings that it is almost impossible for them to become detached. By contrast, even though revealed in parts on certain occasions, the Qur'an is as equally universal and objective when dealing with particular issues as it is exact and precise when dealing with universal matters. It uses precise expressions even while describing the beginning of creation and the end of time, and humanity's creation and life in the other world. Just as it sometimes draws universal conclusions from particular events, it sometimes goes from universal principles to particular events. This typical Qur'anic style cannot be found in any human work and is, therefore, another sign of its Divine origin.

- No author has ever written a book in his or her field that is as accurate as the Qur'an is in such varied fields as religion and law, sociology and psychology, eschatology and morality, history and literature, and so on. The Qur'an also contains the principles of all branches of knowledge, either in summary or in detail, and not even one piece of this knowledge has ever been contradicted. What more is needed to prove its Divine origin?

- Can any author claim that his or her work is absolutely correct and will remain so forever? Scientific conclusions change constantly. The Torah and Gospels undergo continuous alteration. Even a superficial study of Bibles published in different times and languages shows these alterations. Yet the Qur'an's truths retain their freshness or, in the words of Said Nursi, "as time grows older, the Qur'an grows ever younger." No mistake or contradiction has ever been found in it, and ever since the beginning of its revelation it has remained unchanged and displayed its uniqueness. It continues, even now, to conquer new hearts and reveal its hidden unlimited treasures, to bloom like a heavenly rose with countless petals.

- Based on your knowledge and reputation for honesty, can you speak on behalf of the president, the prime minister, and all other ministers; of associations for writers, lawyers, and workers; and of the board of university lecturers and scientists? Can you claim to represent them as perfectly as each would want you to? Can you legislate for all the affairs of the country? This is just what the Prophet achieved through the Qur'an. How can you claim that an unlettered person, who was totally apolitical until he was 40, could achieve such results without Divine inspiration and support?

• The Prophet is admonished in the Qur'an. If he were its author, would he give such a noticeable place to the grave slander against his wife? Would he not hide the revelation ordering him to marry Zaynab (discussed above), rather than publicize it, if it did not come from God? 'A'isha said later that if the Prophet could have concealed any part of the Qur'an, he would have concealed this.

His uncle Abu Talib, who raised him since he was 8 and protected him for 10 years after his declaration of Prophethood, never embraced Islam. The Prophet loved his uncle deeply and desired his conversion, but was told that: *You guide not whom you love, but God guides whom He wills. He is best aware of those who are guided* (28:56). If he were the Qur'an's author, he could have claimed that Abu Talib had embraced Islam.

• Many verses begin with "They ask you" and continue with "Say (in answer)." These were revealed to answer questions asked by Muslims and non-Muslims, especially the Jews of Madina, about allowed or prohibited matters, the distribution of war gainings, (astrological) mansions of the moon, Judgment Day, Dhul-Qarnayn (an ancient believing king who made great conquests in Asia and Africa), the spirit, and so on. One without an all-encompassing knowledge cannot answer such questions. But his answers satisfied everybody. This shows that he was taught by God, the All-Knowing.

• The Prophet was very austere and shunned worldly gain, fame, rulership, wealth, and pleasure. Also, he endured great hardship and persecution. To claim that he invented the Qur'an means that Muhammad the Trustworthy, as he was commonly known, was the greatest liar and cheat history has ever known. Why would he falsely claim Prophethood and expose himself and his family to severe deprivation and persecution? Such an accusation, as well as that of saying that he wrote the Qur'an, are totally groundless and lack evidence.

- The Jews and Christians were very strong opponents. Eventually, he had to fight the Jews of Madina several times and expel them. Despite this, the Qur'an mentions Prophet Moses about 50 times and Jesus many times; it mentions Muhammad's name only four times. Why should a person who falsely claims Prophethood mention the Prophets of his opponents? Can there be any reason other than jealousy, prejudice, selfishness, and other negative emotions for denying Muhammad's Prophethood?

- The Qur'an also refers to certain facts of creation only recently established by modern scientific methods. How, except for Divine authorship, could the Qur'an be correct on matters which the people listening to it had no idea? For example, if the Qur'an were a regular book, could it have contained: *Do not the unbelievers realize that the heavens and the earth were one unit of creation before we split them asunder?* (21:30).

Whether the Qur'an refers explicitly or implicitly to scientific facts, and the exact relationship between the Qur'an and modern science, are matters of considerable controversy among Muslim intellectuals. Therefore, we will discuss this subject at some length.

SCIENCE AND RELIGION

Science considers any fact, established through empirical methods, to be scientific. Therefore, assertions not established through observation and experiment are only theories or hypotheses.

As science cannot be sure about the future, it does not make definite predictions. Doubt is the basis of scientific investigation. However, Prophet Muhammad, who was taught by the All-Knowing, made many decisive predictions. Most have come true already; the rest are waiting for their time to come true. Many Qur'anic verses point to recently discovered and established scientific facts. As pointed out earlier, the Qur'an mentions many important issues of creation and natural phenomena that even the most intelligent person living fourteen centuries ago could not have known. Furthermore, it uses the Prophets' miracles to allude to the farthest reaches of science, which originated in the Knowledge of the All-Knowing One.

Does the Qur'an contain everything? The Qur'an describes humanity and the universe. It declares:

> With Him are the keys of the Unseen. None but He knows them. And He knows what is in the land and the sea. Not a leaf falls but with His Knowledge, not a grain amid the darkness of the earth, nothing of wet or dry but (it is noted) in a Manifest Book. (6:59)

Ibn Mas'ud says that the Qur'an provides information on everything, but that we may not be able to see everything in it. Ibn 'Abbas, the "Interpreter of the Qur'an" and "Scholar of the Umma," asserts that if he loses his camel's rein, he can find it by means of the Qur'an. Jalal al-Din al-Suyuti, a major scholar who lived in Egypt in the 15th century, explains that all sciences or branches of knowledge can be found in the Qur'an.

How can a medium-sized book, which also contains a great deal of repetition, contain everything we need to know about life, science, social conduct, creation, past and future, and so on?

Before explaining this important matter, we should point out that to benefit from the Qur'an, which transcends time and location and is not bound by its audience's intellectual level, we have to prepare ourselves to do so. We should have firm belief in it and do our best to implement its principles to our daily life. We must refrain from sin as much as possible. As the Qur'an declares we only get what we strive for (53:39), we should, like a deep-sea explorer, dive into its "ocean" and, without becoming tired or bored, continue studying it until we die.

Moreover, we need a good command of Arabic and sufficient knowledge of all branches of the natural and religious sciences. A good interpretation necessitates cooperation among scientists from all natural and social sciences, and religious scholars who are experts on Qur'anic commentary, *hadith*, *fiqh* (Islamic jurisprudence), theology, and spiritual sciences. While reciting and studying the Qur'an, we should regard ourselves as being its first addressee, consciously aware that each verse addresses us directly. If we consider, for example, its historical accounts of the Prophets and their peoples as unrelated to us, we will derive no benefit.

According to its nature and significance, worth and place in existence, everything has its own place in the Qur'an. The Qur'an contains everything, but not to the same degree. It pursues four purposes: to prove the existence and Unity of God, Prophethood, bodily resurrection, and worship of God and justice.

To realize its purposes, the Qur'an draws our attention to God's acts in the universe, His matchless art displayed through creation, the manifestations of His Names and Attributes, and the perfect order and harmony seen in existence. It mentions certain historical events, and establishes the rules of personal and social good conduct and morality, as well as the principles of a happy, harmonious social life. In addition, it explains how to worship and please our Creator, gives us some information about the next life, and tells us how to gain eternal happiness and be saved from eternal punishment.

Everything is contained in the Qur'an, but at different levels. Therefore, not everything is readily apparent. The Qur'an's main duty is to teach about God's perfection, essential qualities, and acts, as well as our duties, status, and how to serve Him. Thus, it contains them as seeds or nuclei, summaries, principles, or signs that are explicit or implicit, allusive or vague, or suggestive. Each occasion has its own form, and is presented in the best way for making each Qur'anic purpose known according to the existing requirements and context. For example:

Human progress in science and industry has brought about such scientific and technological wonders as airplanes, electricity, motorized transport, and radio and telecommunication, all of which have become basic and essential for our modern, materialistic civilization. The Qur'an has not ignored them and points to them in two ways:

- The first is, as will be explained below, by way of the Prophets' miracles.
- The second concerns certain historical events. In other words, the wonders of human civilization only merit a passing reference, an implicit reference, or an allusion in the Qur'an.

For example, if an aircraft told the Qur'an: "Give me the right to speak and a place in your verses," the aircrafts of the sphere of Divine Lordship (the planets, the Earth, the moon) would reply on the Qur'an's behalf: "You may take a place here in proportion to your size." If a submarine asked for a place, the submarines belonging to that sphere, the heavenly bodies "swimming" in the atmosphere's vast "ocean" would say: "Compared to us, you are invisible." If shining, star-like electric lights demanded the right to be included, the electric lights of that sphere (lightning, shooting stars, and stars adorning the sky's face) would reply: "Your right to be mentioned and spoken about is proportional to your light."

If the wonders of human civilization demanded a place based on the fineness of their art, a fly would reply: "O be quiet! Even my wing has more right than you. If all of humanity's fine arts and delicate instruments were banded together, the delicate members of my tiny body would still be more wonderful and exquisite. The verse: *Those upon whom you call, apart from God, shall never create (even) a fly, though they banded together to do it* (22:73), will silence you."

The Qur'an's viewpoint of life and the world is completely different from the modern one. It sees the world as a guesthouse, and people as temporary guests preparing themselves for eternal life by undertaking their most urgent and important duties. As that which is designed and used mostly for worldly purposes only has a tiny share in servanthood to and worship of God, which is founded upon love of truth and otherworldliness, it therefore has a place in the Qur'an according to its merit.

The Qur'an does not explicitly mention everything necessary for our happiness in this world and the next for another reason: Religion is a divine test to distinguish elevated and base spirits from each other. Just as raw materials are refined to separate diamonds from coal and gold from soil, religion tests conscious beings to separate precious "ore" in the "mine" of human potential from dross.

Since the Qur'an was sent to perfect us, it only alludes to those future events pertaining to the world, which everyone will see at the appropriate time, and only opens the door to reason to the degree necessary to prove its argument. If everything was explicit, the test would be meaningless, for the truth of the Divine obligations would be readily apparent. Given that we would then be unable to deny or ignore them, the competition behind our testing and trials would be unnecessary, for we would have to confirm their truth. "Coal" spirits would remain with and appear to be no different from "diamond" spirits.

As the great majority of people are always "average," the Qur'an uses a style and language that everyone can understand. An ordinary person and a great scientist can benefit from the Qur'an, regardless of his or her specialization. A most suitable way to do this is through symbols, metaphors and allegories, comparisons and parables. Those well-versed in knowledge (3:7) know how to approach and benefit from the Qur'an, and conclude that it is the Word of God.

Earlier civilizations would neither have benefited from nor understood Qur'anic accounts of modern scientific and technological discoveries, so why mention them? Also, scientific "truths" change constantly and therefore are not eternal.

God Almighty gave us intelligence, and the Qur'an urges us to use it to study ourselves, nature, and surrounding events. If it mentioned modern scientific and technological discoveries or everything pertaining to life, nature, history, and humanity, creating us in our present form would have been pointless. God created us as the best pattern of creation, and gave us many intellectual faculties. But if everything were clear, we would not need these, for we would already know everything.

Finally, if the Qur'an contained explicit references to everything we want to know, it would be so large that its complete recitation would be impossible. We would be unable to benefit from its spiritual enlightenment, and would become really bored while reciting it. Such results contradict the reasons for the Qur'an's revelation and its purposes.

THE CONCEPT OF SCIENCE AND TECHNOLOGY

Despite the disasters caused by science and technology, their mistaken approach to the truth, and their failure to bring happiness, we cannot condemn them outright and become pure idealists. Science and technology do not bear the full responsibility for humanity being devalued, human feelings being diminished, and certain human virtues, along with health and the ability to think, being seriously weakened. Rather, the fault lies with scientists who avoid their responsibilities, who cause science to develop in a materialistic and almost purely scientific atmosphere, and then let it be exploited by an irresponsible minority. Many worrying conditions probably would not exist if scientists had remained aware of their social responsibility, and if the Church had not forced it to develop in opposition to religion.

Flowing to the future like a rapid flood full of energy and vitality, and sometimes resembling a dazzling garden, the natural world is like a book to study, an exhibition to behold, and a trust from which we can benefit. We are responsible for studying the meaning and content of this trust so that we and future generations may benefit from it. If we wish, we can call this relationship "science."

Science can also be described as comprehending what things and events tell us, what the Divine laws reveal to us, and striving to understand the Creator's purpose. Created to rule creation, we need to observe and read, to discern and learn about our surroundings so that we can find the best way to exert our influence and control. When we reach this level, by the decree of the Exalted Creator, everything will submit to us and we will submit to God.

There is no reason to fear science. The danger does not lie with science and the founding of the new world it will usher in, but rather with ignorance and irresponsible scientists and others who exploit it for their own selfish interests.

If true science directs human intelligence toward eternity without expecting any material gain, undertakes a tireless and detailed study of existence to discover absolute truth, and follows the methods required to reach this aim, what can we say about modern science other than it cannot fulfill our expectations. Although usually presented as a conflict between Christianity and science, the conflicts during the Renaissance were mainly between scientists (not science per se) and the Catholic Church. Copernicus, Galileo, and Bacon were not anti-religious; in fact, we could say that their religious commitment drove them toward scientific truth.

The religious thought springing from eternality, and the resulting love and zeal accompanied by feelings of poverty and impotence before the Eternal, All-Powerful and All-Knowing Creator, enabled the Muslim world's great five-century scientific advance until the close of the twelfth century. The driving concept of science as based on Divine Revelation was represented almost perfectly by illustrious figures who, imbued with eternality, tirelessly studied existence to attain eternity. Their commitment to Divine Revelation caused It to diffuse a light that engendered a new concept of science in human souls.

If Islamic civilization had not been so badly damaged by the horrific Mongol and numerous destructive Crusader invasions, the world would be very different today. If the Islamic concept of science as being approved and appropriated by the community, as if it were part of the Divine Message and pursued as an act of worship, had continued to flourish, our world would be more enlightened, its intellectual life richer, its technology more wholesome, and its sciences more promising. All Islamic science sought, based on eternality, was to benefit humanity by helping us to aspire for the other world and to handle things responsibly for the sake and pleasure of God Almighty. (See Chapter VI Endnote: Qur'anic Perspective of the Universe)

Only the love of truth, defined as approaching existence not for material advantage or worldly gain but to observe and recognize it as it really is, gives true direction to scientific studies. Those with such love will achieve their goal; those who do not have such love, who are led by worldly ambitions, material aspiration, ideological prejudice and fanaticism, either will fail or turn science into a deadly weapon to be used against humanity.

Intellectuals, educational institutions, and mass media must strive to deliver modern science from the current lethal atmosphere of materialism and ideological fanaticism. To redirect science toward human values, scientists' minds must be freed of ideological superstition and fanaticism, and their souls purified of desire for worldly gain and advantage. This will enable them to secure true freedom of thought and engage in pure science. Their centuries-long battle against the clergy and corrupt concepts formed in the name of religion, and their subsequent denunciation of religious people as backward, narrow-minded, and fanatic should serve as a warning to scientists not to fall into the same trap.

Intellectual and scientific despotism arise from a group's own self-interest and power-seeking, ideology and fanaticism. Such groups can be found among both scientists and clerics. Despotism is despotism, whether it arises from restricting reason to corrupt and distorted religious conceptions and clerical domination or its scientific counterpart. Islam continually urges humanity to study nature, the exhibition of Divine works, to reflect on creation and what has been created, and to approach it responsibly in order to benefit humanity.

When studied without prejudice and preconception, the Qur'an shows that it promotes love of science and humanity, justice and order. The Qur'an is full of verses urging us to study nature, which it sees as a place of exhibition of Divine works. It also urges us to reflect upon creation and the created, to approach it responsibly, and to use it to everybody's benefit. According to Islam, the whole point of seeking knowledge is to discover the meaning of existence so that we can reach the Creator and benefit humanity and all creation. We are to combine that knowledge with belief, love and altruism. Humanity has seen such an ideal in practice: the exemplary life of Prophet Muhammad and the conduct of many of its representatives who perfected their thoughts and deeds.

So what is there to fear from science? Planned acts based on knowledge sometimes cause bad results, but certainly ignorance and disorganization always cause bad results. Instead of opposing the products of science and technology, we must use them to bring happiness to humanity. Herein lies the essence of our greatest problem, for we cannot take measures against the Space Age or erase atomic or hydrogen bomb-making knowledge.

Although science might be a deadly weapon in the hands of an irresponsible minority, we should not hesitate to adopt both it and its products and then use them to establish a civilization in which we can secure our happiness in this world and the next. It is pointless to curse machines and factories, because machines will continue to run and factories to operate. Science and its products will begin to benefit us only when people of truth and belief begin to direct our affairs.

We have never suffered harm from a weapon in the hands of angels. Whatever we have suffered has come from those who still believe that only might is right. This situation will continue until we build a world on faith and science.

DOES THE QUR'AN ALLUDE TO SCIENTIFIC DEVELOPMENTS?

Before answering this question, we should point out one important fact: Considering science as opposed to religion and scientific study as separate from and independent of the Qur'an is just as mistaken as trying to reduce the Qur'an to a science textbook by showing that every new scientific theory or fact can be found in it.

For example, some have claimed, especially in Turkey, that *dabbet al-ard* (a little moving creature) mentioned in Qur'an 27:82 is the virus that causes AIDS. However, this is a hasty conclusion for several reasons: the Qur'an is silent about this particle's nature; if we accept this assertion, we also must accept other venereal disease-causing bacteria or viruses; and, we cannot know whether new and more lethal viral diseases will appear in the future.

The context in which *dabbet al-ard* appears suggests that it will emerge toward the end of this world, when almost no one believes in God. So, we must not show haste in trying to find some type of correspondence between a Qur'anic verse and every new development in science and technology.

Scientific theories are usually like clothes, for both are discarded after a while. Trying to show that every new scientific fact or theory can be found in the Qur'an displays an inferiority complex and makes science more important than the Qur'an. Each Qur'anic verse and expression has a universal content. Therefore, any time-specific interpretation can address only one aspect of that universal content.

Every interpreter, scientist, and saint prefers a particular aspect as a result of his or her spiritual discovery or intuition, personal evidence, or natural disposition. Besides, we accept both Newton's physics and Einstein's physics as science and therefore true. Although in absolute terms both may be false, there certainly must be some truth in both.

Causality is a veil spread by God Almighty over the rapid flux of existence so that we can plan our lives to some degree. This means that Newton's physics and Einstein's physics are only relatively true. In short, while pondering on the Qur'anic verses, we should consider the relative truths found in existence and our lives, which are much more numerous than the unchanging absolute truths.

Qur'anic expressions have multiple meanings. For example, consider the verses: *He let forth the two seas that meet together, between them a barrier, they do not overpass* (55:19-20). These verses indicate all the pairs of "seas" or realms, spiritual and material, figurative and actual, from the realms of Lordship and servanthood to the spheres of necessity and contingency, from this world to the Hereafter (including this visible, corporeal world and all unseen worlds), the Pacific and Atlantic oceans, the Mediterranean and Red seas, salt water and sweet water in the seas and underground, and such large rivers as the Euphrates and Tigris that carry sweet water and salty seas to which they flow. All of these, together with many others I do not need to mention here, are included in these verses, either literally or figuratively.

So even if a Qur'anic verse or expression appears to point exactly to an established scientific fact, we should not restrict its meaning to that fact. Rather, we should consider all other possible meanings and interpretations as well.

On the other hand, sometimes the Qur'an does point or allude to specific scientific developments and facts. Being the Divine Revelation that includes *everything wet or dry* (6:59), it cannot exclude them. Indeed, it refers to them directly or indirectly, but not in the manner of science and materialistic or naturalistic philosophy.

The Qur'an is not a science textbook that has to expound upon cosmological or scientific matters; rather, it is the eternal interpretation of the Book of the Universe and the interpreter of all natural and other sciences. It comments upon the visible and invisible worlds, and discloses the spiritual treasures of the Divine Beautiful Names in the heavens and the Earth. The Qur'an is the key leading to an understanding of the hidden realities behind events taking place in nature and human life, and is the tongue of the hidden worlds in the manifest world.

The Qur'an is like the sun shining in the spiritual and intellectual sky of Islam. It is the sacred map of the next world; the expounder of the Divine Attributes, Names, and acts; and the educator of humanity that guides us to truth and virtue. It is a book of law and wisdom, worship and prayer, Divine commands and prohibitions. Fully satisfying our spiritual and intellectual needs, it leaves no theological, social, economic, political, or even scientific issue undiscussed, whether in brief or in detail, directly or through allusion or symbols.

The Qur'an considers creation only for the sake of knowing its Creator; science considers creation only for its own sake. The Qur'an addresses humanity; science addresses only those who specialize in it. Since the Qur'an uses creation as evidence and proof to guide us, its evidence must be easily understandable to all of us non-specialists. Guidance requires that relatively unimportant things should be touched on briefly, while subtle points should be discussed as completely as possible through parables and comparisons. Guidance should not change what is obvious, so that people are not confused. If it did, how could we derive any benefit?

Like everything else, science has its source in one of God Almighty's Beautiful Names. The Name All-Healing shines on medicine; geometry and engineering depend on the Names All-Just, All-Shaping, and All-Harmonizing; and philosophy reflects the Name All-Wise. As pointed out above, the Creator refers in the Qur'an to everything that He has allowed us to learn and use for our material and spiritual progress.

The Qur'an's primary aims are to make God Almighty known, to open the way to faith and worship, and to organize our individual and social life so that we may attain perfect happiness in both worlds. To achieve this aim, it refers to things and events, as well as scientific facts, in proportion to their importance. Thus the Qur'an provides detailed explanations of the pillars of faith, the fundamentals of religion, the foundations of human life, and essentials of worship, but only hints at other relatively less significant things. The meaning of a verse may be compared to a rosebud: it is hidden by successive layers of petals. A new meaning is perceived as each petal unfolds, and people discover one of those meanings according to their capacity and are satisfied with it.

Examples

One way the Qur'an hints of technological advances and marks their final development is by mentioning the miracles of the Prophets.

* It encourages us to fly in the air and alludes implicitly to the fact that one day we will make spaceships and aircraft: *And to Solomon (We subjugated) the wind; its morning course was a month's journey, and its evening course was a month's journey* (34:12).

* It invites us to learn how to cure every illness: (Jesus said): *I also heal the blind and the leper, and bring to life the dead, by the leave of God* (3:49), and hints that one day we will be so successful that people will find it hard to believe that they will actually die.

- The verse: *Said he who possessed knowledge of the Book: "I will bring it (the throne of the Queen of Sheba) to you (Solomon in Jerusalem) before ever your glance returns to you"* (27:40), foretells that one day images or even physical items will be transmitted instantly through knowledge of the Divine Book of the Universe, just as those with knowledge of the Book of Divine Revelation can bring things from a long distance in the blink of an eye.

- The Qur'an symbolically informs us that it might be possible to identify a murderer by some cells taken from his body at the time of death: A murderer was revealed in the time of Moses, by smiting the slain man with part of a cow that God Almighty ordered the Children of Israel to slaughter (2:67-73).

Below are further examples to illustrate the Qur'an's allusions to scientific facts and developments.

- The Creator, Who is not bound by the human concept of time, informs us that, in a general sense, the future will be the age of knowledge and information, as well as an age of faith and belief: *Soon We shall show them Our signs in the outer world and in their own souls, until it becomes manifest to them that this is truth. Is it not enough that your Lord witnesses all things?* (41:53).

From the very early days of Islam, Sufis have interpreted this verse as a sign and assurance of the spiritual wisdom for which they strive. But if the verse is read in the context of scientific progress, a progress significantly initiated and advanced by Muslims, the mere fact of the verse will be seen to be a miracle.

Everything within the fold of human thinking and research affirms the Creator's Oneness, as the true nature and interrelationship of microcosm and macrocosm come to be further disclosed and better understood. When we see hundreds of books on this point, we understand that what was Divinely revealed is near at hand. Even now we feel that we shall soon hear and even understand testimonies and praises to God through thousands of nature's tongues:

> The seven heavens and the Earth, and all things therein,
> declare His Glory. There is not a thing but celebrates His
> praise. And yet you do not understand how they declare His
> Glory. Truly He is Oft-Forbearing, Most Forgiving. (17:44)

We already understand something of this verse's import.
The smallest atoms as well as the largest nebulae speak to
us, in the language of their being, of their submission to the
One God and so glorify Him. However, those who can listen to and understand this universal praise are very few.

- What the Qur'an reveals about the embryo's formation and
developmental phases in the uterus is striking. Consider the
following:

> O mankind! If you have a doubt about the Resurrection,
> (consider) that We created you out of dust, then out of
> sperm, then out of a leech-like cloth, then out of a lump of
> flesh, partly formed and partly unformed, in order that We
> may manifest (what We will) to you. (22:5)

In another verse, this development is explained in greater
detail, and the distinct phases are emphasized more clearly:

> Man We created from a quintessence (of clay). Then We
> placed him as (a drop of) sperm in a place of rest, firmly
> fixed. Then we made the sperm into a clot of congealed
> blood. Then of that clot We made a lump (embryo); then
> we made out of that lump bones and clothed the bones
> with flesh. Then We developed out of it a new (distinct,
> individual) creature. (23:12-14)

- What the Qur'an says about milk and its production is as
brilliant as the drink itself, and our understanding of it has
brought us great benefits: *And verily in cattle (too) will you
find an instructive sign. From what is from their bodies, between
excretions and blood, We produce, for your drink, milk, pure and
agreeable to those who drink it* (16:66).

The Qur'an narrates the process in remarkable detail:
part-digestion and absorption of what is ingested as food,
and then a second process and refinement in the glands. Milk

is a wholesome and agreeable source of human nourishment, and yet its owner rejects it as useless.

- The Qur'an reveals that all things are created in pairs: *Glory be to God, who created in pairs all things, of what the earth produces, of themselves, and of which they have no knowledge* (36:36).

  Everything that exists has a counterpart, whether opposite or complementary. The complementarity of human, animal, and certain plant genders has long been known. But what about the pairs of things of which we have no knowledge? This may refer to a whole range of entities, inanimate as well as animate. In the subtle forces and principles of nature within (and among) animate or inanimate entities, there are many kinds of pairs. All things, as our modern instruments confirm, occur in twos.

- The Qur'an recounts, in its own unique idiom, the first creation of the world and its living inhabitants: *Do not the unbelievers see that the heavens and the earth were joined together (as a single mass), before We clove them asunder? We made from water every living thing. Will they not then believe?* (21:30).

  This meaning of the verse is clear, and should not be obscured with hypotheses as to whether the primary material in creation is an ether or a large cloud, a huge nebula or a mass of hot gas, or something else. The Qur'an states that every living thing was created of water. Whether the water itself was caused by gases and vapors rising from the ground, condensing, and then returning as rain to form seas and prepare a suitable environment for life, or by some other process, is relatively unimportant.

  The verse explicitly presents the universe as a single miracle of creation. Each thing in it is an integral part of that miracle, and contains signs that prove its claim. Everything is interconnected, just like the leaves of a massive tree. They are all different, but resemble each other and are linked to a common root. The verse also emphasizes water's vitality and significance, for it constitutes three-fourths of the body mass of most living creatures.

- The sun has a special and significant place. The Qur'an reveals its most important aspects in four words, whose full meaning cannot be rendered easily: *And the sun runs its course* (mustaqarr) *determined for it. That is His decree, the Exalted in Might, the All-Knowing* (36:38).

  Given the context, mustaqarr may mean a determined orbit, a fixed place of rest or dwelling, or a determined route in time. We are told that the sun follows a predetermined course toward a particular point. Our solar system is heading toward the constellation Lyra at an almost inconceivable speed: Every second we come ten miles closer (almost a million miles a day). Our attention also is drawn to the fact that when the sun finishes its appointed task, it will abide by a command and come to rest. (See Chapter VI Endnote: The Meaning of the First Command "Read!")

  Such is the richness of the Qur'an, which explains many truths in so few words. Here, in only four words, many vague things were clarified at a time when people generally believed that the sun made a daily circuit around the Earth.

- Another inspiring and eloquent Qur'anic verse concerns the universe's expansion, mentioned in only four words: And the firmament: We constructed it with power and skill, and We are spreading it (51:47-48).

  The verse reveals that the distance between celestial bodies is increasing, which means that the universe is expanding. In 1922, the astronomer Hubble claimed that all galaxies, except the five closest to Earth, are moving further away into space at a speed directly proportional to their distance from the Earth. According to him, a galaxy one million light years distant is moving away at a speed of 168 km/year, a galaxy two million light years distant at twice that speed, and so on. Le Maître, a Belgian mathematician and priest, later proposed and developed the theory that the universe is expanding. No matter how we try to express this reality, whether through Hubble's coefficient or a future theory, the Revelation is unmistakably clear on the reality itself.

- The Qur'an provides some indication of the invisible operation of various laws as attraction and repulsion, rotation and revolution: *God is He Who raised the heavens without any pillars that you can see* (13:2).

All celestial bodies move in order, balance, and harmony. They are held and supported by invisible pillars, some of which are repulsion or centrifugal forces: *He holds back the sky from falling on earth, except by His leave* (22:65).

At any moment, the heavens could fall upon the Earth. That the All-Mighty does not allow this to happen is yet another instance of the universal obedience to His Word. Modern science explains this as a balance of centripetal and centrifugal forces. What is of far greater importance, however, is that we turn our minds to that obedience and to the Divine Mercy that holds the universe in its reliable motion, rather than deciding to follow Newton's or Einstein's theories about the mechanical and mathematical terms of that obedience.

- Previously, some Qur'anic commentators thought travel to the moon, once considered a very remote possibility, could be found in: *By the moon's fullness! You shall surely travel from stage to stage* (84:18-19).

  Earlier commentators took this as a figurative reference to our spiritual life, an ascent from one stage to the next, and from one heaven to another. Others interpreted it as referring to change in general, from one state to another. Later interpreters gave ambiguous meanings, because the literal meaning did not agree with their beliefs about travelling such distances. But in fact, the more appropriate sense of the words following the oath by the moon given the verse's immediate context is that of really travelling to the moon, whether literally or figuratively.

- The Qur'anic description of the Earth's geographical shape and change in that shape are particularly interesting: *Do they not see how We gradually shrink the land from its outlying borders? Is it then they who will be victors?* (21:44).

  The reference to shrinking from its borders could relate to the now-known fact that the Earth is compressed at the poles, rather than to the erosion of mountains by wind and rain, of coastal areas by the sea, or of the gradual desertification of agricultural land.

At a time when people generally believed that the Earth was flat and stationary, the Qur'an explicitly and implicitly revealed that it is round. More unexpectedly still, it also says that its precise shape is more like an ostrich egg than a sphere: *After that He shaped the Earth like an egg, whence He caused to spring forth the water thereof, and the pasture thereof* (79:30-31).

The verb *daha'* means "to shape like an egg," and its derived noun *da'hia* is still used to mean "an egg." As this scientific fact may have appeared incorrect to scientists living before the advent of modern science, some interpreters misunderstood the word's meaning. They understood it as "stretched out," perhaps fearing that its literal meaning might be difficult to understand and thus mislead people. Modern scientific instruments recently established that the Earth is shaped more like an egg than a perfect sphere, and that there is a slight flattening around the poles as well as a slight curving around the equator.

- As a last example, consider what the Qur'an says about the sun and the moon: *We have made the night and the day as two signs; the sign of the night We have obscured, while the sign of the day We have made to enlighten you* (17:12).

According to Ibn 'Abbas, the *sign of the night refers to the moon, and the sign of the day to the sun. Therefore, from the sign of the night We have obscured*, we understand that the moon once emitted light just as the sun does, and that for some reason God took away its light, causing it to darken or become obscured. While the verse accurately recounts the moon's past, it also points to the future destiny of other heavenly bodies.

Many other verses are related to what we now call scientific facts. Their existence indicates that our quest for knowledge is a portion of Divine Mercy graciously bestowed by our Creator. Indeed, Divine Mercy is one of the Qur'an's names. All the truth and knowledge that it contains is beyond our ability to recount or even to hold in our mind.

We must remember, however, that while the Qur'an alludes to many scientific truths, it is not a textbook of science or scientific explanations. Rather it is, and has always been understood by believers to be, the book of guidance that teaches us the way to right belief and right action so that we may be worthy of Divine Mercy and Forgiveness. It is our responsibility to ensure that the pursuit of scientific and other kinds of knowledge is conducted in the light of the Qur'an, which so encourages and supports it. Such an approach results in knowledge that will not engender arrogance and self-pride, for such feelings lead to mental desolation and human degradation, not to mention the degradation of the Earth, our temporary home and Divinely given trust.

WHY WE REFER TO SCIENCE AND SCIENTIFIC FACTS

We refer to science and scientific facts when explaining Islam because some people only accept scientific facts. Materialists and both non- and anti-religious people have sought to exploit science to defy religion and give their ideas more prestige than they deserve. Through this approach, they have misled and corrupted the minds of many people. Therefore, we must learn how to talk with them in their own terminology to prove that science and technology do not contradict Islam. We have to turn their arguments against them by evaluating them and then using them to guide people to the right way.

Such an approach is entirely permissible, for how can we dispute what such people say if we are not well-versed in their facts and ideas? The Qur'an urges us to reflect and study, to observe the stars and galaxies. They impress upon us the Magnificence of the Creator, exhort us to wander among people, and direct our attention to the miraculous nature of our organs and physical creation.

From atoms to the largest beings, from the first human being's appearance on Earth until our final departure, the Qur'an places all creation before our eyes. Touching upon a multitude of facts, it tells us that *those who truly fear God, among His servants, are those who have knowledge* (35:28), and so encourages us to seek knowledge, to reflect and research. However, we must never forget that all such activities must comply with the spirit of the Qur'an. Otherwise, even though we claim to be following its advice and command, actually we will be moving away from it.

Science and its facts can and should be used to explain Islamic facts. But if we use them to show off our knowledge, whatever we say cannot influence our hearers in the right way, if at all. Bright and persuasive words and arguments lose their effectiveness if we have the wrong intention: they get as far as the listeners' eardrums and no further. Similarly, if our arguments seek to silence others instead of persuading them, we actually will be blocking their way to a correct understanding. And so our efforts will fail, and our goals remain unachieved.

However, if we try to persuade with a full and proper sincerity, even those who need such arguments to believe will receive their portion and benefit. Sometimes a sincere argument may be far more beneficial than one in which you spoke rather more freely and eloquently. Our primary aim when introducing science and scientific facts, in accordance with our audience's level of understanding, must be to win the pleasure of God.

Science cannot be regarded as superior to religion, and substantial Islamic issues cannot use science or modern scientific facts to justify or reinforce religion's credibility. If we adopt such techniques, we are proclaiming that we have doubts about the truths of Islam and need science to support them. In addition, we cannot accept science or scientific facts as absolute. Making science the decisive criteria for the Qur'an's authenticity or Divine origin, thereby placing science over the Qur'an, is absurd, abhorrent, and completely impermissible. Such arguments and allusions to science have, at best, a secondary and supportive use. Their only possible value is that they might open a door onto a way that certain people simply would not know exists.

Science is to be used to awaken or stir some minds that otherwise might remain asleep or unmoved. It is like a feather duster used to brush the dust off the truth and the desire for truth, which lie hidden in unstirred consciences. If we begin by saying that science is absolute, we shall end up seeking to fit the

Qur'an and Hadith to it. The result of such an undertaking can only be doubt and confusion, especially when we cannot reconcile the Qur'an and Hadith with some present scientific assertions that may be proven false in the future.

Our position must be clear: The Qur'an and hadith are true and absolute. Science and scientific facts are true (or false) only to the degree that they agree (or disagree) with these sources. Even definitely established scientific facts cannot be pillars to uphold the truths of faith; rather, they can be accepted only as instruments giving us ideas or triggering our reflection on God, Who establishes the truths of faith in our conscience. To expect that this does or even could take place through science is a grave error: faith comes only by Divine guidance.

Anyone who fails to grasp this has fallen into an error from which it is hard to recover. Such people look for and gather evidence from the universe and, trying to make it speak eloquently in the Name of God, remain unconscious servants to nature and nature worshippers. They study and speak of flowers, of the verdancy and spring of nature, but not the least greenness or bud of faith sprouts in their conscience. They may never even feel the existence of God within their conscience. In appearance they do not worship nature, but in reality that is what they are doing.

A man or a woman is a believer (*mu'min*) owing to the faith (*iman*) in his or her heart, not to the great amount of knowledge in his or her head. After we have understood as much as we can about the objective and subjective evidence we have gathered, we must break our dependence on the outer circumstances, qualities, and conditions of such evidence. Only by doing this will we be able to make any spiritual progress. When we abandon this dependence and follow our heart and conscience within the Qur'an's light and guidance, then, if God wills, we will find the enlightenment for which we are looking. As the German philosopher Immanuel Kant once said: "I felt the need to leave behind all the books I have read in order to believe in God."

Undoubtedly, the grand Book of the Universe and the book of humanity's true nature, as well as their commentaries, have their proper place and significance. But after we use them, we should put them aside and live with our faith, as it were, face to face. This might sound rather abstract to those who have not gone deep into the experience of faith and conscience. But for those whose nights are bright with devotion, and who acquire wings through their longing to aspire to their Lord, the meaning is clear.

ENDNOTE: Qur'anic Perspective of the Universe

According to Islam, the universe resembles a book written by God, a palace built by Him to make Himself known to conscious beings—primarily us. The universe essentially exists in God's Knowledge in meaning. Creation means that through His Will, He specifies or gives a distinct character and form to that meaning as species, races, families, or individuals. Then, through His Power, He clothes each in matter so that it can exist in this time-and-space constrained material realm. After a thing ceases to exist, it continues to live in God's Knowledge and in the memories of those who saw it and through its offspring (if any). For example, a dead flower continues to exist in God's Knowledge, in the memories of those who saw it, and in its seeds.

Everything has five stages or degrees of existence. First, and essentially, it exists in the Creator's Knowledge as meaning. Even if God Almighty did not create it (in the material realm), it would exist in His Knowledge as meaning, for meaning constitutes the essential existence of everything. Then, it exists in the Divine Will as a form or a plan; as a material object in the material realm; as a memory and through its offspring (if any); and, finally, its eternal existence in the other world. God Almighty will use the debris of this world to construct the other one. There, animals will continue their existence, each species through a representative of its own species, while each human being will find the eternal life designed for him or her according to how he or she lived while in this world.

The universe, which science studies, manifests God's Names and therefore has some sort of sanctity. Everything in it is a letter from God Almighty inviting us to study it and acquire knowledge of Him. Thus, the universe is the collection of those letters or, as Muslim sages call it, the Divine Book of Creation issuing primarily from the Divine Attributes of Will and Power. The Qur'an, which issues from the Divine Will of Speech, is the universe's counterpart in written form. Just as there can be no conflict between a palace and the paper describing it, there can be no conflict between the universe and the Qur'an, for they are two different expressions of the same truth.

Similarly, humanity is a Divine book corresponding to the Qur'an and the universe. This is why the term used to signify a Qur'anic verse also means events occurring within human souls and phenomena occurring in nature.

The Meaning of the First Command "Read!"

It is interesting that the first revelation of the Qur'an was: *Read, in and with the name of your Lord Who created. He created man of an embryo suspended. Read, and your Lord is the Most Munificent, Who taught by the Pen, taught man what he knew not* (96:1-3).

The Qur'an ordered people to read when the local civilization to which it was revealed had almost nothing to read. What does this apparent contradiction tell us? Nothing less than that we are to read, in the sense of studying, the universe as the Book of Creation and its written counterpart, the Qur'an. We are to observe the universe, perceive its meaning and content, and use the resulting knowledge to deepen our appreciation of the beauty and splendor of the Creator's system and the infinitude of His Might. And so we are obliged to penetrate the universe's manifold meanings, discover the Divine laws of nature, and establish a world in which science and faith complement each other so that we can be God's vicegerent and attain true bliss in both worlds.

God Almighty has two kinds of laws. One is the Shari'a, which comprises His laws issuing from His Attribute of Speech, governs humanity's religious life, and serves as the basis for reward or punishment, which are usually given in the afterlife. The second is the Divine laws governing creation and life as a whole, which issue from His Attribute of Will and are generally (but mistakenly) called "the laws of nature and life." The reward or punishment for them is usually given in this world. For example, patience and persever-ance are rewarded with success, while indolence brings privation. Industry brings wealth, and steadfastness victory.

The Qur'an insistently draws our attention to natural phe-nomena, which are the subject matter of science, and urges their study. During the first 5 centuries of Islam, Muslims united sci-ence and religion, intellect and heart, material and spiritual. Later on, however, it was the West that pursued scientific knowledge and therefore showed an (unconscious) obedience to the Divine laws of nature. The West dominated the Muslim world because the latter no longer understood or practiced Islam correctly in their daily lives, and because they neglected scientific investiga-tion and the study of nature. All of this amounted to disobeying the Divine laws of nature. (Tr.)

> The sun moves (in its course) to a resting-place for it. (36:38)

Before elucidating other meanings and connotations, remember that earlier peoples' sense-derived information led them to believe that the sun moved around a motionless Earth. Science and obser-vation later showed that the Earth spins on its own axis and orbits the sun, which is relatively motionless. First, since people see the sun moving, the Qur'an mentions it as moving. Second, the Qur'an mentions the sun here to illustrate the magnificent order prevailing throughout the universe as a sign of God's Might and Knowledge:

> A sign for them is the night. We strip it of the day, and behold! they are in darkness. And the sun moves (in its course) to a resting-place for it. That is the measuring and ordaining of the All-Mighty, the All-Knowing. And for the moon We have appointed mansions till it returns like an old shriveled palm-leaf. It is not for the sun to overtake the moon, nor does the night outstrip the day. They float, each in an orbit. (36:37-40)

We understand from this context that the sun's function is vital. The word *mustaqarr* (stability) applies to is course and the place in which stability is secured. So, the statement can mean that the sun has a central position in the universe's order. Second, the preposition used here, *li*, has three meanings: for, to, and in. Therefore, the exact meaning of this statement is: The sun moves following a route or course to a fixed place determined for it for the purpose of its (system's) stability.

Recently, solar astronomers have observed that the sun is not motionless; rather it quivers, shakes, and continually rings like a well-hit gong [M. Bartusiac, "Sounds of the Sun," *American Scientist* (January-February 1994): 61-68]. The resulting vibrations reveal vital information about its deep interior and hidden layers, information that affects calculations of the universe's age. Also, knowing exactly how the sun spins internally is important in testing Einstein's theory of general relativity. Like so many other significant findings in astronomy, this one was totally unexpected. Some astronomers have commented that it is as if the sun were a symphony orchestra, with all its instruments being played simultaneously. At times, all the vibrations combine to produce a net oscillation on the solar surface that is thousands of times stronger than any individual vibration.

Commenting on the Qur'anic verse: *The sun moves to a resting-place for it*, several decades before this totally unexpected discovery, Said Nursi wrote:

> As the word "moves" points to a style, the phrase "in its course" demonstrates a reality. The sun, like a vessel built of gold, travels and floats in the ocean of the heavens comprising ether and defined as a stretched and tightened wave. Although it quivers and shakes in its course or orbit, since people see it running, the Qur'an uses the word "travel" or "float." However, since the origin of the force of gravity is movement, the sun moves and quivers in its orbit. Through this vibration, which is the wheel of its figurative movement, its satellites are attracted to it and preserved from falling and scattering. When a tree quivers, its fruits fall. But when the sun quivers and shakes, its fruits—its satellites—do not fall.

Again, wisdom requires that the sun should move and travel on its mobile throne (its course or orbit) accompanied by its soldiers (its satellites). For the Divine Power has made everything moving, and condemns nothing to absolute rest or motionlessness. Divine Mercy allows nothing to be condemned to inertia, which is the cousin of death. So the sun is free; it can travel, provided it obeys the laws of God and does not disturb others' freedom. So it may actually be travelling, as its travelling may also be figurative. However, what is important according to the Qur'an is the universal order, the wheel of which is the sun and its movement. Through the sun, the system's stability and orderliness are ensured. (Tr.)

NOTES

CHAPTER I
THE EXISTENCE AND UNITY OF GOD

1 On the Qur'an's Divine authorship, consult M. Fethullah Gülen, *Questions This Modern Age Puts to Islam 1* (London: Truestar, 1993), 53-97.

2 Adapted from the Second Station of Said Nursi, *The Words*, "The Twenty-second Word" (Izmir, Turkey: Kaynak, 1997).

3 Reported in *Discover*, 20 August 1993.

4 Suppose you take ten pennies and mark them from 1 to 10. Put them in your pocket and give them a good shake. Now try to draw them out in sequence from 1 to 10, putting each coin back in your pocket after each draw. Your chance of drawing No. 1 is 1 in 10. Your chance of drawing 1 and 2 in succession would be 1 in 100. Your chance of drawing 1, 2, and 3 in succession would be 1 in 1,000. Your chance of drawing 1, 2, 3, and 4 in succession would be 1 in 10,000 and so on, until your chance of drawing from no. 1 to no. 10 in succession would reach the unbelievable figure of one chance in 10 billion.
The object in dealing with so simple a problem is to show how enormously figures multiply against chance.
So many essential conditions are necessary for life on our Earth that it is mathematically impossible that all of them could exist in proper relationship by chance on any one Earth at one time. Therefore, there must be in nature some form of intelligent direction. If this be true, then there must be a purpose. Morrison, *Man Does Not Stand Alone*, 13.

5 Ibid., 14, 16-19, 22, 24-27, 76-77.

6 Ibid., 65.

CHAPTER 2
THE INVISIBLE REALM OF EXISTENCE

1 Said Nursi, *The Words*, "The 29th Word," 2 (Izmir, Turkey: Kaynak AS, 1997), 196-97.

2 In traditional Islamic literature, every mention of the Prophet is followed by a phrase of blessing, usually "peace and blessings be upon him." In the case of the Companions and other pious Muslims, the phrase "may God be pleased with him (or her)" is used. Both of these are religious obligations. We have not followed this practice in

this book, as it is foreign to American literary style. This is not meant as a sign of disrespect, for they are assumed to be there.

3   This does not imply that God creates something imperfect. Rather, everything in the world has imperfection because its substance cannot receive God's manifestations in perfect form. Since death leads to a more perfect life than the previous one, death may be more perfect than life itself.

4   The Ahl al-Sunna wa al-Jama'a, meaning the People of Sunna and Community, are the great majority of Muslims who follow the way of the Prophet and Companions. Other groups of Muslims, which can be called fractions, differ from them with respect to either matters of belief (e.g., the Mu'tazila and Jabriya) or viewing the Companions' role in religion (e.g., the Kharijites and Shi'a) because of political inclinations and influences from ancient philosophies. (Tr.)

5   For many of his predictions, see, Said Nursi, *The Letters* (London, UK: Truestar, 1994), 1:111-30; Gülen, *The Messenger of God: Muhammad - An Analysis of the Prophet's Life* (The Light Inc., New Jersey, 2005).

6   Some maintain that the Qur'an, in 7:172 and 23:14, alludes to the fact that our spirits were created long before Adam and Eve came to the world. According to a *hadith*, each person's spirit is breathed into him or her when he or she is about a 6-week old embryo in the mother's womb.

7   The king said: "[In my dream] I saw seven fat cows devoured by seven lean ones, and seven green ears of corn and (seven) dry (ears of corn). O my courtiers, tell me the interpretation of my dream, if you understand the meanings of dreams." They replied: "A jumble of dreams. We are not skilled in interpreting jumbled dreams." ... (Joseph) said: "You shall sow, as usual, for seven years. Leave in the ear the corn you reap, except a little which you may eat. After that will come seven years of severity, which will consume all but a little of what you have stored for them. After that will come a year in which the people will have abundant water and in which they will press (juice, oil, etc.)." (12:43-44, 47-49.)

8   During dreams, the spirit continues this connection through a cord.

9   This is an official of the highest rank, whom God employs to veil His provisioning of all creation. (Tr.)

10 Said Nursi says that they have partial will-power, as shown by their response to God's proclaiming to them that He would choose a vicegerent on the Earth. This partial willpower, however, does not cause or enable them to disobey God's orders. As such, their willpower is weaker than our willpower.

11 We do not know what the Qur'an means by God's Throne or how it is carried. (Tr.)

12 We are not certain whether the Qur'an means energy or something like X-rays when it talks of such a smokeless, penetrating, and scorching fire. (Tr.)

13 The Companion did not know that the man was Satan. (Tr.)

14 We do not know how they eat our foods or drink our beverages. (Tr.)

15 Founder of the Qadiyani (also known as Ahmadiyya) sect, which most Muslims say is either heretical or non-Islamic.

CHAPTER 3
DIVINE DECREE AND DESTINY, AND HUMAN FREE WILL

1 Such foreknowledge and prerecording are apparent, because past and future time are relevant only to humanity. They cannot, and do not, apply to God. As He "sees" everything simultaneously, there is no such thing as "fore-" or "pre-" when speaking of Him.

2 Islam does not accept the deistic concept of God, namely, that He created the universe and left it to run itself. We are contained by time and space, and therefore are limited in the following ways: we cannot draw exactly true conclusions about the relation between the Creator and the creation, we cannot perceive eternity, and we have little true information about this world. God is beyond all time and space, infinite and eternal. He holds the universe in His "hand" and controls and manages it as He wills. However, so that we might glimpse His actions and acquire some knowledge of Him and His Attributes, He allows those of His manifestations related to creation to be limited by time and space. If He did not, life could not exist and we could acquire no knowledge of Him and the universe. Therefore, what we have said about His Will and Destiny should be considered in light of the fact that we can talk about these matters only from within the bounds of this life (limited by time, space, and matter) and of our very existence.

3 We are included in the same mirror, but we are conscious of both the mirror and of what is reflected in it.

4 Muttaqi al-Hindi, *Kanz al-'Ummal*, Hadith No. 3123; Ibn 'Asakir, *Tarikh al-Dimashq*, 5:168.

5 Such events are meant to benefit both believers and unbelievers. For the latter, there is the added benefit of warning. We must endure such trials patiently, for they are usually followed by good and bring perfection in this life and much reward for the next life.

6 *Sahih al-Bukhari*, "Bad'u l-Wahy," 1; *Sahih al-Muslim*, "'Imara," 155.

7 Ibn Sa'd, *Al-Tabaqat al-Kubra'*, 2.142; Ibn Ishaq, *Al-Sirat al-Nabawiyya*, 2:402.

8 Bukhari, *Jihad*, 102; Muslim, *Fada'il al-Sahaba*, 35. "Red camels" is a metaphor used by medieval Arabs for the most precious thing one can have. (Tr.)

9 Muslim, *Zakat*, 69; Ibn Maja, *Muqaddima*, 203.

CHAPTER 4
THE RESURRECTION AND THE AFTERLIFE

1 Ibn Kathir, *Tafsir*, 3:539 (quoting from Ibn 'Asakir's *Tarikh al-Dimashq*).

2 *Kanz al-'Ummal*, 3.141, Hadith No. 5878.

3 Ibn Ishaq, *Al-Sirat al-Nabawiyya* (Beirut: 1955), 2:642; Ibn Sa'd, *Al-Tabaqat al-Kubra'* (Beirut), 2:204.

4 Bukhari, *Anbiya'*, 8:48; Muslim, *Janna*, 56; Tirmidhi, *Qiyama*, 3.

5 Ahmad ibn Hanbal, *Musnad*, 3:154. (Related by Anas.)

[6] Bukhari, *Riqaq,* 45; Muslim, *Janna,* 59; Nasa'i, *Jana'iz,* 118. (Related by Abu Hurayra. *Bukhari* and *Muslim.*)

[7] Bukhari, *Shahada,* 27; Muslim, *'Aqdiya,* 4; Abu Dawud, *Adab,* 87.

[8] You see that trees come to life again and grow green. Your bones resemble dry branches, yet you refuse to recognize that your bones can be similarly reanimated and regard it as utterly improbable.

[9] Bukhari, *Adab,* 18; Muslim, *Tawba,* 22.

[10] Obviously, this example does not apply to those regions of the world that do not experience winter.

[11] For many other examples, see: Safvet Senih, *Ilim Acisindan Kader* (Destiny from the Perspective of Science) (Izmir, Turkey: Caglayan AS, 1985), 16-17.

[12] For the sources of the information given in this section, as well as information on the universality of belief in the Resurrection, see Chapter 5.

CHAPTER 5
PROPHETHOOD AND MUHAMMAD'S PROPHETHOOD

[1] Taken from the Turkish translation of the Bible, published in Istanbul in 1885.

[2] For example, most of the idols at the Ka'ba toppled over; the Sassanid Emperor's palace shook and cracked, and its fourteen pinnacles collapsed; the small Persian lake of Sawa sank into the ground; and the fire worshipped by Istakhrabad's Magians was extinguished (it had been lit continually for 1,000 years. (Tr.)

[3] See his *Man, This Unknown,* published during the 1930s.

[4] *Sahih al-Muslim,* "Janna," 76, 77.

[5] *Sahih al-Bukhari,* "Manaqib," 22; *Sunan Abu Dawud,* "Jihad," 97.

[6] *Bukhari,* "Salat," 63; *Muslim,* "Fitan," 70, 72; Ibn Hanbal, *Musnad,* 12:161, 164.

[7] The hadith is in this strain: "You will be the first of my family to join me after my death." *Sunan Ibn Maja,* "Jana'iz," 65; Muslim, *Fada'il al-Sahaba,* 15; Ibn Hanbal, 3.197.

[8] *Bukhari,* "Jihad," 95, 96; *Abu Dawud,* "Malahim," 10; *Ibn Maja,* "Fitan," 36.

[9] Hakim, *Mustadrak,* 3:75. Also related by Tirmidhi, Ibn Hanbal and, Ibn Maja.

[10] Hakim, 4:445; Ibn Hanbal, 4:303; also related by Muslim, Tirmidhi, and Ibn Maja.

[11] *Abu Dawud,* "Sunna," 8; *Sunan al-Tirmidhi,* "Fitan," 48; Ibn Hanbal, 4:273.

[12] Hakim, 3:100; Ibn Hanbal, 6:114; *Ibn Maja,* 5:188; *Tirmidhi.*

[13] Abu Nu'aym, *Hilyat al-Awliya',* 1:94; *Bukhari* and *Muslim.*

[14] Suyuti, *Jami' al-Saghir,* 6:24; *Bukhari, Muslim,* and *Tirmidhi.*

[15] Hakim, 3:453; also related in Muslim, *Sunan* by Ibn Hanbal and *Tirmidhi.*

[16] Hakim, 4:422; Bukhari, *Tarikh al-Saghir,* 139; Ibn Hanbal, 4:335.

[17] *Bukhari,* "Manaqib," 27; *Muslim,* "Kitab Sifat al-Munafiqin wa Ahkamihim," 44.

[18] *Bukhari,* "Ayman," 22; *Muslim,* "Ashriba," 142.

[19] *Bukhari,* "At'ima," 6; *Muslim,* "Ashriba," 175.

[20] *Sunan al-Nasa'i,* 1:60; *Bukhari,* 4:233; *Muslim,* Hadith No. 2279.

[21] *Bukhari,* "Shurut," 15.

22 *Bukhari*, "Fada'il al-Sahaba," 9; *Muslim*, "Fada'il al-Sahaba," 34.

23 *Tirmidhi*, "Da'awat," 119; *Ibn Hanbal*, 4:138; *Ibn Maja*, "Iqama," 189.

24 *Musnad Ibn Hanbal*, 1:348.

25 *Bukhari*, "Nikah," 10:22.

26 *Muslim*, "Salam," 45; *Abu Dawud*, "Diyat," 6.

27 *Musnad Ibn Hanbal*, 4:112.

28 *Bukhari*, "Adab," 39; *Muslim*, "Fada'il," 48; *Ibn Hanbal*, 3:147.

29 *Muslim*, "Fada'il," 2; *Sunan al-Darimi*, "Muqaddima," 4.

30 *Bukhari*, "Manaqib," 25; Ibn Hanbal, *Musnad*, 1:460.

31 *Muslim*, "Fada'il," 50.

32 *Tirmidhi*, Hadith No. 3630; Hakim, 2:607.

33 *Bukhari*, "Maghazi," 31, 33; *Muslim*, "Fada'il," 13.

34 *Muslim*, "Sifat al-Munafiqin," 38.

35 Bukhari, 2:35; Bayhaqi, *Sunan*, 6:147.

36 *Bukhari*, "Istisqa'," 7; *Muslim*, "Istisqa'," 1.

37 *Tirmidhi*, "Manaqib," 18; Ibn Hanbal, *Musnad*, 2:95.

38 *Bukhari*, "'Ilm," 17; *Muslim*, "Fada'il," 137.

39 *Muslim*, "Fada'il," 143.

40 Ibid., 159.

41 *Bukhari*, "Iman," 37.

42 *Bukhari*, "Maghazi," 18; *Muslim*, "Fada'il," 46-47.

43 *Bukhari*, "Maghazi," 11.

44 *Musnad*, 1:455.

45 *Bukhari*, "Abwab 'Amal fi al-Salat," 2; *Muslim*, "Kusuf," 3.

46 *Bukhari*, "Adab," 46; *Muslim*, "Tahara," 3.

47 *Muslim*, "Zuhd," 74.

48 *Bukhari*, "Manaqib," 25; *Tirmidhi*, "Manaqib," 6; *Nasa'i*, "Jumu'ah," 17.

49 *Musnad Ibn Hanbal*, 3:65.

50 For example, Prophet Solomon had *700 wives, princesses, and 300 concubines* (I Kings 11:1-3).

51 *Bukhari*, "Tawhid," 22.

52 *Bukhari* and *Muslim*.

53 Ibn Hanbal, *Musnad*, 6:277.

CHAPTER 6
THE HOLY QUR'AN

1 *Sahih al-Bukhari*, "Fada'il al-Qur'an," 21; *Sunan Abu Dawud*, "Witr," 14.

2 Ibn Hanbal, *Musnad*, 4.201.

INDEX